NEW TESTAMENT

EVERYDAY BIBLE STUDY SERIES

NEW TESTAMENT

EVERYDAY BIBLE STUDY SERIES

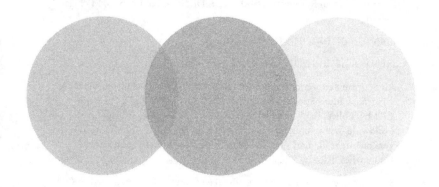

LUKE

SCOT MCKNIGHT

QUESTIONS WRITTEN BY

BECKY CASTLE MILLER

New Testament Everyday Bible Study Series: Luke

Requests for information should be addressed to:
HarperChristian Resources, 3900 Sparks Dr. SE, Grand Rapids, Michigan 49546

ISBN 978-0-310-12930-1(softcover)

ISBN 978-0-310-12931-8 (ebook)

HarperChristian Resources titles may be purchased in bulk for church, business, fundraising, or ministry use. For information, please e-mail ResourceSpecialist@ChurchSource.com.

First Printing January 2023 / Printed in the United States of America

CONTENTS

LUKE

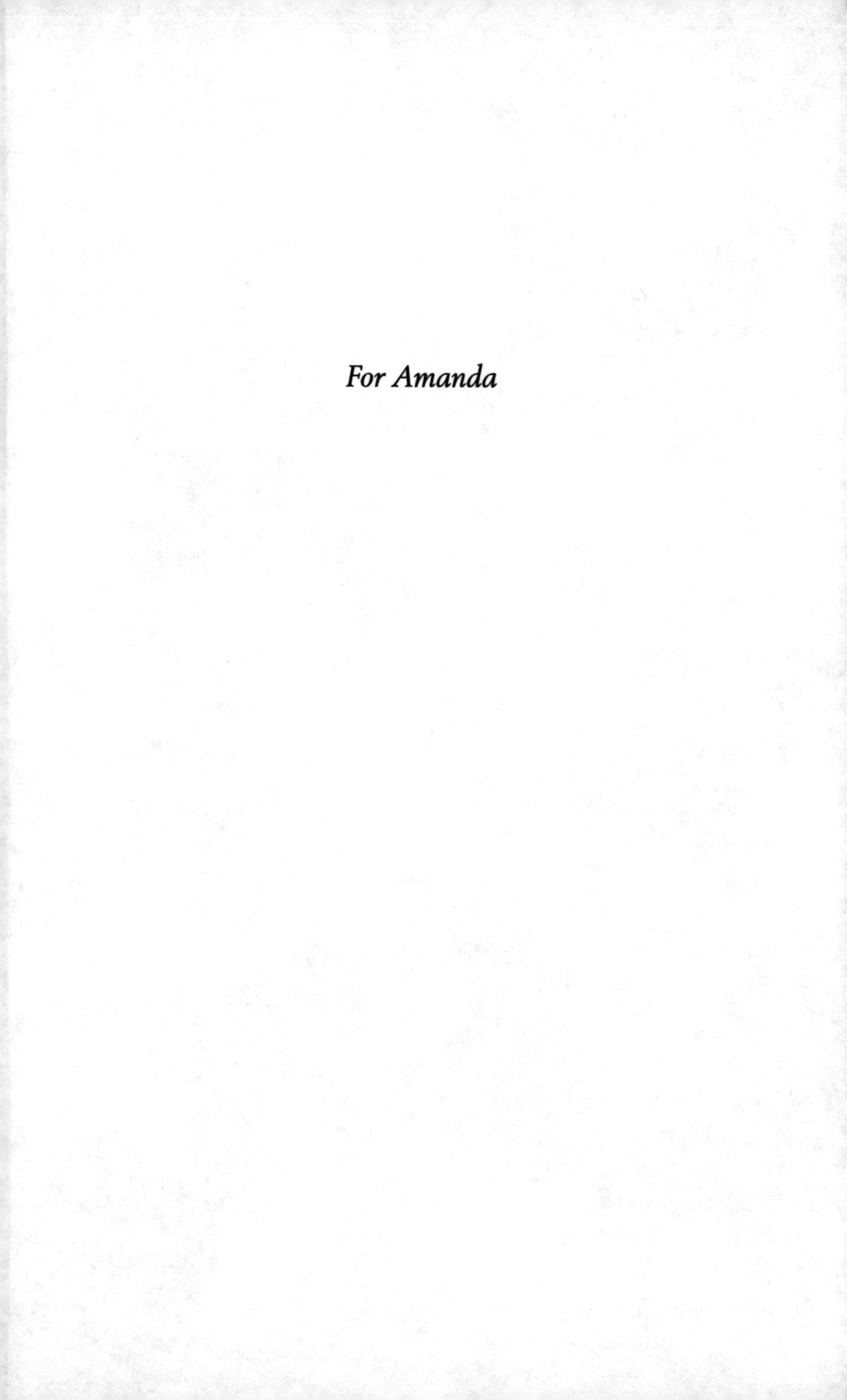

For Amanda

GENERAL INTRODUCTION

Christians make a claim for the Bible not made of any other book. Or, since the Bible is a library shelf of many authors, it's a claim we make of no other shelf of books. We claim that God worked in each of the authors as they were writing so that what was scratched on papyrus expressed what God wanted communicated to the people of God. Which makes the New Testament a book unlike any other book. Which is why Christians are reading the NT almost two thousand years later with great delight. These books have the power to instruct us and to rebuke us and to correct us and to train us to walk with God every day. We read these books because God speaks to us in them.

Developing a routine of reading the Bible with an open heart, a receptive mind, and a flexible will is the why of the *New Testament Everyday Bible Studies*. But not every day will be the same. Some days we pause and take it in and other days we stop and repent and lament and open ourselves to God's restoring graces. No one word suffices for what the Bible does to us. In fact, the Bible's view of the Bible can be found by reading Psalm 119, the longest chapter in the Bible with 176 verses! It is a meditation on eight terms for what the Bible is and what the Bible does to those who listen and read it. Its laws (*torah*) instruct us, its laws (*mishpat*) order us, its statutes direct us, its precepts inform us, its decrees guide us, its command compel us, its words speak to us, and its promises comfort us, and it is no wonder that the author can sum all eight up as the "way" (119:3, 37). Each of those terms still speaks to what happens when we open our minds to the Word of God.

Every day with the Bible then is new because our timeless and timely God communes with us in our daily lives in our world and in our time. Just as God spoke to Jesus in Galilee and Paul in Ephesus and John on Patmos. These various contexts help up hear God in our context so the *New Testament Everyday Bible Studies* will often delve into contexts.

Most of us now have a Bible on our devices. We may well have several translations available to us everywhere we go every day. To hear those words we are summoned by God to open the Bible, to attune our hearts to God and to listen to what God says. My prayer is that these daily study guides will help each of us become daily Bible readers attentive to the mind of God.

INTRODUCTION: READING THE GOSPEL OF LUKE

The Gospel of Luke is a biography. Now for the twister that tells the truth: this biography is the gospel. The book itself is not just a biography, but this biography of Jesus is the gospel itself. Biography is gospel, and the gospel is a biography.

The Gospel of Luke is about Jesus every paragraph. Luke wants his reader, whom he names Theophilus, to know about Jesus, so he writes this Gospel. Be prepared to learn lots about Jesus in this Gospel. Biographies of the ancient world did not engage in what today we would call psychological analysis of a person's character. However, character was the core idea of ancient biographies: they presented a person's life in order to record significant events in a person's life, to praise the person, to present that person's teaching, or to elucidate that person's character as worthy of imitation. (And more.) How then was character presented? By actions, by what the person did, and by sayings, what they taught or said or how they debated opponents. This is exactly how Acts summarizes Luke: what "Jesus began to do and to teach" (Acts 1:1). In the Gospel of Luke what Jesus does and what is done to him are the indicators of character, and the fundamental ideas connected to Jesus are his labels (Lord, Son of God, Son of Man, etc.) and his actions (healing, exorcising demons, showing compassion, feeding others, calling and sending disciples, etc.). By far the subject of the most verbs in this Gospel is Jesus, revealing the book as a biography as well as revealing the character of Jesus. Every separate paragraph in the Gospel can be entitled "Jesus does or says" or "So-and-so said" or "did this to Jesus."

But Luke did something the other Gospel authors did not do. He wrote a follow-up to the Gospel we call the Acts of the Apostles. His biography of Jesus became a biography also of the early church with special emphasis on Peter and Paul. Luke unleashes a Christian theory of history, a history that begins in Israel's story and continues in Jesus' story and then moves on into church history (González, *The Story Luke Tells*, 1–28).

The Jesus of Luke's Gospel unleashes the kingdom of God as a holistic redemption. Holistic redemption forms the spine to this Gospel. Jesus is the subject of Luke's Gospel, but the Jesus of this biography is one who launches the kingdom of God and that means holistic redemption. He redeems in all sorts of ways—spiritually, physically, socially, politically—and he redeems all sorts of people—Jews and gentiles, women and men, the powerful and the powerless—and in doing so Jesus sets the standard for the church to become, as Paul said, "all things to all people." At the heart of this holistic redemption is the theme of coming home to the table for fellowship with God, with family, with friends, with neighbors—and yes, with the whole world eventually. Meals are the preeminent expression of being at home, and this Gospel will have plenty of meal settings (Matthew Croasmun, Miroslav Volf, *The Hunger for Home*). And this redemption is empowered by a favorite theme in Luke's Gospel: the Spirit of God. We all know about the Spirit in the Book of Acts, but an attentive reader will notice just how often Luke brings in the Spirit to his Gospel, too.

Only a holistic redemption fits the pattern of Scripture's expectations for the messianic kingdom. It begins on the basis of the truths of Mary's song, which is about her son, Jesus, the Son of God, the Son of the Most High, the messiah, and the Lord. He is the one who brings this redemption. This redemption cannot be reduced to ethics, morality, or even what we call social justice. Its foundation is a Person, and in that Person holistic redemption explodes into living realities. Those who follow this Person suddenly realize they are on mission with Jesus, as Luke tells his great story.

Luke might say to us today, "Go and do Luke-wise" (Thanks Steve Walton for that clever expression based on Luke 10:37.)

WORKS CITED IN THE STUDY GUIDE

(Throughout the Guide you will find the author's name and title as noted in this book listing with page numbers whenever I cite something from it):

Richard Burridge, *What are the Gospels?*, 3d ed. (Waco: Baylor University Press, 2020). (Burridge, *Gospels*)

Matthew Croasmun, Miroslav Volf, *The Hunger for Home: Food and Meals in the Gospel of Luke* (Waco, Texas: Baylor University Press, 2022). (Croasmun-Volf, *Hunger for Home*)

Stephanie Buckhanon Crowder, "Luke" in *True to Our Native Land*. (Crowder, "Luke")

Justo González, *Luke* (Louisville: Westminster John Knox, 2010). (González, *Luke*)

Justo González, *The Story Luke Tells: Luke's Unique Witness to the Gospel* (Grand Rapids: Wm. B. Eerdmans, 2015). (González, *The Story Luke Tells*)

Joel B. Green, *The Gospel of Luke* (Grand Rapids: Wm. B. Eerdmans, 1997). (Green, *Luke*)

F. Scott Spencer, *Luke* (Grand Rapids: Wm. B. Eerdmans, 2019). (Spencer, *Luke*)

Ben Witherington III and Amy-Jill Levine, *The Gospel of Luke* (Cambridge: Cambridge University Press, 2018). (Levine-Witherington, *Luke*)

REDEMPTION WRITING

Luke 1:1–4

[1] Many have undertaken to draw up an account of the things that have been fulfilled among us, [2] just as they were handed down to us by those who from the first were eyewitnesses and servants of the word. [3] With this in mind, since I myself have carefully investigated everything from the beginning, I too decided to write an orderly account for you, most excellent Theophilus, [4] so that you may know the certainty of the things you have been taught.

This most elegant sentence sounds like the prefaces of other noteworthy histories in the Greco-Roman world. The introduction functioned as the inside flyleaf on a dust-jacket. Luke's first four verses are only one sentence in Greek. The aim of these four verses was to attract the attention of all who heard it being read.

Several features of this preface stand out:

First, Luke acknowledges that "many people" have written up "accounts" about the life of Jesus, the Gospel of Mark being one that Luke knew. Second, those "events" (or "matters") were part of Israel's story now "fulfilled among us" in the life, death, resurrection, and ascension of Jesus. Third, the accounts wrote up what could be learned from "eyewitness reports." One can imagine an evening dinner among such Christians concluding with story time that began with, "Can anyone tell us something they remember Jesus saying or doing?" By the time Luke wrote his Gospel those reports were "circulating." These eyewitnesses became witnesses to the saving significance of Jesus in their storytelling. Luke describes them with another expression that is strangely translated in the NIV, which has "handed down to us" (1:2). This is more accurately translated as "servants of the word." Yes, they were early disciples, but their discipleship here is one of witnessing about Jesus and becoming agents of the gospel by speaking about Jesus.

Fourth, Luke, as a professional historian "carefully investigated everything" that shows up in this Gospel. Such language not only connects Luke to other historians, but he also makes a claim to have done his homework. His investigation now completed, he wrote "an accurate account." This expression could be translated "orderly" or "sequentially ordered" narrative. It suggests that other accounts were disorganized or, more accurately, below Luke's research standards. Fifth, Luke wrote the Gospel and Acts of the Apostles for someone with the name "Theophilus," which means "one who loves God." This, then, could be the patron who funded Luke's work, or it could be a man named Theophilus, or it could be a moniker for what a Christian should be: a lover of God. He adds "most honorable" to this person's status.

Noticeably, and finishing off this beautiful sentence, Luke wrote the Gospel (and Acts) so his reader could be "certain of the truth" of what the person learned in his catechism classes (the Greek term for "taught" is *katēchizō*). Luke composes a persuasive and sequentially ordered story about Jesus that reveals how he has fulfilled the story of Israel so his reader(s) can be assured of what they know about Jesus and the gospel.

Luke's account is a biography according to ancient standards. This biography, however, tells the gospel so that we can now say that the gospel is the biography of Jesus.

Questions for Reflection and Application

1. Why did Luke write his Gospel?

2. How did Luke go about this work?

3. Which theory about the identity of Theophilus do you think is correct?

4. If you were to write a biography of Jesus, how would you approach it, and what would you focus on?

5. What do you hope undertaking this study will do for you?

TWO REDEMPTION WITNESSES

Luke 1:5–25

[5] *In the time of Herod king of Judea there was a priest named*
Zechariah, who belonged to the priestly division of Abijah; his wife
Elizabeth was also a descendant of Aaron. [6] *Both of them were righ-*
teous in the sight of God, observing all the Lord's commands and
decrees blamelessly. [7] *But they were childless because Elizabeth was*
not able to conceive, and they were both very old.

[8] *Once when Zechariah's division was on duty and he was*
serving as priest before God, [9] *he was chosen by lot, according to*
the custom of the priesthood, to go into the temple of the Lord and
burn incense. [10] *And when the time for the burning of incense came,*
all the assembled worshipers were praying outside.

[11] *Then an angel of the Lord appeared to him, standing at the*
right side of the altar of incense. [12] *When Zechariah saw him, he*
was startled and was gripped with fear. [13] *But the angel said to him:*
"Do not be afraid, Zechariah; your prayer has been heard. Your
wife Elizabeth will bear you a son, and you are to call him John.
[14] *He will be a joy and delight to you, and many will rejoice because*
of his birth, [15] *for he will be great in the sight of the Lord. He is never*
to take wine or other fermented drink, and he will be filled with the
Holy Spirit even before he is born. [16] *He will bring back many of the*

people of Israel to the Lord their God. 17 And he will go on before the Lord, in the spirit and power of Elijah, to turn the hearts of the parents to their children and the disobedient to the wisdom of the righteous—to make ready a people prepared for the Lord."

18 Zechariah asked the angel, "How can I be sure of this? I am an old man and my wife is well along in years."

19 The angel said to him, "I am Gabriel. I stand in the presence of God, and I have been sent to speak to you and to tell you this good news. 20 And now you will be silent and not able to speak until the day this happens, because you did not believe my words, which will come true at their appointed time."

21 Meanwhile, the people were waiting for Zechariah and wondering why he stayed so long in the temple. 22 When he came out, he could not speak to them. They realized he had seen a vision in the temple, for he kept making signs to them but remained unable to speak.

23 When his time of service was completed, he returned home. 24 After this his wife Elizabeth became pregnant and for five months remained in seclusion. 25 "The Lord has done this for me," she said. "In these days he has shown his favor and taken away my disgrace among the people."

Stories of our families shape our families so much one can say the family is a story.

Behind Jesus was his mother, Mary. Behind Jesus was also a witness we call John the Baptist. Behind that witness were John's parents, Zechariah the priest and Elizabeth his wife. The events described in this passage—Zechariah's time to serve in the temple, the appearing of an angel (and they are not cute little pudgy cherubs) to him about the pregnancy of his "very old" (1:7) wife, the nature of the son she would birth, the seemingly innocent but evidently doubt-expressing question Zechariah asked, his divine silencing, and the words of gratitude for her pregnancy by Elizabeth—must have been told as a threaded story around the table in their home. That story shaped John, shaped Mary, shaped Jesus, and has now shaped how Christians tell the story of God's redemption in the Lord Jesus.

Events, not just words, can rhyme. To listen to the stories of Zechariah and Elizabeth, and then to listen to the stories of Jesus and Mary, is to hear their rhyming.

A Temple Story

The inner temple formed the center of the temple, which formed the center of Jerusalem, which formed the center of Israel. In the very center of Israel's holiest place, a fresh redemption for Israel began. Criticism of the temple is not to be found in this text. In fact, the sanctity of the temple is contrasted with the faith failure of a priest. Jesus will be dedicated in the temple; the elderly Anna and Simeon will declare the identity of Jesus in the temple area; and Jesus will return to the temple at twelve. All these events are found in chapters one and two of Luke.

The time is set: Herod (the Great) is king. The location and the family are holy: Zechariah is a priest, which means in the line of Aaron, in the specific family of Abijah (see 1 Chronicles 24:1–20), and his wife is in the family of Aaron, too. They married inside the order. They were "righteous," which means they knew the Torah and observed it faithfully. It does not mean they were sinless (1:6). They were childless and now beyond the age of giving birth (1:7). One hears echoes in this story about Elizabeth with other childless women: Sarah (Genesis 18:9–15), Rebekah (25:21), Rachel (30:22–24), and Hannah (1 Samuel 1).

A priest worked in the temple two weeks a year, but this year was different. As the lot fell to Zechariah to burn incense in the temple "all the assembled worshipers were praying outside" in the temple courts (1:9–10). Such a luck of the lot was a lifetime experience itself, but he got more than that: he encountered "an angel of the Lord" and responded as most would—it scared him in an overwhelming sense. Angels appear in the Bible especially at history-altering moments, and often enough people respond in fear (1:29; 24:38). Angels in the Bible are powerful spiritual beings that evoke fear—not charm.

God sent this angel to Zechariah to reveal a miracle baby who has a special redemptive mission (1:11–17). What is revealed? (1) His prayer for a baby has been heard; (2) the baby will be a son he is to name "John" (Yohanan in Hebrew); (3) he will be a "joy and delight to you" and to "many"'; (4) he will be "great in the sight of the Lord," which indicates the significance of God's vocation for John; (5) he will abstain from alcohol (cf. Leviticus 10:9; Numbers 6:3) and, even before his birth, (6) "he will be filled with the Holy Spirit." The angel's not done: he will (7) lead many to convert back to the Lord (cf. Malachi 3:1), (8) he will carry on in this conversion mission in a way that reminds of Elijah, and the angel sums this up as a twofold conversion—turning parents to their children and the disobedient "to the wisdom of the righteous" (cf. Malachi 4:5–6). All this suggests a people wandering from God in need of turning back to God, and the angel sums it all up with (9) "to make ready a people prepared for the Lord."

Very few parents get such a complete job description for their son, but one has to wonder how many would respond as Zechariah did.

A Trust Story

The revelation of John's mission provokes Zechariah to ask for proof, which drops him into a story about trust. And perhaps too into a lack of concern for the body that mattered most here: Elizabeth's! No sooner had the words spilled from his lips than the angel identifies himself as Gabriel (most angels were males in the Jewish tradition), and then reveals the good news about the birth of a son, and then all of a sudden moves from nice guy to tough guy: "you will be silent," Gabriel tells him. Why? Because Zechariah "did not believe" (1:19–20).

This all seems a bit harsh, but there is a family history at work in a moment like this. God had often challenged Israel's leaders to trust (think of Abraham, think of Sarah). But an angel appearing in the inner court of the temple, an angel speaking to Zechariah, and an angel informing him about a miracle baby should have been enough for the priest to take a big gulp of air and say, "OK, Lord, you know what you're doing."

Trusting someone requires a history of trustworthiness of the person making a claim, in this case an angel; it requires listening to the words that are promised or uttered; it entails believing their truthfulness; and it finds completion only in acting upon those words as reliable. In acting, one learns the transforming power of trusting. Faith entails risk if the words are not true.

A Miracle Story

Zechariah returned to his home in the hill country of Judea (cf. 1:39), Elizabeth conceived and "remained in seclusion" for almost half a year (1:23–24). We don't know why this occurred, but it does mean her first interaction is with Mary, whose story begins in our next passage. Elizabeth's trusting witness contrasts with her husband's, who doubted. God has shown her "favor," she confesses, and has "taken away" the common "disgrace" of childlessness (1:25). The miracle here is a menopausal woman conceives by the power of God.

Questions for Reflection and Application

1. What does McKnight mean when he says stories can rhyme?

2. How does Zechariah's response compare with Elizabeth's?

3. Why is Zechariah disciplined for not trusting but Mary is not (cf. 1:29, 34)?

4. What stands out to you most about the miraculous plan for John's life?

5. What stories does your family tell about itself?

REDEMPTION STORY

Luke 1:26–38

26 In the sixth month of Elizabeth's pregnancy, God sent the angel Gabriel to Nazareth, a town in Galilee, 27 to a virgin pledged to be married to a man named Joseph, a descendant of David. The virgin's name was Mary. 28 The angel went to her and said, "Greetings, you who are highly favored! The Lord is with you."

29 Mary was greatly troubled at his words and wondered what kind of greeting this might be. 30 But the angel said to her, "Do not be afraid, Mary; you have found favor with God. 31 You will conceive and give birth to a son, and you are to call him Jesus. 32 He will be great and will be called the Son of the Most High. The Lord God will give him the throne of his father David, 33 and he will reign over Jacob's descendants forever; his kingdom will never end."

34 "How will this be," Mary asked the angel, "since I am a virgin?"

35 The angel answered, "The Holy Spirit will come on you, and the power of the Most High will overshadow you. So the holy one to be born will be called the Son of God. 36 Even Elizabeth your relative is going to have a child in her old age, and she who was said to be unable to conceive is in her sixth month. 37 For no word from God will ever fail."

38 "I am the Lord's servant," Mary answered. "May your word to me be fulfilled." Then the angel left her.

Have you ever wondered how much Mary told Jesus about events like these? Have you ever wondered how we got such stories? I have. My answer to the first question is "Quite often, probably," and the second one is, "From Mary" (McKnight, *Real Mary*). By the way, "Mary" translates *Mariam*.

A Baby Son Story

Six months behind the Zechariah and Elizabeth story about redemption, the story of redemption continues with Mary of Galilee. The stories rhyme. Same angel (Gabriel), different location (Nazareth of Galilee), and a different woman (Mary), who is engaged to a Davidic ancestor named Joseph (1:26–27). Same message of redemption. Mary was probably fifteen to twenty years old. The angel greets her with "Rejoice" (NIVhas "Greetings") but then affirms her with words from the deep wells of God's grace: "you who are highly favored," with the sense of "you have been deeply graced" because in some special sense "The Lord is with you" (1:28). Her disturbance at the appearing of an angel is like Zechariah's (1:12).

This joy, grace, and the divine presence will take on physical form when she gives "birth to a son" (1:31), and she (notice that the father is not told this) is to name him "Jesus," which in Hebrew is either *Yeshu* or *Yeshua*, which means YHWH redeems or saves. What she learns next starts slow and builds. The son will be "great," and he will be called "Son of the Most High God," and he will rule on "the throne of his father David," and his rule and kingdom will be "forever" and will "never end"! Mary knows her son will save Israel as its king, and he will rule an eternal kingdom (1:31–33). (In what follows the word "kingdom" will be used frequently, and a brief description of the five elements of kingdom can be found at 9:1–17, pp. 142.)

A Miraculous Conception Story

Mary's question is neither naïve nor doubting. Yes, she was disturbed by the angelical vision (1:28), but the implication of her question, "How will this be since I am a virgin?" (1:34), requires that we think she perceives an imminent pregnancy before marriage and consummation. The answer to her question occurs in 1:35–37. If God can become human (John 1:1–14), God can miraculously impregnate. "The one miracle greater than that of a postmenopausal woman conceiving is that of a virgin conceiving" (Levine-Witherington, *Luke*, 33). Yet Mary knows her body is hers. "This is her body, and she would like to know how it is going to be used" (Spencer, *Luke*, 42).

The angel explains the divine impregnation of Mary as "the Holy Spirit will come upon you" and the "Most High will overshadow you" (1:35). God envelops Mary as miracle and protection (Spencer, *Luke*, 39–40). Mary's pregnancy before her marriage to Joseph surely raised questions in her social circles (notice Mark 6:3's "Mary's son" and not Joseph's), so this account in Luke probably counters accusations. The act of God in Mary results in "the Son of God" (Luke 1:35). Son of God was a common enough term for the Roman emperor and for a king in Israel (Psalm 2).

The angel sweeps any doubt away by revealing to Mary that she has company in the births of redemption. Her relative Elizabeth has experienced a similar miracle (Luke 1:36).

A Trust Story

Mary's words are some of the most profound in the entire Bible. First, she identifies herself, and I translate: "Look! God's slave." The "I am" can be applied but she may have looked into the eyes of Gabriel to say, "Look at me. What more do you want? I'm God's slave, and I will do what God wants." She signs off with, and again I paraphrase, "May it be to me in a manner consistent with your word that I will conceive as a virgin by an act of God" (1:38). This is no passive surrender; this is an active acceptance of God's redemption through her baby boy. Let us think realistically: a woman pregnant before marriage was scrutinized and judged, her engaged partner, Joseph, shamed as well. Mary will suffer for her son before her son suffers for her. She knows what her future will look like, and she accepts it because she aches for God's holistic redemption.

Mission accomplished; the angel returns to the throne room of God.

Scott Spencer expresses this so completely I record his words here and ask you to ponder them: "Mysteriously, but materially, Mary's entire embodied being, not least her amniotic waters, will be swept up and over in the dynamic crosswinds of trinitarian vitality" (Spencer, *Luke*, 40). Just wow.

These small vignettes in Luke 1–2 began as family stories. Mary was at times the only source of information for these stories. She becomes the witness behind the redeemer who informed the redeemer what the angel had revealed about the mission of Jesus to redeem Israel as its king. Galileans were known storytellers.

Mary was perhaps the best storyteller of all, that is, after her son.

Questions for Reflection and Application

1. How does the conception announcement of Jesus "rhyme" with the conception announcement of John?

2. What have you been taught about Mary before? How does this section challenge or confirm your prior understanding?

3. How do you think Luke may have gathered Mary's reminiscences in his research?

4. How do you think Mary's storytelling might have impacted Jesus as he was growing up?

5. What can you learn from Mary's example in responding to God's invitation?

FOR FURTHER READING

Scot McKnight, *The Real Mary: Why Protestant Christians Can Embrace the Mother of Jesus* (Brewster, Mass.: Paraclete, 2016).

REDEMPTION SONG

Luke 1:39–56

39 At that time Mary got ready and hurried to a town in the hill
country of Judea, 40 where she entered Zechariah's home and greet-
ed Elizabeth. 41 When Elizabeth heard Mary's greeting, the baby
leaped in her womb, and Elizabeth was filled with the Holy Spirit.
42 In a loud voice she exclaimed: "Blessed are you among women,
and blessed is the child you will bear! 43 But why am I so favored,
that the mother of my Lord should come to me? 44 As soon as the
sound of your greeting reached my ears, the baby in my womb
leaped for joy. 45 Blessed is she who has believed that the Lord
would fulfill his promises to her!"

46 And Mary said:

"My soul glorifies the Lord
47 and my spirit rejoices in God my Savior,
48 for he has been mindful
of the humble state of his servant.
From now on all generations will call me blessed,
49 for the Mighty One has done great things for me—
holy is his name.
50 His mercy extends to those who fear him,
from generation to generation.
51 He has performed mighty deeds with his arm;

he has scattered those who are proud in their inmost
thoughts.
[52] *He has brought down rulers from their thrones*
but has lifted up the humble.
[53] *He has filled the hungry with good things*
but has sent the rich away empty.
[54] *He has helped his servant Israel,*
remembering to be merciful
[55] *to Abraham and his descendants forever,*
just as he promised our ancestors."

[56] *Mary stayed with Elizabeth for about three months and then returned home.*

I like to imagine Mary singing her special song about her special son when she looked into his eyes, nursed him, clothed him, changed him, and taught him to talk, pray, and sing. After all, there are echoes of this song in Jesus' special prayer, which we call "The Lord's Prayer." Her song is called the Magnificat because the Latin version begins with *Magnificat* ("magnifies"; the NIV has "glorifies"). Dietrich Bonhoeffer, in 1933, described this song as "the most passionate, the wildest, and one might almost say the most revolutionary Advent hymn that has ever been sung" (*Collected Sermons* 1.116).

The Occasion for the Song

Upon Mary's greeting the family in the muted Zechariah's home, some two days journey south from the Galilee, John the Baptist leaped in Elizabeth's womb, which was the palpable experience of being "filled with the Holy Spirit" (1:41).

So inspired, Elizabeth uttered a triple blessing on Mary in words famous now among Roman Catholics: "Blessed are you among women, and blessed is the child you will bear! But why am I so favored, that the mother of my Lord should come to me? As soon as the sound of your greeting reached my ears, the baby in my womb leaped for joy. Blessed is she who has believed that the Lord would fulfill his promises to her!" (1:45).

Mary is the one blessed here and is called "the mother of my Lord" (1:43). Her focus aside, the narrative begins to shift our attention away from the miracle baby John to the virginally conceived baby Jesus, and it also shifts our minds from the significance of John to the superior significance of Jesus.

We can speculate about why Mary "hurried" to the hills of Judea but that's all it is: speculation. Scandal shows no hints here, though eventually some would set rumors loose. Justo González, a wonderful theologian and historian, wonders if Mary didn't hurry to be with Elizbeth out of "solidarity" (González, *Luke,* 22).

A Song for the Son of Redemption

Mary's song evokes dozens of lines and terms from Israel's Scriptures, and you might look some up in your study Bible's cross references. Especially Hannah's song in 1 Samuel 2:1–10. There are so many echoes of Bible passages we are stunned by the depth and richness of Mary's grasp of the Bible's redemption story. In fact, Mary's song expresses the heart of the gospel. As Barbara Brown Taylor once said, "The church's central task is an imaginative one. By that I do not mean a fanciful or fictional task, but one in which the human capacity to imagine—to form mental pictures of the self, the neighbor, the world, the future, to envision new realities—is both engaged and transformed." Some pages later she connected such an imagination to faith in these words: "In faith, we imagine ourselves whole, imagine ourselves in love with our neighbors, imagine ourselves bathed and fed by God, imagine the creation at peace, imagine the breath of God coinciding with our own, imagine the heart of God beating at the heart of the world" (Taylor, *The Preaching Life*, 41, 53). Mary's faith produced Mary's imagination, and her imagination fed her faith.

This woman of faith's song begins with a personal witness, and her witness evokes the emotion of relief through vindication: "My soul" and "my spirit" and "his servant" and "call me blessed" (ignored by most Protestants) and "for me." A slight shift happens in verse fifty when we read, "to those who fear him," but this too is about Mary's own experience of awe before her God.

Following her personal testimony of God answering her prayers for the redemption of her people, Mary's song suddenly turns into metaphors for God's redemption. Each of the metaphors invites our imaginations to consider the redemption God works in Jesus from different angles. Here they are: "performed mighty deeds" and "scattered those who are proud" and "brought down rulers" and "lifted up the humble [or poor]" and "filled the hungry" and "sent the rich away empty" and "helped his servant Israel" according to the Abrahamic promise.

We must pause to adjust our vision (McKnight, *Real Mary*, 15–24). We have been enculturated to think of redemption as both (almost exclusively) individual and (almost entirely) spiritual. Not for Mary. Notice how physical and political and national and social her sense of redemption is. Rulers dethroned, the poor enthroned, the hungry filled with food, and the rich sent packing. This is a "political manifesto" (Levine-Witherington, *Luke*, 42), a prediction of a great reversal in redemption. I was once told that during a particularly turbulent time, a South American country banned Roman Catholics from singing this song. It features daily in the monastery life. So politically threatening was the imagination of this song it was banned! Have we tamed it? (The answer is "Yes.")

All these fulfill the promise to Abraham. Just open your Bibles to watch these redemptive blessings reverberate when John himself preaches (3:7–14), when Jesus preaches (4:16–30) and then explains himself to John (7:18–23), all of which will come to fruition in Luke's second book, Acts (2:42–47; 4:32–35).

It took courage to sing this song. Again, Bonhoeffer says it right: "This is not the gentle, tender, dreamy Mary as we often seen her portrayed in paintings. . . . [she is] passionate, carried away, proud, enthusiastic." Her song is a "hard, strong, relentless hymn about the toppling of thrones and the humiliation of the lords of this world, about the power of God and the powerfulness of humankind" (*Collected Sermons*, 116). Her first Christmas is unlike any other, and it is radically different from ours.

This courageous woman's song about the son of redemption is a song about holistic redemption. Only a holistic redemption fits the pattern of Scripture's expectations for the messianic kingdom. And here's the foundation of it all: Mary's song is about her son, Jesus, the Son of God, the Son of the Most High, the messiah, and the Lord. He is the one who brings this redemption. This redemption cannot be reduced to ethics, morality, or even what we call social justice. Its foundation is a Person, and in that Person holistic redemption explodes into living realities.

Questions for Reflection and Application

1. How does the Mary depicted in this section compare to the Mary often depicted in Christian art, especially around Christmas?

2. What are the tangible, political, holistic themes in Mary's song?

3. Look up Hannah's song in 1 Samuel 2:1–10. What parallels (or "rhymes") do you see with Mary's song?

4. What words in this passage describe God? Compare this song to Psalm 136. What similarities do you find?

5. What emotions do you notice in this narrative and particularly in the Magnificat?

FOR FURTHER READING

Dietrich Bonhoeffer, *The Collected Sermons of Dietrich Bonhoeffer* (ed. Isabel Best; Minneapolis: Fortress, 2012).

Scot McKnight, *The Real Mary: Why Protestant Christians Can Embrace the Mother of Jesus* (Brewster, Mass.: Paraclete, 2016).

Barbara Brown Taylor, *The Preaching Life* (Lanham, Maryland: Cowley, 1993).

REDEMPTION WITNESSES, AGAIN

Luke 1:57–80

57 When it was time for Elizabeth to have her baby, she gave birth
to a son. 58 Her neighbors and relatives heard that the Lord had
shown her great mercy, and they shared her joy.

59 On the eighth day they came to circumcise the child, and
they were going to name him after his father Zechariah, 60 but his
mother spoke up and said, "No! He is to be called John." 61 They
said to her, "There is no one among your relatives who has that
name." 62 Then they made signs to his father, to find out what he
would like to name the child. 63 He asked for a writing tablet, and
to everyone's astonishment he wrote, "His name is John."

64 Immediately his mouth was opened and his tongue set free,
and he began to speak, praising God. 65 All the neighbors were
filled with awe, and throughout the hill country of Judea people
were talking about all these things. 66 Everyone who heard this won-
dered about it, asking, "What then is this child going to be?" For the
Lord's hand was with him.

67 His father Zechariah was filled with the Holy Spirit and
prophesied:

68 *"Praise be to the Lord, the God of Israel,*
because he has come to his people and
redeemed them.
69 *He has raised up a horn of salvation for us*
in the house of his servant David
70 *(as he said through his holy prophets of long ago),*
71 *salvation from our enemies*
and from the hand of all who hate us—
72 *to show mercy to our ancestors*
and to remember his holy covenant,
73 *the oath he swore to our father Abraham:*
74 *to rescue us from the hand of our enemies,*
and to enable us to serve him without fear
75 *in holiness and righteousness before him all our days.*
76 *And you, my child, will be called a prophet of the*
Most High;
for you will go on before the Lord to prepare the way
for him,
77 *to give his people the knowledge of salvation*
through the forgiveness of their sins,
78 *because of the tender mercy of our God,*
by which the rising sun will come to us from heaven
79 *to shine on those living in darkness*
and in the shadow of death,
to guide our feet into the path of peace."

80 *And the child grew and became strong in spirit; and he lived*
in the wilderness until he appeared publicly to Israel.

Luke's Gospel shifts from John to Jesus. Readers and hearers notice how their stories rhyme with one another. In this text we get the birth of John, the naming of John, and a redemption song about John. In the next chapter we will read about the birth of Jesus, the naming of Jesus, and then even more redemptive songs about Jesus. These songs, marked off in the NIV as poetry, are some of the most powerful articulations of holistic redemption in the whole Bible.

A reminder: Luke is a biography about Jesus. It is about us when the Gospel of Luke presents teachings of Jesus about discipleship. But when the stories are about Jesus, or in this passage about the forerunner to Jesus, we read most faithfully when we keep our attention on him (and off ourselves). If we are asking "What's in this passage for me?" we might be asking the wrong question.

The Son

The baby Baptist boy is born to the (previously) barren Elizabeth, which immediately leads to his circumcision as the covenant entrance into Israel (1:57–59; cf. Genesis 17:11–12). This is the earliest record of naming a son at his circumcision, though it is common in later rabbinic texts (Levine-Witherington, *Luke*, 43). Children were often named after a close relative, but what stands out here is the choice of the name "John" (or *Yohanan*, which means "God has shown his favor"), and we should assume that Zechariah had communicated this to Elizabeth before her insistence (1:60–61). Neighbors and family resisted naming the son "John," so God restored Zechariah's voice, and he confirmed his wife's naming the boy "John." The ending of his muted voice impressed neighbors in a way that they perceived this son was going to be someone special (1:62–66). Noticeably, John does not follow in the footsteps of his father as a priest but becomes a prophet of the Messiah.

The Song

Like Mary's Magnificat, this song has a name, too: Benedictus (again, too, because the first word in the Latin version is *benedictus*). In Mary's visit it is Elizabeth who was filled with the Spirit (1:41). Now Zechariah is both "filled with the Holy Spirit and prophesied" (1:67). Prophesy means to utter God-revealed, Spirit-prompted speech for the people of God.

The theme for his song is God's redemption in all its dimensions. Notice, too, that he prophesies in the past tense (as did Mary): "he has come . . . and redeemed them" and "he has raised up a horn of salvation" and that is "salvation from our enemies and from the hand of all those who hate us" and this means "to show mercy and to remember his holy covenant." It goes on to "rescue us from . . . enemies" and "to enable us to serve him without fear" of those enemies. Notice here the holistic element of liberation (cf. Psalm 18:2–3). Justo González calls Luke's presentation of holistic redemption the "great reversal" (González, *The Story Luke Tells*, 29–44).

Only after he has given a full sketch of holistic redemption does Zechariah prophesy about his son. He prophesies that he will be a "prophet of the Most High" (Luke 1:76)—as the Most High came upon Mary (1:35)—and John will "prepare the way for" the Lord (1:76). He, too, will preach a redemptive, educational message: "knowledge of salvation through the forgiveness of their sins" (1:77). When one connects forgiveness, the people of God, and a prophet to come, the forgiveness is holistic too: not just personal but corporate and national (Jeremiah 31:31–34; 33:6–9, 11). This merciful redemption will lead, as well, "into the path of peace" (Luke 1:79). What Zechariah did not know was that this son of redemption of his would be decapitated, as the one to whom he pointed would be crucified.

The fitting end to the song's prophetic words about the son describe John growing and becoming "strong in spirit/ Spirit" and living "in the wilderness until he appeared publicly to Israel" (1:80). Luke has John where he wants him: in the wilderness, being made ready to announce the arrival of the One to come. As Scott Spencer reminds us, "John will not spring from Elizabeth fully formed and ready to reform Israel. He must grow into his Spirit-anointed vocation through rigorous Nazirite discipline." That is, "Spirit-dynamism and self-discipline go hand in hand" (Spencer, *Luke*, 62).

Questions for Reflection and Application

1. How do the naming and vocation of John go against cultural conventions and expectations?

2. How does Zechariah paint a picture of holistic liberation and redemption with his song?

3. What Old Testament passages and themes come to mind as you read the Benedictus?

4. How does prophecy function in this passage?

5. What do you learn about John, the forerunner of Jesus, in this passage?

REDEMPTION'S SON

Luke 2:1–20

[1] In those days Caesar Augustus issued a decree that a census should be taken of the entire Roman world. [2] (This was the first census that took place while Quirinius was governor of Syria.) [3] And everyone went to their own town to register.

[4] So Joseph also went up from the town of Nazareth in Galilee to Judea, to Bethlehem the town of David, because he belonged to the house and line of David. [5] He went there to register with Mary, who was pledged to be married to him and was expecting a child. [6] While they were there, the time came for the baby to be born, [7] and she gave birth to her firstborn, a son. She wrapped him in cloths and placed him in a manger, because there was no guest room available for them.

[8] And there were shepherds living out in the fields nearby, keeping watch over their flocks at night. [9] An angel of the Lord appeared to them, and the glory of the Lord shone around them, and they were terrified. [10] But the angel said to them, "Do not be afraid. I bring you good news that will cause great joy for all the people. [11] Today in the town of David a Savior has been born to you; he is the Messiah, the Lord. [12] This will be a sign to you: You will find a baby wrapped in cloths and lying in a manger."

[13] Suddenly a great company of the heavenly host appeared with the angel, praising God and saying,

[14] "Glory to God in the highest heaven,
and on earth peace to those on whom his favor rests."

[15] When the angels had left them and gone into heaven, the shepherds said to one another, "Let's go to Bethlehem and see this thing that has happened, which the Lord has told us about."

[16] So they hurried off and found Mary and Joseph, and the
baby, who was lying in the manger. [17] When they had seen him,
they spread the word concerning what had been told them about
this child, [18] and all who heard it were amazed at what the shep-
herds said to them.

[19] But Mary treasured up all these things and pondered them in
her heart. [20] The shepherds returned, glorifying and praising God
for all the things they had heard and seen, which were just as they
had been told.

This is the Christmas story many of us hear at a Christmas service or read on Christmas Day. It deserves to be read aloud with skill. I love to hear this text read. The birth of Jesus, as we have said a few times, rhymes with the story of John's birth, and we do a real disservice if we fail to read this passage slowly and thoughtfully. Let's not get ahead of ourselves by wondering what it means for us. It's a story about Jesus.

From Nazareth to Bethlehem

The opening verses of chapter two connect the birth of Jesus, who is Messiah (and Messiah means king and king means emperor), to Rome's current emperor, Augustus. The birth of Jesus is part of world, not just local, history. This more than suggests that the emperor is one of the rulers who will be brought down by the birth of king Jesus (1:52).[1]

Standing right behind the emperor theme is a taxation theme. Taxation filled the vaults of the powers that be. The names in 2:1–3, then, are oppressors, and those who suffer the most are the poor—like Joseph and Mary.

In submission to emperor and taxation, Joseph and Mary travel to Bethlehem where, ironically, Jesus' birth fulfills a messianic hope and promise. King David, who was everyone's image of a future Messiah, was from Bethlehem (2:4; see Micah 5:2). Surprising to many of us, Jesus' birth occurs before Joseph and Mary are officially married: "Mary, who was pledged to be married to him" (Luke 2:5).

The KJV's "no room in the inn" line, which has a history of all sorts of speculation in sermons, inaccurately translates the Greek term *kataluma*. That term does not mean "inn" as in a hotel but "guest room" in the very home in which they were staying. That is, the guest room did not have sufficient space for a birth, so Mary and Joseph went downstairs to the stable where they could find some privacy, where the animals were kept, and she laid her son in a feeding trough. There is no reason whatsoever to criticize some non-existent innkeeper or pretend this had something to do with a woman's impurity.

The Gospel of the Angel

Bethlehem was known for its sheep and shepherds. To some shepherds an unnamed angel of the Lord appears accompanied by splendorous light, something that evokes the presence of God so overwhelming the shepherds were "terrified" (2:8–9). The angel gospels the shepherds. Here are the big terms to consider: "I *gospel great joy*, what will be for *all* the people (my translation), that a *Savior* has been born today who is *Messiah the Lord*, in the *City of David*" (2:10–11). You can't really get a better heavenly message than that and, truth be told, you can't be any more overt about some kind of message to Rome, that is, to Augustus. Or about fulfilling promises (cf. Isaiah 9:6). These terms express the holistic redemption of the kingdom of God. The "sign" is now explained—in Bethlehem they'll find a baby "lying in a manger" (2:12).

Because of the Christmas gospel God should be praised, that is, because "on earth" God has given his Messiah-Son to bring "peace to those on whom his favor rests" (2:14). Again, we need to resist turning this "peace" into exclusively inner, personal peace. Peace is an earthy, social contagion propagated by redemption and justice.

Mary Pondering

So the shepherds come into Bethlehem and find it just as the angel said, turning them into gospeling shepherds. They find the baby with Joseph and Mary. The history of art about Mary is that she's a pensive, pious, even poker-faced young woman draped in blue and white. She was not. That image derives in part from "treasured up all these things and pondered them in her heart" (2:19). Mary was interpreting, tossing together, or puzzling this specific shepherd-event in light of the previous angel's messages to her and to Elizabeth. One thing was clear: her son was destined to become the King of Israel, the Messiah. A lot was going on, more than a mind could handle.

World history indeed!

I close with an amazing statement that takes us to the deepest level of the Christmas story–God became human for us: "Through the Son, the invisible God is made visible. Through the Son, the unknowable God is made known. Through the Son, the incomprehensible love of God is made tangible" (Strawbridge, Mercer, Groves, *Love Makes No Sense,* 18).

Questions for Reflection and Application

1. How does this section challenge ideas you have heard about the nativity story in the past?

2. What are the holistic, earthy implications of this baby king's birth?

3. How do the shepherds' reactions to the angels compare to Zechariah and Mary's angelic responses?

4. Have you thought of this text as a "gospeling" passage before? Why or why not?

5. What do you learn about Jesus in this passage?

FOR FURTHER READING

Jennifer Strawbridge, Jarred Mercer, Peter Groves, *Love Makes No Sense: An Invitation to Christian Theology* (London: SCM, 2019).

TWO MORE REDEMPTION WITNESSES

Luke 2:21–39

*21 On the eighth day, when it was time to circumcise the child, he
was named Jesus, the name the angel had given him before he was
conceived. 22 When the time came for the purification rites required
by the Law of Moses, Joseph and Mary took him to Jerusalem to
present him to the Lord 23 (as it is written in the Law of the Lord,
"Every firstborn male is to be consecrated to the Lord"), 24 and to
offer a sacrifice in keeping with what is said in the Law of the Lord:
"a pair of doves or two young pigeons."*

*25 Now there was a man in Jerusalem called Simeon, who was
righteous and devout. He was waiting for the consolation of Israel,
and the Holy Spirit was on him. 26 It had been revealed to him by
the Holy Spirit that he would not die before he had seen the Lord's
Messiah. 27 Moved by the Spirit, he went into the temple courts.
When the parents brought in the child Jesus to do for him what the
custom of the Law required, 28 Simeon took him in his arms and
praised God, saying:*

> *29 "Sovereign Lord, as you have promised,*
> *you may now dismiss your servant in peace.*

30 For my eyes have seen your salvation,
31 which you have prepared in the sight of all
nations:
32 a light for revelation to the Gentiles,
and the glory of your people Israel."

33 The child's father and mother marveled at what was said
about him. 34 Then Simeon blessed them and said to Mary, his
mother: "This child is destined to cause the falling and rising of
many in Israel, and to be a sign that will be spoken against, 35 so
that the thoughts of many hearts will be revealed. And a sword will
pierce your own soul too."
36 There was also a prophet, Anna, the daughter of Penuel, of
the tribe of Asher. She was very old; she had lived with her hus-
band seven years after her marriage, 37 and then was a widow until
she was eighty-four. She never left the temple but worshiped night
and day, fasting and praying. 38 Coming up to them at that very
moment, she gave thanks to God and spoke about the child to all
who were looking forward to the redemption of Jerusalem.
39 When Joseph and Mary had done everything required by
the Law of the Lord, they returned to Galilee to their own town of
Nazareth.

Joseph and Mary were observant Jews and, like most, knew how to usher Jesus into a life as an observant covenant son. First, on the eighth day he had to be circumcised (2:21), and second, thirty-two days later Mary needed to be purified[1] (not from sin, Leviticus 12:2–6), and third, along with that, Jesus could be presented (like Samuel, 1 Samuel 2:24; also Exodus 12; 13:11–15) in the temple with an offering (2:22–24). Everything sounds so observant until two senior citizens interrupt Joseph and Mary's temple worship with Spirit-prompted words.

Simeon and Anna are two of my favorite characters. One of them turned into an indelible tune for me when Michael Card wrote his beautiful song about Simeon ("Now That I've Held Him in My Arms"). Each in their own way, prompted by the Spirit that was at work in Mary, Elizabeth, and Zechariah, witness to redemption in Jesus.

Each of these two gendered word-witnesses can be shaped by one word. Both words, however, need some spelling out, but remember that both words are about what Jesus will accomplish.

Simeon's Word of Witness: Consolation

Luke pins heavy biblical terms on Simeon: he is "righteous" because he's known for being observant to the law, and he is "devout" in the sense that his conduct is deeply affirmed (2:25). But our focus is on this expression: "he was waiting [longingly, expectantly] for the *consolation* of Israel" (2:25). The word "consolation" for some of us will evoke empathy for those who have lost a loved one. The term in Luke evokes for its readers Isaiah 40's famous words: "Comfort, comfort my people" and "Speak tenderly" to her because "her hard service" in Babylon's exile "has been completed" and "her sin has been paid for." In fact, she has experienced "double for all her sins" (40:1–2). The famous "in the wilderness prepare a way for the LORD" comes next and that sends us into Luke chapter three for John the Baptist, and we are off and running sprints to keep up with Luke.

So we have to look at this term. Not only does it evoke Isaiah's promise that the exile would end, that Judah would return to the Land and to Jerusalem, but also that language became popular for the arrival of the kingdom of God.

Simeon himself saw in this baby the end of all exiles and the inauguration of the kingdom. But there's more: this term evokes the Holy Spirit as the "Paraclete" (John 14–16), which suggests the Spirit, who Luke tells us is "on him" (Luke 2:25), integrates Isaiah's "consolation" into one's personal and community life. That Spirit divulged to Simeon he'd get to see with his own eyes "the Lord's Messiah" before he died (2:26).

When he did see the baby boy he sang a new redemption song, which we call *Nunc dimittis* ("now dismiss") with the theme that he's ready to die because his dream has come true (2:29). His words "dismiss . . . in peace," another weighty biblical term, points to peace on earth (2:14). The baby is "salvation" in a Jewish body, but the redemption this baby brings is "for all nations" (2:30). The salvation of the Messiah is both "revelation" of something new for "Gentiles" and "glory" for God's elect people Israel (2:31–32).

The Spirit unveils a dark side to this Messiah's redemption: he will cause "the falling and rising of many" and he will be "spoken against" (we'll get to that over and over in this Gospel), and he will unveil "thoughts of many hearts" and then he thrusts a dagger into Mary: "a sword will pierce your own soul too" (2:33–35).

These words portend the whole Gospel of Luke.

Anna's Word of Witness: Redemption

Luke is schooling us, his readers, on what redemption means. If we read carefully we will see that the salvation Jesus is to bring is holistic, and the major emphases are social and political, justice and liberation. Luke's stories may be brief, but they have deep roots in the Old Testament prophets.

What the prophet Anna, widowed for either 77 or 84 years, said, unfortunately, is not recorded. We get the gist of her constant presence in the temple instead. That gist can be reduced to one word that says all that Simeon sang. Luke 2:38 says she "gave thanks to God," though that translation only glimpses the sophisticated term Luke used. His term suggests "openly confessing" or "announcing" or "acknowledging," which she did to "all" those who like Simeon were longing for the kingdom of God. Luke's words are "the redemption of Jerusalem," and once again I suggest we can do better than the term "redemption." The word evokes Isaiah. The term means "liberation" from captivity, from exile, from bondage, and from unfulfilled expectations. That idea of liberation sends us straight back a page to Zechariah's song when he prophesied of "salvation from our enemies" (1:71).

Anna's message is about the "child." She is a witness to others about Jesus and what will be accomplished through Jesus.

These two witnesses prophesy vital information about what Jesus will accomplish: he will launch the kingdom of God by liberating people from captivities. I must say this: we have sanitized the language of Luke in these two witnesses, resulting in more of a comfortable faith instead of a liberating revolution. Our brothers and sisters who are marginalized hear the words of these two witnesses in ways that many white Christians do not hear. Nor does the theme of liberation from oppression enter into our heads when we talk about these two senior citizens.

It's time we began.

Let's join these two senior citizen witnesses.

Questions for Reflection and Application

1. In what ways did Mary and Joseph properly observe the law following Jesus' birth?

2. What does "consolation" mean in Simeon's story?

3. What does "redemption" mean in Anna's story?

4. What would change for you if you began to understand salvation as holistic liberation?

5. Image your reaction to meeting and holding the baby Jesus. What might you have experienced/thought/prayed/sung?

FOR FURTHER READING

Michael Card, "Now That I've Held Him in My Arms," from *Legacy*, produced by John W. Thompson, Randy Scruggs; words by Michael Card (1983).

REDEMPTION REVEALED IN THE TEMPLE

Luke 2:40–52

*40 And the child grew and became strong; he was filled with wis-
dom, and the grace of God was on him.*

*41 Every year Jesus' parents went to Jerusalem for the Festival
of the Passover. 42 When he was twelve years old, they went up to
the festival, according to the custom. 43 After the festival was over,
while his parents were returning home, the boy Jesus stayed behind
in Jerusalem, but they were unaware of it. 44 Thinking he was in
their company, they traveled on for a day. Then they began looking
for him among their relatives and friends. 45 When they did not
find him, they went back to Jerusalem to look for him. 46 After
three days they found him in the temple courts, sitting among the
teachers, listening to them and asking them questions. 47 Everyone
who heard him was amazed at his understanding and his answers.
48 When his parents saw him, they were astonished. His mother
said to him, "Son, why have you treated us like this? Your father
and I have been anxiously searching for you."*

*49 "Why were you searching for me?" he asked. "Didn't you
know I had to be in my Father's house?" 50 But they did not understand what he was saying to them.*

[51] *Then he went down to Nazareth with them and was obedi-*
ent to them. But his mother treasured all these things in her heart.
[52] *And Jesus grew in wisdom and stature, and in favor with God*
and man.

The account of Jesus going to the temple at twelve (before the *bar mitzvah* ceremony existed, by the way) extols his precociousness. Like other major figures in the ancient world, a great man had a great beginning. Words about Jesus here sound like words about Samuel (1 Samuel 2:26), but it would be the later apocryphal gospels that would fill in all sorts of legendary details about Jesus, like making some mud doves, fluffing them a bit with his hands, and then sending them away flying. In spite of how many of us would write a story about Jesus by beginning with profuse descriptions of his childhood, these are the only words written in the Gospels about Jesus between the birth stories and his public ministry. What do we learn?

Jesus Developed

Many think of Jesus as emerging from Mary's womb fully developed and (probably) capable of a discourse or two! Christian art often has baby Jesus making the peace sign and perhaps the sign of the Trinity.

Not so.

Twice in our passage Luke tells us Jesus "became strong" and "grew . . . in stature," that is, from a little body to an adult male body. If Jesus were normal in size for his time, he would have been somewhere around five feet six inches. British medical artist Richard Neave made a drawing in color of Jesus that has found acceptance with many scholars of the Gospels. His growth meant he was potty-trained (however that was done) and fed and learned to talk and cook and fish and learned the trade of a hand-working artisan.

But the central hub here is Jesus "was filled with wisdom" (2:40) and "grew in wisdom" (2:52). Notice, too, that "the grace of God was on him" (2:40) and that he grew "in favor with God" and other humans (2:52). These words surround the story of Jesus in the temple as an introduction to shape what readers see in the temple story, but also as the conclusion to what they are to draw from that story. Jesus at the temple as a twelve-year-old reveals a wise, growing young man. One more term clarifies it all: "obedient" (2:51), a term often translated as "submissive" (e.g., Ephesians 5:21). It means he lived within the expectations and traditions of a son and parents.

Jesus Revealed

His parents were observant of the law of Moses, so they went annually to Jerusalem for the week-long celebration of Israel's liberation from Egypt at Passover (2:41–42). It was a three-day walk from Nazareth to Jerusalem, most often down the Jordan Rift Valley (through Scythopolis, a gentile city, and turning for the climb up to Jerusalem just south of Jericho). Pilgrims traveled in caravans, which explains what happened.

At their night stop, one day into their return from Jerusalem, Joseph and Mary realized Jesus was not with them (2:44). You just have to say it: What's it like to lose the Messiah? Probably the next day, they returned to Jerusalem but did not find him for "three days," and that could mean they searched three days and only then found him, or three days refers to the period from when they discovered his absence. Doesn't matter, they found him, and where was a revelation.

The temple almost forms into a "character" for Luke in chapter two: his parents take him to the temple, Simeon sings a song about Jesus in the temple, and Anna announces who Jesus is in the temple. The parents may take Jesus back to Nazareth, but Luke rushes ahead to Jesus being revealed in the temple. And what is the temple? The place of God's presence with Israel. Where is Jesus? In the heart of divine presence, and for Luke he is present as the divine presence.

His "sitting among the teachers" perhaps evokes the posture of a teacher (notice Matthew 5:1), while "listening" and "asking them questions" perhaps suggest the posture of a student. We ought not make too much of the posture. The point is this: a twelve-year-old engaged with leading intellectuals of Jerusalem! He is a "full participant" (Levine-Witherington, *Luke*, 71). Think of your teenage son or daughter sitting in a room with Tish Harrison Warren, N.T. Wright, and Esau McCaulley in a graduate seminar room at name-your-seminary. Luke wants us all to know everyone who was listening was beside themselves over his understandings. This is Jesus listening, asking, learning. Remember, the introduction and conclusion to this passage are about Jesus' growing in wisdom.

Even mom and dad were impressed, or were they? What do you think? Would you connect their "astonished" with his brilliance or with his absence from them? I think they were angry, so much so that his mother blurts out a question—a question from mothers can be more exclamation than interrogation! (Amen?) Their anxiety is palpable and understandable, and you would have done the same thing. He puts forth two questions, and these are the first words uttered by Jesus in this Gospel:

"Why were you searching for me?"
"Didn't you know I had to be in my Father's house?"

The NIV's "in my Father's *house*" stretches the expression. Literally, it reads "among those [matters, concerns, people] of my Father." He needed to be in the middle of Jerusalem's leading thinkers because his redemptive mission would impact the heart of Israel, namely, the temple itself.

No surprise that they didn't comprehend. What he did was a sign of some sort of who he was (son of God the Father) and what his redemptive mission was all about (temple restoration, theological vision), and what he said cracked a door for them to see inside. So, they collected their son and headed home, where he would spend his time growing in size and wisdom. All the while, like you and I reading this biography about Jesus, Mary is collecting information about him that expands what Gabriel, Simeon, and Anna have said to her (2:51).

Questions for Reflection and Application

1. In what ways did Jesus grow and develop during the time of his life not covered by the Gospels?

2. What is significant about Luke's use of the temple location?

3. How does this scene foreshadow Jesus' future mission and work?

4. How do you think Mary and Joseph perceived and understood this experience?

5. What are some ways you can nurture your own growth in wisdom?

FOR FURTHER READING

Richard Neave, behind a paywall at: https://www.popularmechanics.com/science/health/a234/1282186/

REDEMPTION'S PREDECESSOR

Luke 3:1–20

[1] *In the fifteenth year of the reign of Tiberius Caesar—when Pontius*
Pilate was governor of Judea, Herod tetrarch of Galilee, his brother
Philip tetrarch of Iturea and Traconitis, and Lysanias tetrarch of
Abilene—[2] *during the high-priesthood of Annas and Caiaphas, the*
word of God came to John son of Zechariah in the wilderness.

[3] *He went into all the country around the Jordan, preaching a*
baptism of repentance for the forgiveness of sins. [4] *As it is written in*
the book of the words of Isaiah the prophet:

> *"A voice of one calling in the wilderness,*
> *'Prepare the way for the Lord,*
> *make straight paths for him.*
> [5] *Every valley shall be filled in,*
> *every mountain and hill made low.*
> *The crooked roads shall become straight,*
> *the rough ways smooth.*
> [6] *And all people will see God's salvation.'"*

[7] *John said to the crowds coming out to be baptized by him,*
"You brood of vipers! Who warned you to flee from the coming

wrath? 8 Produce fruit in keeping with repentance. And do not begin
to say to yourselves, 'We have Abraham as our father.' For I tell
you that out of these stones God can raise up children for Abraham.
9 The ax is already at the root of the trees, and every tree that does
not produce good fruit will be cut down and thrown into the fire."

10 "What should we do then?" the crowd asked.

11 John answered, "Anyone who has two shirts should share
with the one who has none, and anyone who has food should do
the same."

12 Even tax collectors came to be baptized. "Teacher," they
asked, "what should we do?"

13 "Don't collect any more than you are required to," he told
them.

14 Then some soldiers asked him, "And what should we do?"

He replied, "Don't extort money and don't accuse people
falsely—be content with your pay."

15 The people were waiting expectantly and were all wonder-
ing in their hearts if John might possibly be the Messiah. 16 John
answered them all, "I baptize you with water. But one who is more
powerful than I will come, the straps of whose sandals I am not
worthy to untie. He will baptize you with the Holy Spirit and fire.
17 His winnowing fork is in his hand to clear his threshing floor and
to gather the wheat into his barn, but he will burn up the chaff with
unquenchable fire." 18 And with many other words John exhorted
the people and proclaimed the good news to them.

19 But when John rebuked Herod the tetrarch because of his
marriage to Herodias, his brother's wife, and all the other evil
things he had done, 20 Herod added this to them all: He locked John
up in prison.

The right response to John's message was grit and grime, hands and feet, words and acts. Sure, he had a theology and ideas and thought things out, but he grounded them in breathing behaviors. His theology was not classroom discussion but dust-forming deeds. Repentance is the right response,

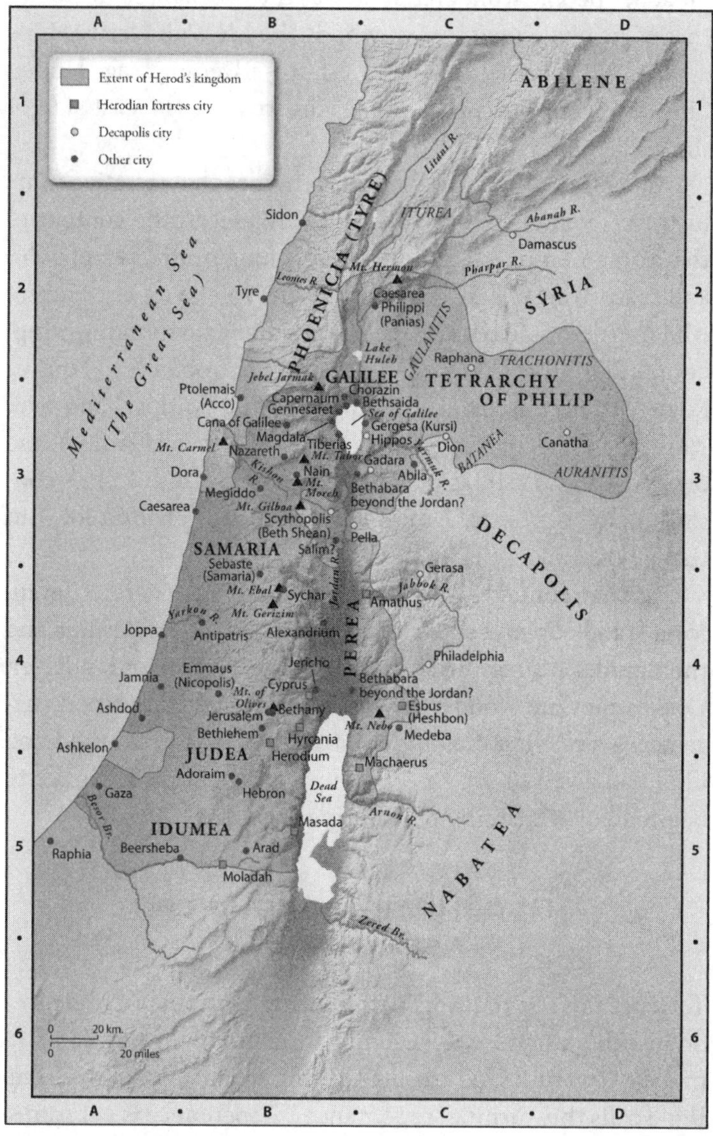

Map by International Mapping

but it means nothing until we see it turned into conduct, and John does that in our passage. He was so powerful as a preacher people wondered if he was the Messiah, so he denies that as he gives a witness to who is the Messiah (Jesus). One cannot be surprised that John's sharp-edged message landed him in a Herodian prison in Machaerus (on the east side of the Dead Sea).

Once again Luke anchors and rhymes the narrative in its historical context, in the birth of Jesus set in the context of the Roman empire, and in the preaching ministries of John and Jesus who talked "kingdom" with an eye on the empire (the murderous Tiberius Caesar) and their surrounding kingdoms (2:1; 3:1–2). We meet the governor of Judea (Pontius Pilate), the tetrarchs over Galilee (Herod Antipas) and over Iturea and Traconitis (Herod Philip; north of Galilee) and over Abilene (Lysinias; north of Damascus). Plus Luke's context includes priests: Annas and Caiaphas. That's a lot, but that's how Luke rolls in 3:1–2.

In that context, none of it explored in concrete detail, John stands up and speaks out in the Judean wilderness and then guides his converts to get baptized in the Jordan River. One cannot but wonder how many thought the location suggested Israel's first crossing over the Jordan to enter the Land God had given them. If so, John gave the people a chance to begin all over again by re-entering the Land.

Redemption Requires Repentance

To trust in God requires turning from trusting in ourselves or in others or in our accomplishments or in power or in money. To trust God means turning from self to God. The Bible calls this turning "repentance." Repentance is not something that follows from trusting or believing or having faith or getting baptized. No, true faith requires repentance, and true repentance is like faith, a life-long process. No better words have ever been written about this than those by Dietrich Bonhoeffer:

> Cheap grace is preaching forgiveness without repentance; it is baptism without the discipline of community; it is the Lord's Supper without confession of sin; it is absolution without personal confession. Cheap grace is grace without discipleship, grace without the cross, grace without the living, incarnate Jesus Christ (Bonhoeffer, *Discipleship*, 44).

John's theology is a prophet's. Luke summarizes his message with "preaching a baptism of repentance for the forgiveness of sins" (3:5). First, he is *preaching*, which means he is publicly announcing a message from God. When Luke summarizes John's ministry down at 3:18, he summarizes it as "gospeling the people" (my translation). Second, the content of his preaching is *repentance*. A term that can be translated "convert," repentance draws on the prophets' image of turning or turning around in order to return to God. That term itself explains why John required *baptism* if people wanted *forgiveness of sin*. Baptism, which in the Jewish world took place as often as almost daily in order to rid a person of any impurity, was performed commonly in a step-pool or what we call a *mikveh*. These sacred pools are found in all ancient Jewish villages.

John warns his audiences that they cannot appeal to their ethnic heritage to get clean before God. In fact, he warns them that divine judgment is imminent (3:7–10). Warning of hellfire has become a rhetorical trick for some preachers, which unfortunately produces more people walking away from God than to God. These warnings, however harshly they confront us in our world, are not to shame us but to reform us. As Alan Jacobs, a wonderful essayist, once put it: "Certainly, it is because of our sin that we must be spoken to in such a harsh language; but we are being spoken to, not destroyed" (Jacobs, *Shaming the Devil,* 69).

Forgiveness from sins evokes for a prophet a national and personal act of God's grace following divine discipline for sin. John's message then is that if people want to participate in the ushering in of the kingdom of God, then they will have to get into the Jordan River (immersion is probably in mind). Luke extends John's theology when he connects John to the "voice of one calling in the wilderness," a text of the prophet Isaiah (40:3–5) who was preaching the end of exile and return to the Land. And this very text was a theme text for the Essenes who lived at the Qumran Community, just a few miles from where John was preaching. One has to at least raise the possibility that John the Baptist either knew of this community or was somehow connected to them. After all, his father and the founders of that community were priests.

Repentance Is Real

If his message is repentance, what does that look like? Does he mean feel deep sorrow and contrition? Perhaps. But for John repentance has its feet on the ground, and it is both group-specific and behavioral. First, John's repentance is not generalized into a one-act-for-all but becomes specific, and the groups represent two of the more despised groups of society–which gives this entire baptism scene a socio-political setting.

1. For the *general populace* it means economic distribution (3:10–11).
2. For *tax collectors* it means taxing no more than is required (3:12–13).

3. For *soldiers* it means to stop extorting money and swearing falsely (3:14).

Notice how important money and greed are to John's theology. Genuine repentance will be experienced in the pocketbook by a manifestation of generosity and a striving for just equality. Yes, this is distributive justice and yes, his idea of repentance is social and communal and systemic. This very theme of economic justice was also predicted in the Magnificat by Mary (1:46–55).

One's Mission in Redemption Is Only a Moment in Time

John the Baptist has been wildly underestimated in Christian circles. He had a good push from the start with a father who was a priest, and he became a star in the wilderness of Judea. That both tax collectors and soldiers were coming to John for baptism must have made some think the Messiah himself was just over the horizon! Perhaps it was John! John denies that he is the Messiah by pointing to the One who is, the One who is greater than he is (3:15–17).

Luke sets us up for John's denial when he makes John the "voice" who prepared the way "for the Lord" and for "God's salvation" (3:4, 6). John says as much now when he says he baptizes with mere "water" (3:16) but the about-to-appear Messiah will baptize "with the Holy Spirit and fire" (3:16). He also reveals to the people that the Messiah will affect a judgment on both "wheat" and "chaff" (3:17).

John is but a moment. His mission is to gather crowds, call them to repent, baptize them in the Jordan, and to point everyone to the coming Messiah, Jesus. And then get out of the way.

He did that, with a parting shot for one specific tetrarch.

Repentance's Rough Side

Luke quickly summarizes that John "rebuked" a "tetrarch" because his marriage was against the law of Moses and because of all the "other evil things he had done" (3:19). Unlike many preachers and would-be influencers today, he had the backbone to stand up for God's ways, and he used his voice to denounce the sins of corrupted powers. John got locked up while the preachers of our day get some glory. It takes courage to speak against political leaders and calling them to repent can get rough.

A lurking, looming shadow covered this entire passage once Tiberius Caesar, the governor Pilate, and the tetrarchs were mentioned. We now know why: by the end of our passage John was headed for a beheading at the sword of the Roman-appointed powers.

Holistic redemption is not a pie in some sweet by and by. This single episode in the biography of Jesus pushes us to turn the page.

Questions for Reflection and Application

1. What is the social and political context in which Luke sets his Gospel? How does this context help us understand and interpret the story?

2. What is the fuller understanding of repentance and forgiveness given in this section?

3. How does John's theology of repentance impact economic forces?

4. Which Christian "influencers" today do you see speaking truth to power in the bold way John does here?

5. What particular, specific repentance might God be calling you toward in your life?

FOR FURTHER READING

Dietrich Bonhoeffer, *Discipleship* (DBW 4; Minneapolis: Fortress, 2001). Formerly titled *The Cost of Discipleship.*

Alan Jacobs, *Shaming the Devil: Essays in Truthtelling* (Grand Rapids: Wm. B. Eerdmans, 2004).

REDEMPTION AND THE SON OF GOD

Luke 3:21–38

*21 When all the people were being baptized, Jesus was baptized too.
And as he was praying, heaven was opened 22 and the Holy Spirit
descended on him in bodily form like a dove. And a voice came
from heaven: "You are my Son, whom I love; with you I am well
pleased."*

*23 Now Jesus himself was about thirty years old when he began
his ministry. He was the son, so it was thought, of Joseph,*

the son of Heli,
24 the son of Matthat,
the son of Levi, the son of Melki,
the son of Jannai, the son of Joseph,
25 the son of Mattathias, the son of Amos,
the son of Nahum, the son of Esli,
the son of Naggai, 26 the son of Maath,
the son of Mattathias, the son of Semein,
the son of Josek, the son of Joda,
27 the son of Joanan, the son of Rhesa,

the son of Zerubbabel, the son of Shealtiel,
the son of Neri, [28] the son of Melki,
the son of Addi, the son of Cosam,
the son of Elmadam, the son of Er,
[29] the son of Joshua, the son of Eliezer,
the son of Jorim, the son of Matthat,
the son of Levi, [30] the son of Simeon,
the son of Judah, the son of Joseph,
the son of Jonam, the son of Eliakim,
[31] the son of Melea, the son of Menna,
the son of Mattatha, the son of Nathan,
the son of David, [32] the son of Jesse,
the son of Obed, the son of Boaz,
the son of Salmon, the son of Nahshon,
[33] the son of Amminadab, the son of Ram,
the son of Hezron, the son of Perez,
the son of Judah, [34] the son of Jacob,
the son of Isaac, the son of Abraham,
the son of Terah, the son of Nahor,
[35] the son of Serug, the son of Reu,
the son of Peleg, the son of Eber,
the son of Shelah, [36] the son of Cainan,
the son of Arphaxad, the son of Shem,
the son of Noah, the son of Lamech,
[37] the son of Methuselah, the son of Enoch,
the son of Jared, the son of Mahalalel,
the son of Kenan, [38] the son of Enosh,
the son of Seth, the son of Adam,
the son of God.

A person's life is not solitary. Jesus, like anyone else ever born, learned life from his mother and father, from his siblings (at least five; Mark 6:3), from his neighbors, from his community, from those from whom he learned and from those with whom he disagreed. As well, from his relatives, three of whom were Zechariah, Elizabeth, and their son John the Baptist. John was baptizing repentant persons in the Jordan River, perhaps evoking entering into the Land (all over again), the consequence of the baptism being specific changes of conduct, especially changes for economic justice. Those baptized became nothing less than a movement of some sort in the diverse spectrum of Jewish groups, like the Essenes, Pharisees, and Sadducees. The Baptist movement did not go away quickly, for his followers are still at work some three decades later in Ephesus (cf. Acts 19:1–7).

From this passage forward, Luke's biography shifts entirely into constant concentration on Jesus, the Lord, the Savior, the Son of God, the Messiah. In all this he is one of us and not one of us, he is like us and he is not like us, and his story is our story but our story is not his story. All of this happens in our passage.

Jesus Like Us

Now notice this: Jesus was baptized into John's baptism. For you and me it may be a bit odd to think about, and perhaps feel a bit irreverent, but Jesus got baptized into a "baptism of repentance for the forgiveness of sins." That's what John's baptism was (Luke 3:3). If Jesus was sinless, and I think he was (Hebrews 4:15), then he does what we call a "vicarious act." He vicariously repented for us, he vicariously got baptized for us, and he vicariously entered the water, and he vicariously experienced the overwhelming presence of the Spirit for us—all as a unique person but still representing us in that very action. Either that or we have a few other options: this was a public symbolic action of joining the vision of John or he wasn't sinless. The first one makes more sense to me, though the second one compels at times.

Jesus Not like Us

Yes, he was unique so his baptism-like-ours was simultaneously a baptism-unlike-ours. Maybe we, too, are praying when baptized (3:21), but more likely we're paying attention to the baptizers and the audience and the water and doing the right thing. And nervous or looking around to see if our loved ones are watching (or videoing it).

But there are some distinctives about Jesus' baptism. Only he experienced heaven opening up, only he had the Spirit descend on him "in bodily form like a dove" (3:22), that is, like Noah's dove (Genesis 8:8–12), and especially only for him does the Father quote Psalm 2:7 with an echo of Isaiah 42:1, texts that affirm the identity of Jesus as God's Son who is empowered by the Spirit to do the work of the Messiah. All the wonderings that have been muttering around in our heads since the days of Zechariah's muteness, Elizabeth's miracle baby, Mary's angelic visitations and song, along with Zechariah's song and Simeon's song and Anna's prophetic words, not to discount Jesus' own words in the temple (Luke 1–2), now come into one term for Jesus: *Son*. *My* son, the one and only Son "whom I love; with you I am well pleased" (3:22). Here are those texts from the Old Testament:

> I will proclaim the LORD's decree:
>
> He said to me, "You are my son;
> today I have become your father."
> (Psalm 2:7)
>
> "Here is my servant, whom I uphold,
> my chosen one in whom I delight;
> I will put my Spirit on him,
> and he will bring justice to the nations.
> (Isaiah 42:1)

His baptism-like-ours transcends our baptism because it is a baptism-unlike-ours. Our baptism is nothing if it is not a baptism into his own baptism. He is the paradigmatic baptized person into whom we are baptized. The apostle Paul will develop this at length in Romans 6, and you might want to read it to make sense of why Jesus was baptized and what our baptism signifies. We enter into the waters with Jesus, we go down in death with him, and we rise from the waters into new life with him. Father, Son, and Spirit engage the moment of baptism.

We learn nothing about what Jesus looked like, how tall he was, what color his eyes and hair were. Nothing. Instead, in one crisp sentence, Luke informs us that Jesus began his public ministry at "about thirty" years of age (3:23). That's the one detail: he was about thirty.

Jesus like All of Us

Genealogies have to be one of the most (well, admit it) boring sections of the Bible. I remember when I was a high schooler reading the Bible through the first time (in my Morocco leather King James Scofield Bible). It was so nice to get to 1 Chronicles to realize the first nine chapters were almost entirely genealogical lists. I had been reading four chapters a day and felt a little bit guilty (I was a Baptist) for knocking off two days in a few minutes.

A few thoughts about Luke's genealogy. First, the genealogy runs backward from Jesus the son of Joseph, "so it was thought" (3:23),[1] all the way back through David (especially) and then on to Adam. More than 75 names. Matthew's genealogy is different as it moves forward from Abraham through David to Jesus, in fourteen generation collections. *There is more than one way for a biographer to write up a genealogy.* Once you get past your father or mother, depending on where you start, you can begin choosing grandparents and uncles and aunts. Luke chose to make Jesus the Second Adam or the True Human of all Humans, but at the same time Jesus is the Davidic Messiah.

He's like us: he gets baptized, and he has a genealogy.

He's unlike us: his baptism is wildly different, and his genealogy is not the same as ours. Except that we are in union with him, so his genealogy becomes ours by faith, as does his baptism.

Questions for Reflection and Application

1. In what ways does Luke show that Jesus is like us here?

2. How does Luke show that Jesus is not like us?

3. What does Luke tell us by the way he arranges and presents Jesus' genealogy?

4. Reflect on your baptism, if you have been baptized. How was it similar to or different from Jesus' baptism?

5. So far, what has Luke told us about who Jesus is? (We'll look at this question every few chapters throughout this study to help keep track of Luke's progressive revelation of Jesus.)

REDEMPTION THROUGH THE WILDERNESS

Luke 4:1–13

1 Jesus, full of the Holy Spirit, left the Jordan and was led by the
Spirit into the wilderness, 2 where for forty days he was tempted by
the devil. He ate nothing during those days, and at the end of them
he was hungry.

3 The devil said to him, "If you are the Son of God, tell this
stone to become bread."

4 Jesus answered, "It is written: 'Man shall not live on bread
alone.'"

5 The devil led him up to a high place and showed him in an
instant all the kingdoms of the world. 6 And he said to him, "I will
give you all their authority and splendor; it has been given to me,
and I can give it to anyone I want to. 7 If you worship me, it will all
be yours."

8 Jesus answered, "It is written: 'Worship the Lord your God
and serve him only.'"

9 The devil led him to Jerusalem and had him stand on the
highest point of the temple. "If you are the Son of God," he said,
"throw yourself down from here. 10 For it is written:

" 'He will command his angels concerning you
to guard you carefully;
11 they will lift you up in their hands,
so that you will not strike your foot against a stone.' "

12 Jesus answered, "It is said: 'Do not put the Lord your God to the test.' "

13 When the devil had finished all this tempting, he left him until an opportune time.

Salvation has a unique scheme: Out of love God forgives us, not because we earn it but because his Son, Jesus, has accomplished it for us. We acquire that salvation by grace (alone), through faith (alone), in Christ (alone). The foundation for Christ's saving work is his impeccable, divine nature and his obedient, faithful life. Which is why we may need some re-education on how to read the narrative about Jesus' tests. In particular, our divining secrets for how best to resist temptations in our life blunts the power of this short narrative about Jesus in the wilderness with the devil.[1] In fact, it removes it from God's plan of salvation into a kind of moralism. This passage is not about us. It is about Jesus. Rather, it reveals something about Jesus: that he is the Son of God and, as the Son of God, is tested in the wilderness as Israel was tested in the wilderness. With one colossal difference: Israel failed over and over while Jesus proved faithful three times.

Luke's Set-up Helps

Jesus, Luke tells us, was "full of the Holy Spirit" and was "led by the Spirit" into the "wilderness," where he was "tempted" (or "tested"; same word in Greek) by the "devil" for "forty days." Luke wants us to know this is a divinely appointed event; that a contest takes place between God's Son and the arch-rival of God, the devil; that Jesus needed the power of the Spirit to accomplish the Father's mission; and that Jesus was tested in the wilderness for forty days corresponding to Israel's forty years of being tested. We are reading a beautifully constructed, briefer-than-brief short story. Luke provides the precise words needed for us to know what happens.

The Old Testament Texts

We tend to read the Bible and ignore the cross references, which is fine if you are as aware of the Old Testament as Jesus and the first century Christians were. If we are not, and most of us aren't, we need to slow down and check out the cross references. In my copy of the NIV (Heritage Bible, Passaggio Setting) three references from Deuteronomy are provided: Deuteronomy 8:3, then 6:13, then 6:16, each in italics in the Bible text above. Each of these references is from Israel's wilderness testing where God disciplined Israel to trust him, to obey him, and to learn to do what was right. Luke wants you and me to imagine Jesus experiencing Israel's former tests. This verse from Deuteronomy also summarizes Jesus' tests: "Remember how the Lord your God led you all the way in the wilderness these forty years, to humble and test you in order to know what was in your heart, whether or not you would keep his commands" (8:2).

Because Luke 3 ended with Adam, some think the three tests are like Adam's tests in the Garden of Eden, and some also think that both Israel and Adam are echoed in our passage. That all the texts come from Deuteronomy, and there are no quotes from Genesis 3, suggests to us that Jesus' tests are to be connected to Israel and not to Adam's Eden experience.

Three Tests

Jesus is tested as God's Son. Notice "if you are the Son of God." The tests form Jesus into God's faithful, obedient Son. His food provisions will be from God, his own desire for God's glorious reign over all creation will happen only through worshiping God, and he will not put God to the test by demanding proofs. Each of these are tests of the one and only Son of God, not humans in general. None of us imagines turning rocks into bread. None of us, except deluded narcissists, think of ruling the whole world. None of us thinks of jumping off high places claiming biblical promises for protection. (I hope.)

Luke narrates Jesus' testings in a different order than one finds in Matthew (4:1–11) though, other than a significant change in the order of tests, the two accounts are nearly identical in wording. Matthew has bread, temple, kingship; Luke has bread, kingship, temple. Luke's emphasis on temple is why Luke makes the temple climactic.

The Proper Responses

The proper responses to this narrative about Jesus are twofold: first, thanksgiving to Jesus for becoming like us and for turning the failures of Israelites into the failure of one Israelite. The second response ought to be applause. We should stand up and give Jesus a big Hallelujah! Baptized and announced as Son, he is tested as Son. As the faithful Son, he can now go public and enter into his kingdom ministry of revealing, healing, teaching, and preaching, and then experience death and resurrection for us so that we can enter into redemption. But we can be redeemed only because Jesus was the faithful Son of God.

The devil, admitting defeat this time, leaves Jesus. Luke sets us up for more, which will only be discovered by reading the Gospel when he says, "until an opportune time" (4:13), and a hint is 22:3!

Questions for Reflection and Application

1. Why does it matter that this passage is about Jesus, not about us?

2. How does Luke make use of texts from Deuteronomy to give depth and historical resonance to his story about Jesus in the wilderness?

3. What are the three tests Jesus faces, and what is the significance of them?

4. With what details does Luke connect Jesus' story to Israel's story here?

5. What is your response to what you learned about Jesus in this section?

REDEMPTION'S KINGDOM VISION

Luke 4:14–44

*14 Jesus returned to Galilee in the power of the Spirit, and news
about him spread through the whole countryside. 15 He was teaching in their synagogues, and everyone praised him.*

*16 He went to Nazareth, where he had been brought up, and on
the Sabbath day he went into the synagogue, as was his custom. He
stood up to read, 17 and the scroll of the prophet Isaiah was handed
to him. Unrolling it, he found the place where it is written:*

> *18 "The Spirit of the Lord is on me,*
> *because he has anointed me*
> *to proclaim good news to the poor.*
> *He has sent me to proclaim freedom for the prisoners*
> *and recovery of sight for the blind,*
> *to set the oppressed free,*
> *19 to proclaim the year of the Lord's favor."*

*20 Then he rolled up the scroll, gave it back to the attendant and
sat down. The eyes of everyone in the synagogue were fastened on
him. 21 He began by saying to them, "Today this scripture is fulfilled
in your hearing."*

22 All spoke well of him and were amazed at the gracious words
that came from his lips. "Isn't this Joseph's son?" they asked.

23 Jesus said to them, "Surely you will quote this proverb to
me: 'Physician, heal yourself!' And you will tell me, 'Do here in
your hometown what we have heard that you did in Capernaum.'"
24 "Truly I tell you," he continued, "no prophet is accepted in his
hometown. 25 I assure you that there were many widows in Israel
in Elijah's time, when the sky was shut for three and a half years
and there was a severe famine throughout the land. 26 Yet Elijah
was not sent to any of them, but to a widow in Zarephath in the
region of Sidon. 27 And there were many in Israel with leprosy in the
time of Elisha the prophet, yet not one of them was cleansed—only
Naaman the Syrian."

28 All the people in the synagogue were furious when they heard
this. 29 They got up, drove him out of the town, and took him to the
brow of the hill on which the town was built, in order to throw him
off the cliff. 30 But he walked right through the crowd and went on
his way.

31 Then he went down to Capernaum, a town in Galilee, and
on the Sabbath he taught the people. 32 They were amazed at his
teaching, because his words had authority.

33 In the synagogue there was a man possessed by a demon,
an impure spirit. He cried out at the top of his voice, 34 "Go away!
What do you want with us, Jesus of Nazareth? Have you come to
destroy us? I know who you are—the Holy One of God!"

35 "Be quiet!" Jesus said sternly. "Come out of him!" Then the
demon threw the man down before them all and came out without
injuring him.

36 All the people were amazed and said to each other, "What
words these are! With authority and power he gives orders to impure spirits and they come out!" 37 And the news about him spread
throughout the surrounding area.

38 Jesus left the synagogue and went to the home of Simon.
Now Simon's mother-in-law was suffering from a high fever, and

they asked Jesus to help her. [39] *So he bent over her and rebuked the fever, and it left her. She got up at once and began to wait on them.*

[40] *At sunset, the people brought to Jesus all who had various kinds of sickness, and laying his hands on each one, he healed them.* [41] *Moreover, demons came out of many people, shouting, "You are the Son of God!" But he rebuked them and would not allow them to speak, because they knew he was the Messiah.*

[42] *At daybreak, Jesus went out to a solitary place. The people were looking for him and when they came to where he was, they tried to keep him from leaving them.* [43] *But he said, "I must proclaim the good news of the kingdom of God to the other towns also, because that is why I was sent."* [44] *And he kept on preaching in the synagogues of Judea.*

Announced by the angel Gabriel, sung about by his mother Mary, located alongside the prophet John (the Baptist), born with a song by angels, sung about by Simeon, prophesied by Anna, recognized by temple leaders, declared by John the Baptist, baptized by the same, and tested by the devil, Jesus is now ready to go public with his ministry. He begins in his hometown and then sets up a kingdom mission shop in Capernaum on the northern tip of the Sea of Galilee.

Our passage begins with his "sermon" in the Nazareth synagogue, which overtly articulates his gospel, and then we read of opposing reactions to him, his power to liberate from the evil one, and his miracles of healing. Each of these puts feet on the ground for his gospel.

His Mission of Redemption: Gospeling

The Spirit who came upon Jesus at his baptism and who led him into the wilderness is the Spirit who empowered him to begin at home (4:14–15). His point of contact with the people was the "synagogue," which was a Jewish assembly hall, a combination of a social hall and a meeting place for synagogue instruction and worship and prayer. People were impressed by Jesus as their local Spirit-empowered preacher.

What happened in his hometown's synagogue has been recorded by Luke. Reading texts from the Tanakh (Torah, Prophets, Writings) required standing (out of reverence), while instructing or preaching about the reading occurred sitting (in submission to the text). Jesus does just that (4:16, 20). In those days a service probably began by reciting the *Shema* ("Hear O Israel," from Deuteronomy 6:4–9), then a doxology ("Blessed be the Name . . ."), then someone read texts from the Scriptures from the Law and the Psalms and then explained them. This reading from Isaiah could indicate the first century service included a reading from a prophet (called now a *haftarah*).

Jesus reads from Isaiah 61:1–2, which is nothing short of a prophecy of the rebuilding, restoring, and renewing of Jerusalem where a world of justice will be formed (61:1–9; read the whole chapter, it's glorious). The prophet's words are electrifying enough, but a nuclear charge comes next in an eight-word sermon: "Today this scripture is fulfilled in your hearing." #micdrop

Isaiah's words provide the template for the mission of Jesus, and these are its seven, perhaps eight, features:

1. God's Spirit empowers Jesus (3:22; 4:1, 14).
2. The Spirit anoints Jesus to be a gospeler.
3. The gospel is for the poor, which means economically destitute, socially low status, spiritually sensitive to God, and aching for the Messiah and kingdom.

4. The gospel is liberation for prisoners, which in Isaiah meant exiles and for Jesus suggests the oppressed of Galilee, possibly people in debtors' prison.
5. The gospel gives sight to the blind–both a curable physical malady and redeemable spiritual blindness.
6. The gospel sets the oppressed free (see #4).
7. The gospel is the Jubilee hope (Leviticus 25:8–13), and Jubilee hope is a radical economic redemption (like the Magnificat song of Mary, and John's repentance themes). It meant divestment and distribution in the direction of justice.
8. Many have noticed Luke cuts off Isaiah 61:2 in the middle of the verse at Luke 4:19, right before Isaiah's "and the day of vengeance of our God." Some think the audience became irate over Jesus not including God's vengeance against gentiles. They find support in Jesus' surprising inclusion of gentiles in Luke 4:24–27. We need to be cautious about what is not said and what is then assumed listeners believed and were thinking. I find this eighth point very unlikely, and also it too easily assumes a nasty theology for the entire assembly.

One word, make that two, sums up Jesus' message: holistic redemption. Hearts and bodies, personal and social and economic. Everything is being turned inside out to the redemptive power at work in Jesus. In a sermon given at Duke Chapel, Myron Augsburger put brilliant words to the centrality of Jesus in the unfolding of history: "This is our faith, that God has interpreted history from its middle in Jesus Christ, and we know the end from the middle because God has known the end from the beginning" (Augsburger, *Sermons*, 127). You might need to read that again, and it's worth it.

What Mary predicted for her Messiah son, what Zechariah predicted through his prophet son, and what John the Baptist required in repentance are now expressed in Jesus' personal affirmation of the words of Isaiah. For Jesus it is the Now Time, or as he said it, "Today."

His Mission of Redemption: Suffering

People responded. Some had questions, like, *How can this local say things like this? He's Joe's boy, right? Wow, we've got a prophet in Nazareth!* One expects Jesus now to be a bit grateful to hear such affirming words, but he hears more than those words.

Jesus is hearing that he needs to heal himself and do mighty works in Nazareth (4:23). As Justo González observed, they expect "special favors," and Jesus is about to tell them that will not happen (González, *Luke,* 66). Which is then ramped up to predict he will be denounced and discredited by them. Then ratcheted up a notch that God has a history of turning toward those with a heart fixed on God. So in the days of Elijah God healed a gentile widow, and in the days of Elisha God cleansed a Syrian, not Israelite, leper (4:24–27). Jesus will not promise his locals any "messianic benefits" (Levine-Witherington, *Luke,* 112).

Jesus hopped lanes after those apparent affirming words in the synagogue (4:22). Suddenly the affirmers are "furious" and "drove him out of the town" and then "took him to the brow of the hill . . . to throw him off the cliff" (4:28–29). The suddenness of their response begs explanation, as does how Jesus somehow escaped the crowd to Capernaum, a two to three day walk through the hills up to the north of the Sea of Galilee.

His Mission of Redemption: Liberating

In Capernaum, on the Sabbath, in the synagogue (remains of which are visible today), Jesus addresses another audience (4:31–32). A demonized man screams that he knows who Jesus really is–"the Holy One of God" (4:34). Jesus silences the man and exorcises the demon. Exorcism is common to the public mission of Jesus and the most frequent of his miracles. The people are "amazed" (4:36), eliciting the essential question probed by all four Gospels: who is this man who can use his words to exorcize "impure spirits" (4:36)? Exorcisms by Jesus form one part of the downfall of Satan (11:17–22) as they liberate a human captured by the devil and its demons. Yes, it is spiritual liberation, but such persons were often labeled and marginalized. So their liberation becomes spiritual, social, and status redemption.

His Mission of Redemption: Healing

The mission of holistic redemption moves next into disability, which we have grown to understand better. Disability refers to the combination of one's body and one's social, cultural, and spiritual location, and therefore access to individual esteem and society (Bird and Gosbell). Between the synagogue of Capernaum and the Sea of Galilee, today, is a Franciscan church. Under it are remains of a first century home, which almost certainly was the home of Simon (Peter). Jesus heals Simon's mother-in-law from a fever, but then at sunset, because word traveled, many carry to Jesus those in need of healings and exorcisms because of their disabilities, and Peter's home becomes a hospital of liberation (4:38–41).

What then was Jesus' gospel mission? Holistic redemption of gospeling, suffering, liberating, and healing. Nothing less will do if we want to get into line with Jesus.

Questions for Reflection and Application

1. What is the gospel Jesus preaches in Nazareth?

2. What does Jesus lay out as his mission? Which of the eight points most stands out to you?

3. How does Luke illustrate the mission and work of Jesus in the narratives that follow his sermon in Nazareth?

4. Which element of holistic redemption have you been most in need of in your life?

5. In what ways are you participating in and continuing the liberating work of Jesus today?

FOR FURTHER READING

Myron S. Augsburger, "The Christian in a Revolutionary Age," in William H. Willimon, editor, *Sermons from Duke Chapel: Voices from a Great "Towering Church"* (Durham: Duke University Press, 2005), 127–137.

Michael Bird interviews Louise Gosbell; https://michaelfbird.substack.com/p/the-apostle-paul-and-disability#details

REDEMPTION CALLS, CLEANSES, AND CURES

Luke 5:1–26

*[1] One day as Jesus was standing by the Lake of Gennesaret, the
people were crowding around him and listening to the word of God.
[2] He saw at the water's edge two boats, left there by the fishermen,
who were washing their nets. [3] He got into one of the boats, the one
belonging to Simon, and asked him to put out a little from shore.
Then he sat down and taught the people from the boat.*

*[4] When he had finished speaking, he said to Simon, "Put out
into deep water, and let down the nets for a catch."*

*[5] Simon answered, "Master, we've worked hard all night and
haven't caught anything. But because you say so, I will let down
the nets."*

*[6] When they had done so, they caught such a large number of
fish that their nets began to break. [7] So they signaled their partners
in the other boat to come and help them, and they came and filled
both boats so full that they began to sink.*

*[8] When Simon Peter saw this, he fell at Jesus' knees and said,
"Go away from me, Lord; I am a sinful man!" [9] For he and all
his companions were astonished at the catch of fish they had taken,
[10] and so were James and John, the sons of Zebedee, Simon's partners.*

Then Jesus said to Simon, "Don't be afraid; from now on you will fish for people."

11 So they pulled their boats up on shore, left everything and followed him.

12 While Jesus was in one of the towns, a man came along who was covered with leprosy. When he saw Jesus, he fell with his face to the ground and begged him, "Lord, if you are willing, you can make me clean."

13 Jesus reached out his hand and touched the man. "I am willing," he said. "Be clean!" And immediately the leprosy left him.

14 Then Jesus ordered him, "Don't tell anyone, but go, show yourself to the priest and offer the sacrifices that Moses commanded for your cleansing, as a testimony to them."

15 Yet the news about him spread all the more, so that crowds of people came to hear him and to be healed of their sicknesses. 16 But Jesus often withdrew to lonely places and prayed.

17 One day Jesus was teaching, and Pharisees and teachers of the law were sitting there. They had come from every village of Galilee and from Judea and Jerusalem. And the power of the Lord was with Jesus to heal the sick. 18 Some men came carrying a paralyzed man on a mat and tried to take him into the house to lay him before Jesus. 19 When they could not find a way to do this because of the crowd, they went up on the roof and lowered him on his mat through the tiles into the middle of the crowd, right in front of Jesus.

20 When Jesus saw their faith, he said, "Friend, your sins are forgiven."

21 The Pharisees and the teachers of the law began thinking to themselves, "Who is this fellow who speaks blasphemy? Who can forgive sins but God alone?"

22 Jesus knew what they were thinking and asked, "Why are you thinking these things in your hearts? 23 Which is easier: to say, 'Your sins are forgiven,' or to say, 'Get up and walk'? 24 But I want you to know that the Son of Man has authority on earth to forgive sins." So he said to the paralyzed man, "I tell you, get up, take your mat and go home." [25] *Immediately he stood up in front of them, took what he had been lying on and went home praising God.* [26] *Everyone was amazed and gave praise to God. They were filled with awe and said, "We have seen remarkable things today."*

It has been said many times because it needs to be repeated: redemption for Jesus cannot be reduced to forgiveness of personal sins so we can go to heaven when we die. In the Gospel of Luke redemption is holistic: forgiveness (check), healing (check), exorcisms (check), restoration to society (check), future kingdom (check). Not just one or two but each and more than even these. In our passage, Simon (Peter) is forgiven and called, the leper is cleansed and sent, and a paralyzed man is cured and praises God. No one is left where they were, for those who experience redemption are drawn into the kingdom mission of Jesus.

The mission of Jesus occurs in the midst of crowded places, and this comes through our text at several places (5:1, 15, 17, 26). Perhaps Luke wants his readers to know Jesus' mighty acts did not occur behind closed doors or out in some barren wilderness. No, what Jesus did was seen by many. In fact, people came to Jesus to hear him speak "the word of God" (5:1).

Redemption Calls

Every person Jesus redeems is called to participate in the kingdom. Some turn their professions into gateways to the kingdom, others are more directly called into the church's ministries. It does not matter: each person is called to exercise their gift in the kingdom. Simon is about to become a kingdom agent himself, and Luke will describe this scene with noticeable brevity.

Simon (not yet Peter until verse 8) fishes the Sea of Galilee. Jesus discovers two boats on the shore, gets down into one of them and, while sitting, teaches a crowd of people. Luke turns rather suddenly to Jesus instructing Simon to take a boat out into the water and drop his fish nets. Simon informs Jesus they had fished all night and caught nothing but, he surrenders, "because you say so, I will let down the nets" (5:5). A haul of fish overwhelms Simon's nets, so he solicits another fishing boat for support. In Luke's economy of words again Simon suddenly confesses his sins! Perhaps this can be explained as Simon being overwhelmed by the presence of Jesus and the power of God at work through Jesus. However explained, self-recognition forms the heart of faith.

Redemption of Peter, still in the boat on the water, turns into Jesus' prophecy that "from now on you will fish for people," and the word used by Luke suggests "catching alive" (5:10). Peter's mission is narrated in the Book of Acts. They get to shore and three men—Simon, James, and John (Andrew is not mentioned here)—and they "left everything and followed" Jesus (5:11).

Redemption Cleanses

Kingdom redemption heals a person of diseases and disabilities and restores such persons to social status. Leprosy had the power to alienate a person from society and status, but as Amy-Jill Levine observes, "contrary to Hollywood and popular preconceptions," the kind I heard in Sunday School class and sermons, the leper "was not confined to a cave or banished from the town" (Levine-Witherington, *Luke,* 140). He had some kind of very serious scaly-skinned symptom and wanted to be healed. Jesus cleans the man's skin with a touch of the hand—this touching does not violate the law but instead is an act of mercy, which is always expected.

Jesus then instructs the man to go "to the priest and offer the sacrifices" as "a testimony to them" (5:14). Jesus, it can be said, was a contagion of redemption empowered by the Spirit (3:22; 4:1, 18) as well as his intimacy with God. Even still, Jesus' kingdom ministry exhausted him, so he sought quiet, thin spaces for recuperation (5:16).

Redemption Cures

We now encounter the first mention of Gospel stereotypes, namely, the "Pharisees and teachers of the law" (5:17). This must be said here and often: the Pharisees were analogous to activist judges because they democratized the law of Moses by articulating rules and procedures that, if done, enabled ordinary Jews to be observant of the law. They are best described as expanders of the law in order to enable others to observe it. They were, in some senses then, progressives (not picayune fundamentalists and brow-beating moral cops). But they did not (always) agree with Jesus, and what they differed on became sources of tension.

They heard of Jesus. They want to know what's up, so they show up in Capernaum where Luke tells us the "power of the Lord was with Jesus to heal the sick" (5:17). Some men can't get a paralyzed man to Jesus because the crowds are too thick (at Simon Peter's home, I envision) so they climb on the roof, dig through it, and lower the man to Jesus. Jesus' response is to say, "Your sins are forgiven," which is one element in the man's redemption (5:20). The Pharisees don't see how any human can declare forgiveness, so they call out Jesus, which gives him the opportunity to respond. (Lesson, don't bait Jesus.)

Sin, sickness, and suffering are intertwined in that world (cf. John 5:14; 9:2; Luke 13:1–5), but it is a very serious mistake to connect them all the time. (Think of Job.) In fact, as Levine and Witherington state with biblical examples, the Jewish people believed they were "under God's special protection" (Levine-Witherington, *Luke,* 145). The challenge comes to Jesus either to speak the word of forgiveness or show the power of God to heal the man (5:23–24). He, Daniel 7's Son of Man, wants them to know he has the power to forgive and heals the man to prove it.

No one remains where they were when they encounter Jesus' kingdom mission. The formerly paralyzed man becomes someone who praises God as the witnessing crowds sing a praise song (5:25–26). Redemption, never leaving the redeemed alone, leads to worship.

Questions for Reflection and Application

1. How does Luke illustrate in this passage each of these elements of redemption? (Forgiveness, healing, restoration, future kingdom.)

2. What do you observe about the calling to discipleship in this section?

3. What do you learn about Jesus and healing in this section?

4. How does this section shift your view of Pharisees and teachers of the law?

5. What all is involved when someone joins Jesus in his kingdom mission of holistic redemption?

THE NEW DAY OF REDEMPTION

Luke 5:27–6:11

27 *After this, Jesus went out and saw a tax collector by the name of*
Levi sitting at his tax booth. "Follow me," Jesus said to him, 28 *and*
Levi got up, left everything and followed him.

29 *Then Levi held a great banquet for Jesus at his house, and*
a large crowd of tax collectors and others were eating with them.
30 *But the Pharisees and the teachers of the law who belonged to*
their sect complained to his disciples, "Why do you eat and drink
with tax collectors and sinners?"

31 *Jesus answered them, "It is not the healthy who need a doc-*
tor, but the sick. 32 *I have not come to call the righteous, but sinners*
to repentance."

33 *They said to him, "John's disciples often fast and pray, and*
so do the disciples of the Pharisees, but yours go on eating and
drinking."

34 *Jesus answered, "Can you make the friends of the bride-*
groom fast while he is with them? 35 *But the time will come when the*
bridegroom will be taken from them; in those days they will fast."

36 *He told them this parable: "No one tears a piece out of a*
new garment to patch an old one. Otherwise, they will have torn
the new garment, and the patch from the new will not match the

old. 37 *And no one pours new wine into old wineskins. Otherwise,*
the new wine will burst the skins; the wine will run out and the
wineskins will be ruined. 38 *No, new wine must be poured into new*
wineskins. 39 *And no one after drinking old wine wants the new, for*
they say, 'The old is better.'"

6:1 *One Sabbath Jesus was going through the grainfields, and*
his disciples began to pick some heads of grain, rub them in their
hands and eat the kernels. 2 *Some of the Pharisees asked, "Why are*
you doing what is unlawful on the Sabbath?"

3 *Jesus answered them, "Have you never read what David did*
when he and his companions were hungry? 4 *He entered the house*
of God, and taking the consecrated bread, he ate what is lawful
only for priests to eat. And he also gave some to his companions."
5 *Then Jesus said to them, "The Son of Man is Lord of the Sabbath."*

6 *On another Sabbath he went into the synagogue and was*
teaching, and a man was there whose right hand was shriveled.
7 *The Pharisees and the teachers of the law were looking for a rea-*
son to accuse Jesus, so they watched him closely to see if he would
heal on the Sabbath. 8 *But Jesus knew what they were thinking and*
said to the man with the shriveled hand, "Get up and stand in front
of everyone." So he got up and stood there.

9 *Then Jesus said to them, "I ask you, which is lawful on the*
Sabbath: to do good or to do evil, to save life or to destroy it?"

10 *He looked around at them all, and then said to the man,*
"Stretch out your hand." He did so, and his hand was completely
restored. 11 *But the Pharisees and the teachers of the law were furi-*
ous [bitter, ignorant] and began to discuss with one another what
they might do to Jesus.

Something altogether new was underfoot with Jesus so it is best to begin our passage with the parable of the wineskins (5:36–39). Here is its essential point: Jesus is new wine for a new day with new implications for a new life. Jesus is not saying, *Hey, guys, let's jet from the law of Moses. Let's create a new community with new rules and laws.* No, he's not saying that at all. He's saying, *I will guide you into a new way of following the law of Moses (and covering the side of his mouth and now whispering, some of the major leaders are not going to like it).* It is dramatically mistaken for Christians to think Jesus junked the law of Moses. He could never do that. He reinterpreted it through a kingdom lens, but he did not abolish or abandon it. Take a peek for the moment at Luke 16:17.

It was as if Jesus had assigned them all to type up a ten-page paper, they all pulled out their manual typewriters, and then Jesus stopped them, handed them a laptop computer, and said, "Now go ahead and write the same paper." It was the same and altogether new at the same time. If you have never typed on an old manual typewriter, I have a word for you: "Go and do likewise."

In our passage we see three (or four) instances of the new day of redemption.

Eating Re-Shaped

Eating has always been an act of mutuality, equality, fellowship, and community. People ate with family and peers, though at times people get invited to dine with folks above their status. Meals were simple (Neel and Pugh, *The Food and Feasts of Jesus*), the evening had few distractions, and stories were tossed from one side of the table to another. Food, family, friends, fellowship.

Jesus spotted a toll collector on the road from Damascus to Egypt that passed right by Capernaum. He was a custom official working for Herod Antipas. We get a fifteen-word account of the toll collector's conversion. His name is Levi (5:27), which is a Jewish name, which means for some (perhaps many) he has betrayed his people. (Matthew's Gospel calls him "Matthew" [Matthew 9:9].) Taxes were imposed on an area, say Galilee, by the authority, say Herod Antipas. He hired tax farmers and custom officials who paid an amount for the task or who made a bid on the area and then collected monies in order to pay the piper. Levi had been hired at a specific rate, and what he collected above that was his to keep. He did not break even.

Like the fishermen in the first story in Luke 5, he too abandoned "everything" to follow Jesus (Luke 5:28). To celebrate his new life, Levi holds a banquet at which some "Pharisees and teachers of the law" griped about Jesus' meal habits. Their question is probably less of a question than an accusation (like many questions): "Why do you eat and drink with tax collectors and sinners?" (5:30).

Jesus' answer is that he has come not for those who restrict the table to their types. No, he has come to call "sinners to repentance" (5:32). His table practice engages those stereotyped as evil, as anti-social, as thieves, and as selfish. He calls such persons to repentance in order to find forgiveness before God and others. Jesus is criticized for his associations. Amy-Jill Levine presses this observation further. These are not so much what we call the marginalized but are more like our "arms dealers, drug pushers, pimps, loan sharks and people who . . . sexually abuse others" (Levine-Witherington, *Luke*, 151). No wonder the authorities had an eye on Jesus.

Eating practices are re-shaped by Jesus. Instead of eating with those like us or equal to us or in the same devotion patterns as us, Jesus eats with the otherwise outcast. This is not un-Jewish, but it did offend some (not all) of Jesus' Jewish contemporaries. In this Jesus establishes a new precedent for meals in his community: all are welcome. Welcoming others to the table re-shapes the practice by embodying equality in the kingdom of God.

Fasting Re-Located

The fasting Jesus talks about here is not in the law of Moses. Fasting had become a two-times-a-week spiritual discipline for some. People fasted for all sorts of reasons: some out of duty, some grieving over something they had done or something that had happened to them, to their family, to their village, or to their nation. Some fasted because of the condition of Israel as Simeon and Anna were apparently doing (Luke 2:25–38). John the Baptist's followers, some of whom were still following John and not Jesus, also fasted as the Pharisees did (5:33). But for some reason Jesus' followers did not join those other groups in their fasting habits and that drew some questions (5:33).

Jesus responds by metaphorically re-locating fasting on God's timetable. Prior to the wedding the "friends of the bridegroom" do not fast; they celebrate (5:34). But, but, but: the bridegroom will someday "be taken from them" and that will be the time for the friends to fast (5:35). That's when we encounter the parable discussed at the top: a new day has been launched.

That day is a day of celebration until the day when Jesus is taken from them, a theme running straight through John 13–17, and with Jesus gone his disciples will grieve, and grieving in the Bible takes form in fasting (McKnight, *Fasting*). Jesus says the time for fasting is not now; now is the time for feasting. Something new, the kingdom of God, is underfoot and fasting gets re-located.

Sabbath Re-Centered

Two sabbath stories re-center the significance of Sabbath. Jesus perceives that for some Sabbath is a do-nothing day. Jesus' disciples plucked some heads of grain from the wheat and ate the kernels on a Sabbath. Some (not all) Pharisees (not Jews in general) thought such an act violated the prohibition to work on the Sabbath (6:1–2). Not all Jews would have disagreed with the disciples' behavior.

Jesus justifies their behavior by appealing to David who ate "consecrated bread" in the "house of God," food reserved exclusively for priests (6:3). Jesus re-centers Sabbath in one short expression: "The Son of Man is Lord of the Sabbath." This expression can have two meanings: first, "son of man" can mean "any human you choose" and, if it means that, Jesus said human hunger is more important than Sabbath restrictions. Second, "son of man" can mean "Son of Man," in which case Jesus is saying *I am the Lord, these are my followers, they can do what the Lord of the Sabbath tells them because all things are new with the kingdom.* Either way, human hunger takes precedence over strict observance for Jesus.

"On another Sabbath" Jesus is teaching in a synagogue while the "Pharisees and teachers of the law" are observing him, seemingly to catch him in a *faux pas*. A man with a "shriveled hand" is present and Jesus summons the man to "stand in front of everyone" (6:8), which he does. Jesus poses a moral dilemma: What's right for Sabbath practice: "to do good or to do evil"? That is, "to save life or to destroy it" (6:9). You have to think no one had the guts to say "evil" or "destroy." So Jesus healed the man right then and there. Luke tells us Jesus' opponents were ignorant about who Jesus was (NIV has "furious") and so plotted to do Jesus in (6:11).

The impact of our passage is clear: with Jesus and the launching of the kingdom, everything is new, not by getting rid of the old but by turning the old into its best version.

Questions for Reflection and Application

1. What is the difference between Jesus abandoning the law of Moses and Jesus reinterpreting it?

2. How does Jesus re-shape Jewish eating practices?

3. How does Jesus re-locate fasting?

4. How does Jesus re-center Sabbath?

5. Do you have any religious traditions in your life that Jesus might want to re-shape? What might the new, best version of that tradition look like for you?

FOR FURTHER READING

Scot McKnight, *Fasting* (Nashville, Tennessee: Thomas Nelson, 2009).

Douglas E. Neel, Joel A. Pugh, *The Food and Feasts of Jesus: Inside the World of First-Century Fare, with Menus and Recipes* (Lanham, Maryland: Rowman & Littlefield, 2012).

REDEMPTION AGENTS: APOSTLES

Luke 6:12–16

12 One of those days Jesus went out to a mountainside to pray,
and spent the night praying to God. 13 When morning came, he
called his disciples to him and chose twelve of them, whom he also
designated apostles: 14 Simon (whom he named Peter), his brother
Andrew, James, John, Philip, Bartholomew, 15 Matthew, Thomas,
James son of Alphaeus, Simon who was called the Zealot, 16 Judas
son of James, and Judas Iscariot, who became a traitor.

We find Jesus praying again, during which time he discerns God wants him to expand the mission by including others, who are called here "apostles" (6:13). There are three other lists of apostles (Mark 3:13–19; Matthew 10:1–4; Acts 1:13), and no two lists are identical, but they are similar enough. What matters is the apostles' task and what they symbolize.

Their *task* is to expand and extend the kingdom to others. Read Luke 9, where the twelve are sent out, and then Luke 10, where the seventy are sent out. That's what "apostles" do—they are sent ones (the Greek term is *apostellō* and it means to send out). They're sent to do kingdom work in new areas.

The *symbol* cannot be missed by first century Jewish folks. There are *twelve* of them, and they represent the twelve tribes of Israel. Twelve suggests both the renewal of God's covenant with Israel as well as the fulfillment of the promise that in the future the twelve tribes would be reunited as they returned from their exiles.

Questions for Reflection and Application

1. Look at the other lists of apostles and compare them to Luke's. (Mark 3:13–19; Matthew 10:1–4; Acts 1:13)

2. What is the task of "apostles"?

3. Flip to Luke 9 and 10 and skim the accounts of Jesus sending out disciples. What do you notice about their task?

4. What do the chosen 12 represent to first century Jews?

5. How do you practice being a sent disciple of Jesus?

THE ETHIC OF REDEMPTION

Luke 6:17–49

17 He went down with them and stood on a level place. A large
crowd of his disciples was there and a great number of people from
all over Judea, from Jerusalem, and from the coastal region around
Tyre and Sidon, 18 who had come to hear him and to be healed of
their diseases. Those troubled by impure spirits were cured, 19 and
the people all tried to touch him, because power was coming from
him and healing them all.

20 Looking at his disciples, he said:

"Blessed are you who are poor,
for yours is the kingdom of God.
21 Blessed are you who hunger now,
for you will be satisfied.
Blessed are you who weep now,
for you will laugh.
22 Blessed are you when people hate you,
when they exclude you and insult you
and reject your name as evil,
because of the Son of Man.

23 "Rejoice in that day and leap for joy, because great is your reward in heaven. For that is how their ancestors treated the prophets.

24 "But woe to you who are rich,
  for you have already received your comfort.
25 Woe to you who are well fed now,
  for you will go hungry.
Woe to you who laugh now,
  for you will mourn and weep.
26 Woe to you when everyone speaks well of you,
for that is how their ancestors treated the false prophets.

27 "But to you who are listening I say: Love your enemies, do
good to those who hate you, 28 bless those who curse you, pray for
those who mistreat you. 29 If someone slaps you on one cheek, turn
to them the other also. If someone takes your coat, do not withhold
your shirt from them. 30 Give to everyone who asks you, and if
anyone takes what belongs to you, do not demand it back. 31 Do to
others as you would have them do to you.

32 "If you love those who love you, what credit is that to you?
Even sinners love those who love them. 33 And if you do good to
those who are good to you, what credit is that to you? Even sinners do that. 34 And if you lend to those from whom you expect
repayment, what credit is that to you? Even sinners lend to sinners,
expecting to be repaid in full. 35 But love your enemies, do good to
them, and lend to them without expecting to get anything back.
Then your reward will be great, and you will be children of the
Most High, because he is kind to the ungrateful and wicked. 36 Be
merciful, just as your Father is merciful.

37 "Do not judge, and you will not be judged. Do not condemn,
and you will not be condemned. Forgive, and you will be forgiven.
38 Give, and it will be given to you. A good measure, pressed down,
shaken together and running over, will be poured into your lap. For
with the measure you use, it will be measured to you."

[39] *He also told them this parable: "Can the blind lead the blind? Will they not both fall into a pit?* [40] *The student is not above the teacher, but everyone who is fully trained will be like their teacher.*

[41] *"Why do you look at the speck of sawdust in your brother's eye and pay no attention to the plank in your own eye?* [42] *How can you say to your brother, 'Brother, let me take the speck out of your eye,' when you yourself fail to see the plank in your own eye? You hypocrite, first take the plank out of your eye, and then you will see clearly to remove the speck from your brother's eye.*

[43] *"No good tree bears bad fruit, nor does a bad tree bear good fruit.* [44] *Each tree is recognized by its own fruit. People do not pick figs from thornbushes, or grapes from briers.* [45] *A good man brings good things out of the good stored up in his heart, and an evil man brings evil things out of the evil stored up in his heart. For the mouth speaks what the heart is full of.*

[46] *"Why do you call me, 'Lord, Lord,' and do not do what I say?* [47] *As for everyone who comes to me and hears my words and puts them into practice, I will show you what they are like.* [48] *They are like a man building a house, who dug down deep and laid the foundation on rock. When a flood came, the torrent struck that house but could not shake it, because it was well built.* [49] *But the one who hears my words and does not put them into practice is like a man who built a house on the ground without a foundation. The moment the torrent struck that house, it collapsed and its destruction was complete."*

This is one of two records of the most important sermon ever preached, though Luke does not locate it on a mountain as Matthew does (5:1). Instead, he has Jesus on a "level place" (Luke 6:17). Luke says Jesus had just been on a mountainous location (6:12), and then descended to some flat place to teach "his disciples" (6:17). The instructions are nothing less than Life for Kingdom People. This famous firehose of a sermon requires that we see the big picture to prevent getting knocked down by its power.

What it also requires is for you and me to consider and ponder if the big ideas of Jesus' kingdom vision are the big ideas in what we consider central to Christian living. Something about Jesus' teachings get under the skin of each of us at different times. He talks about status, about love, about judging, and about character. We might consider some conversations with others about how important these themes are in what we teach about discipleship today.

Kingdom Redemption Is Holistic

Swarming crowds thronged to Jesus (6:17), and one reason was to get healing for their bodies and liberation from "unclean spirits" (6:18). So powerful was Jesus that people sought merely to touch him for their healing (6:19). Out of this throng of the redeemed, Jesus gathers disciples and teaches them how kingdom people conduct themselves.

Kingdom Redemption Flips the Status Story

Four groups of people are blessed and four are warned. The Greek word often translated "woe" is the exclamatory *ouia*, that is, "Oy!," and it does not mean "go to hell." It's the heart cry of the Messiah working to get the attention of specific groups. The groups who find the favor of God, which best translates "blessed" (and is better than "happy" or "congratulations"), are the poor, the hungry, the weeping, and the ones rejected for following Jesus, the "Son of Man" (6:20–23). One sees here the restoration of those who have various forms of disability, that is, who were not as able as others to fulfill social expectations for life. The warned ones are the mirror opposites: the rich, the well fed, the laughers, and the well-regarded. These are terms of no-status and status, and Jesus here flips the social script upside down. Those who think they've got status with God don't, and those who have the status script of the powerful are to hear that such a script is not God's.

Kingdom Redemption Flips the Love Story

Jesus blesses those who are hated because they follow him and warns those who find immediate social acceptance. Now, teaching his disciples about non-retaliation, he urges them to "love" their enemies. He thereby flips the us vs. them, the good vs. bad, the godly vs. the demonized, and the insider vs. the outsider story (6:27–36). It is easy to love those we like or who are like us, and it is a colossal challenge to love those we don't like or who are not like us, but holistic kingdom redemption transforms the former hater into an everyone lover. Followers of Jesus don't seem to have mastered love of enemies any more than those who observe the law of Moses. As Amy-Jill Levine has pointed out, Proverbs 25:21 anticipates this very teaching of Jesus (Levine-Witherington, *Luke*, 180): "If your enemy is hungry, give him food to eat; if he is thirsty, give him water to drink."

Jesus gets specific. Loving one's enemy means when someone slaps you, you respond with the other cheek to shame them; when someone steals your coat you give more of your clothing to shame them. He wants kingdom people to reverse the social script of every society in history: "do to others as you would have them do to you" (6:31). Two warnings: first, this is not about tolerating or especially submitting to abusive behaviors (verbal, physical, social, sexual) and, second, this is not an economic theory of giving up all your possessions. This is hyperbole teaching kingdom people to love the most difficult to love, to be generous, and not to be retaliators.

Holistic redemption expands our capacity to love not only our affinity groups but those outside such groups. Doing good to your friends or giving loans only to those who can easily pay it back do not challenge us the way doing good to enemies or loaning to those who are poor can do. Underneath all this is that, since God loves all humans, kingdom people are to love all humans too.

Jesus opposes loving others because they please us. Or thinking we are loved because we please the one whom we want to love us. The wonderful essayist Nancy Mairs once countered loving-only-the-pleasing approach with God's love:

> So long as I understood [God loving me] as a response to my pleasingness—if I was good, then God would love me (and contrariwise, if I was bad, then God would throw me into hell, the most hateful gesture imaginable)—I couldn't believe in it, since the chances of my ever being good enough to merit the love of God were slenderer than a strand of silk (*Ordinary Time*, 146).

She's right. That is not how God loves, and we are to learn love from how God loves. Holistic kingdom redemption purges of us earning love and loving only those we like or who bring us pleasure. God's love transcends generosity because it flows freely and abundantly from another reality, namely that, since God *IS* love, God always loves us. More than we can know.

Kingdom Redemption Flips the Judging Script

Religious people of a certain sort instinctually judge negatively anyone not in their group. Kingdom redemption transforms people from judges-of-others into gracious agents of forgiveness and welcome. That is, they are transformed into people who behave and think like Jesus (6:37–40). Jesus pushes harder and warns those prone to judge that they may well be ignoring a plank in their own eye while being picky about a speck of dust in the eye of the one they are judging. Jesus' followers know their own sinfulness, their own leaning toward judgmentalism, and he urges them to become agents of grace, love, and forgiveness.

Kingdom Redemption Flips the Character Script

Character wells up into behavior the way fruit grows on trees, and so he says good trees produce good fruit, and bad trees produce bad fruit. Character matters more than fruit. Character is the accumulation in heart, soul, mind, and action of what has entered into us and what we have learned to habituate. Because character is our innermost self, it determines what we do in the here and now. In Willa Cather's wonderful novel, *My Antonía,* we are treated to a honeyed sentence from the comb of life: "The first time I deceived my grandparents I felt rather shabby, perhaps even the second time, but I soon ceased to think about it" (p. 165). There it is: habituated lying forms a character of deception, but habituated truth-telling forms a character of truth.

Good ol' Mr. Rogers, as a result of a lifetime of prayer, loving others, eschewing hate, breaking down barriers, and most of all learning to experience this world as does a child, *did good out of a good character.* That's what Jesus teaches in the last section of the sermon on the "level place." Good character will produce good actions.

Kingdom Redemption Flips Judgment to Practice

Jesus finishes the sermon with a little story-like invitation shaped by a question: "Why do you call me Lord, Lord and do not do what I say?" (6:46). In the evangelical world one is saved by what one believes, by believing the right thing, and by trusting in Jesus. That is, salvation means confessing, believing, and turning to Jesus. That part is true, but it fails if Lordship of Jesus doesn't lead to doing what the Lord says! Jesus wants a life from us that puts into practice his teachings, and this is because redemption is holistic in that it redeems us morally too. A proper foundation is a holistic life of trusting, obeying, and following the Lord, which does not mean sinlessness. Jesus teaches, as does the entire Bible, that the final judgment examines a person's life, and that means what they did and not just what they believed.

Questions for Reflection and Application

1. What is the big idea in Jesus' sermon on "Life for Kingdom People"?

2. How does kingdom redemption flip people's understanding of status?

3. How does kingdom redemption change the perspective on who we should love, and how we should love them?

4. How does Jesus shift understandings of judgement and character into a life of the practice of goodness?

5. How is your character being shaped into the life of one who belongs to the Kingdom People?

FOR FURTHER READING

Willa Cather, *My Antonia* (New York: A.A. Knopf, 1996).

Nancy Mairs, *Ordinary Time: Cycles in Marriage, Faith, and Renewal* (Boston: Beacon, 1993).

REDEMPTION'S JOB DESCRIPTION

Luke 7:1–50

*1 When Jesus had finished saying all this to the people who were
listening, he entered Capernaum. 2 There a centurion's servant,
whom his master valued highly, was sick and about to die. 3 The
centurion heard of Jesus and sent some elders of the Jews to him,
asking him to come and heal his servant. 4 When they came to
Jesus, they pleaded earnestly with him, "This man deserves to have
you do this, 5 because he loves our nation and has built our synagogue." 6 So Jesus went with them.*

*He was not far from the house when the centurion sent friends
to say to him: "Lord, don't trouble yourself, for I do not deserve to
have you come under my roof.*

*7 That is why I did not even consider myself worthy to come to
you. But say the word, and my servant will be healed. 8 For I myself
am a man under authority, with soldiers under me. I tell this one,
'Go,' and he goes; and that one, 'Come,' and he comes. I say to my
servant, 'Do this,' and he does it."*

*9 When Jesus heard this, he was amazed at him, and turning
to the crowd following him, he said, "I tell you, I have not found
such great faith even in Israel." 10 Then the men who had been sent
returned to the house and found the servant well.*

*11 Soon afterward, Jesus went to a town called Nain, and
his disciples and a large crowd went along with him. 12 As he approached the town gate, a dead person was being carried out—the
only son of his mother, and she was a widow. And a large crowd
from the town was with her. 13 When the Lord saw her, his heart
went out to her and he said, "Don't cry."*

*14 Then he went up and touched the bier they were carrying
him on, and the bearers stood still. He said, "Young man, I say to
you, get up!" 15 The dead man sat up and began to talk, and Jesus
gave him back to his mother.*

*16 They were all filled with awe and praised God. "A great
prophet has appeared among us," they said. "God has come to help
his people." 17 This news about Jesus spread throughout Judea and
the surrounding country.*

*18 John's disciples told him about all these things. Calling two
of them, 19 he sent them to the Lord to ask, "Are you the one who is
to come, or should we expect someone else?"*

*20 When the men came to Jesus, they said, "John the Baptist
sent us to you to ask, 'Are you the one who is to come, or should we
expect someone else?' "*

*21 At that very time Jesus cured many who had diseases, sick-
nesses and evil spirits, and gave sight to many who were blind. 22 So
he replied to the messengers, "Go back and report to John what you
have seen and heard: The blind receive sight, the lame walk, those
who have leprosy are cleansed, the deaf hear, the dead are raised,
and the good news is proclaimed to the poor. 23 Blessed is anyone
who does not stumble on account of me."*

*24 After John's messengers left, Jesus began to speak to the
crowd about John: "What did you go out into the wilderness to see?
A reed swayed by the wind? 25 If not, what did you go out to see? A
man dressed in fine clothes? No, those who wear expensive clothes
and indulge in luxury are in palaces. 26 But what did you go out to
see? A prophet? Yes, I tell you, and more than a prophet. 27 This is
the one about whom it is written:*

" 'I will send my messenger ahead of you,
who will prepare your way before you.'

[28] *I tell you, among those born of women there is no one greater*
than John; yet the one who is least in the kingdom of God is greater
than he."

[29] *(All the people, even the tax collectors, when they heard*
Jesus' words, acknowledged that God's way was right, because they
had been baptized by John. [30] *But the Pharisees and the experts in*
the law rejected God's purpose for themselves, because they had not
been baptized by John.)

[31] *Jesus went on to say, "To what, then, can I compare the*
people of this generation? What are they like? [32] *They are like chil-*
dren sitting in the marketplace and calling out to each other:

" 'We played the pipe for you,
and you did not dance;
we sang a dirge,
and you did not cry.'

[33] *For John the Baptist came neither eating bread nor drinking*
wine, and you say, 'He has a demon.' [34] *The Son of Man came eat-*
ing and drinking, and you say, 'Here is a glutton and a drunkard,
a friend of tax collectors and sinners.' [35] *But wisdom is proved right*
by all her children."

[36] *When one of the Pharisees invited Jesus to have dinner with*
him, he went to the Pharisee's house and reclined at the table. [37] *A*
woman in that town who lived a sinful life learned that Jesus was
eating at the Pharisee's house, so she came there with an alabaster
jar of perfume. [38] *As she stood behind him at his feet weeping, she*
began to wet his feet with her tears. Then she wiped them with her
hair, kissed them and poured perfume on them.

[39] *When the Pharisee who had invited him saw this, he said*
to himself, "If this man were a prophet, he would know who is

touching him and what kind of woman she is—that she is a sinner."

40 Jesus answered him, "Simon, I have something to tell you."

"Tell me, teacher," he said.

41 "Two people owed money to a certain moneylender. One owed him five hundred denarii, and the other fifty. 42 Neither of them had the money to pay him back, so he forgave the debts of both. Now which of them will love him more?"

43 Simon replied, "I suppose the one who had the bigger debt forgiven."

"You have judged correctly," Jesus said.

44 Then he turned toward the woman and said to Simon, "Do you see this woman? I came into your house. You did not give me any water for my feet, but she wet my feet with her tears and wiped them with her hair. 45 You did not give me a kiss, but this woman, from the time I entered, has not stopped kissing my feet. 46 You did not put oil on my head, but she has poured perfume on my feet. 47 Therefore, I tell you, her many sins have been forgiven—as her great love has shown. But whoever has been forgiven little loves little."

48 Then Jesus said to her, "Your sins are forgiven."

49 The other guests began to say among themselves, "Who is this who even forgives sins?"

50 Jesus said to the woman, "Your faith has saved you; go in peace."

God loves every human who has walked, who walks, and who will walk on this earth. Not just some, not just those who go to church, not just those who read their Bibles, not just those who cross all the T's and dot all the I's. God loves every human. You and me, too. God loves those we don't like as much as God loves you and me. Jesus proves the love of God.

Toward the end of Luke's sermon Jesus calls kingdom people to be merciful as God is merciful (6:36). And the next chapter in the Gospel of Luke, chapter seven, displays the holistic redemption of Jesus of all sorts of people. In this chapter we meet some of the many faces of redemption: a gentile, a widow, and a "sinful" woman. In the middle of those passages, we overhear a conversation with Jesus about John. But to turn our focus to these characters in the narrative diverts our attention from the central subject: Jesus. Luke is a biography about Jesus, and chapter seven details the Messiah's job description for a gentile, for a widow and son, for John the Baptist, and for a "sinful" woman.

A Gentile

A centurion was a military leader of one hundred troops. Many stereotype such persons as hated by all, and surely there was resentment over taxation and power and presence, but this centurion was known for his positive relationship with Capernaum: "he loves our nation and has built our synagogue" (7:5). Let's start with that: he was loved by the locals. The very synagogue in which Jesus spent so much time was built through this man's support. But he's a gentile, and one may well hear an echo of Simeon here (2:32).

What is the Messiah's job description for a gentile man with a sick slave?

The man had what the NIV translates as "servant," but which should be translated "slave" (the Greek word is *doulos*). That term slightly adjusts our imaginations of this scene, doesn't it? A slave was an owned body, but this Roman centurion loved him, which suggests the slave was treated as a family member. Which tells us more about this centurion. He was a righteous gentile, he perceived Jesus for who Jesus was, and the gentile was humble enough to tell some emissaries that he did "not deserve" for Jesus to enter his home (7:7). Not all Jews had scruples about entering the home of a gentile, so one might instead think the hesitation is because of the luminous status of Jesus. Knowing the power and authority structure of Jesus, he asks them to tell Jesus that he can just speak a word of healing, and it would be done (7:7–8). What a role reversal! As Stephanie Buckhanon Crowder trenchantly remarks, the might of Rome humbles itself before the lowliness of a Galilean (Crowder, "Luke," 167). Jesus affirms the man's perception and draws a line in the dust by stating that "even in Israel" such faith was "not found" (7:9). So he heals the slave, and the emissaries witness the healed slave upon their return (7:10).

There are many features worthy of our attention here, but we want to slow down enough to observe that Jesus sees the face of a Roman centurion and sees the face of that slave as faces of redemption. Jesus does not see "Roman" or "military" or "slave." He sees persons to love. It's in his job description.

A Widow, a Son

Yes, life was often (not always) hard for a widow. In a village visible from the edges of Nazareth called Nain, Jesus encounters a body being carried out of the city to be buried. That body was the son of a widow, so she was struck twice with death. Jesus' telling her not to cry is not a word because she was grieving but a shocking word arresting her attention for another line on his job description. Jesus stopped those carrying the body, and out of the blue told the "young man" to "get up!" (7:11–14). He "sat up and began to talk" as evidence of being raised back to life. Touchingly, "Jesus gave him back to his mother" (7:15).

No surprise here: They were "all filled with awe" and announced that Jesus had to be a "great prophet" whom God had sent to come visit "his people" (7:16). News easily spreads between those Galilean villages. Surely some thought Jesus' act of raising from the dead sounded like Elijah's (1 Kings 17:17–24) and Elisha's actions (2 Kings 4:32–37).

Two new faces of redemption: a widow and a dead son. We might wonder who experienced the greater redemption! Jesus saves (what many call) souls and bodies. Whole persons experience holistic redemption. That's what Jesus does.

Before we get to a third face of redemption, Luke puts on the stage of his story a revealing, full conversation about John the Baptist, which becomes more of a story about Jesus, the holistic redeemer, than about John.

JESUS AND JOHN

Our passage divides neatly into two parts, the first shaped by questions by, as well as about, John (7:18–28), and the second shaped by the divided response to Jesus and John. Along with it all, we hear Jesus' poetic commentary on those who rejected those sent by God (7:29–35).

John disappeared from the narrative after his imprisonment (see 3:20), and we can presume he's imprisoned in Machaerus, a fortified, elevated palace rebuilt by Herod the Great above the eastern shore of the Dead Sea, in what is called Peraea. It reminds one of Masada, a fortress which is on the western shore. One can judge John's influence and charisma because he was nabbed and confined as a political prisoner. John's own "disciples" (7:18) ask Jesus if he's the "one who is to come" because, after all, the one who is to come had said the kingdom would mean prisoners being liberated (4:18–19). Perhaps Jesus thought, *But not just yet, cuz.*

Jesus' response is potent: instead of saying "Yes" or "No," Jesus creates a pastiche of kingdom predictions from Isaiah 29:18–19; 35:5–6; 42:7, 18; and 61:1. His answer in these citations from Scripture all end up clarifying what "the one who is to come" means. Does it mean the Messiah or the forerunner (look at Malachi 3:1)? There is a discovery at Qumran near the Dead Sea, not far from Machaerus, that clearly connects these predictions with the coming Messiah. It has to be quoted:

> For the heavens and the earth shall listen to His Messiah . . .
>
> For the Lord attends to the pious and calls the righteous by name. Over the humble His spirit hovers, and He renews the faithful in His strength. For He will honor the pious upon the throne of His eternal kingdom, setting prisoners free, opening the eyes of the blind, raising up those who are bowed down (cf. Psalm 146:7–8). . . .
>
> And the Lord shall do glorious things which have not been done, just as He said. For He shall heal the critically wounded, He shall revive the dead, He shall send good news to the afflicted (cf. Isaiah 61:1), He shall satisfy the poor, He shall guide the uprooted, He shall make the hungry rich . . .
>
> (4Q521)[1]

You would not be the first person to ask, after reading those lines from Qumran, if John and Jesus did not know what that group believed the Messiah would accomplish. At least it's fair to think they knew what was "in the air" among Jews about what the Messiah would do. And Isaiah's words themselves that Jesus quotes are more than a little clear about the Messiah's job description.

Let's sum this up now: John says are you the one who is to come? And Jesus' answer seems to be a clear affirmation that he is the Messiah. He says to John's messengers, go tell John that *I'm the messianic figure predicted by the prophet Isaiah*. Don't you think John would have at least muttered *How about the Isaiah 61 prediction about liberating the imprisoned?!* (Yes.)

That question, answered by pressing John to consider the acts of the Messiah, Jesus turns to the "crowd" (7:24) with questions about what they expected in John. Did they expect a people-pleasing, well-dressed, high-status man? (Maybe.) Or did they expect a prophet? (For sure.) Surely they wondered why a God-sent prophet would be imprisoned. Jesus quickly chops their ruminations down to size and says John was "more than a prophet" (7:26), and that John was the "messenger" of Malachi 3:1. That is, Jesus is saying, *I am not the "one who is to come." John is. He is the messenger who is to come*. Which makes John the voice in the wilderness preparing the way for the Messiah. No one in Israel's history was as great as John, but—this is one of the most powerful shifts in any New Testament sentence—"The one who is least in the kingdom of God is greater" than even John (7:28).

John is the bridge between Israel's prophets and the Messiah, the messenger of the Messiah, the Voice preparing the people of God for the Messiah. But once the Messiah comes, everything is new, the kingdom is launched, and redemption becomes holistic. John's job description is to witness to Jesus because he is the Subject of this biography about Jesus, a Subject who is Messiah—straight out of Isaiah.

The second part of this conversation turns to the double response: some love the message of John and Jesus while, again hyperbole is being used, "the Pharisees and the experts in the law rejected God's purpose for themselves, because they had not been baptized by John" (7:30). (Not all, but some.) Jesus now explains in poetic, lyrical terms the rejection he is experiencing. He observes a "generation" that finds Jesus playing *Dancing Queen*, and they find his music too upbeat and risqué, and finds John singing *Where Have All the Flowers Gone,* and they find him too morose and even possessed by a demon (7:31–34). Which means, *they're a bunch of contrarians.*

The final words of this section (7:35) pushes a button: God's "wisdom is proved right by *all* her children," which means both John and Jesus especially (2:40) are sent by God to speak the message of doom and the message of celebration. Perhaps you detect an echo of a verse lost from our short-term memory: read again 7:21. Jesus was healing *all* sorts, that is, maybe they too are part of *all* the children of wisdom.

A "Sinful" Woman

The third face of redemption is someone called a "sinful" woman, which has become a gossipy label for a prostitute (7:37). To begin with, the text never says she was a prostitute, and the NIV's translation probably implies that. It reads "a woman . . . who *lived* a sinful life," when the Greek text reads more literally "a woman, who, in that town, was a sinner" or "a women was a sinner in that town." We need to admit that we must imagine prostitute for that to be present, and we might ask why our minds push her into some kind of sexual sin when nothing of the sort is said. Furthermore, very few women chose prostitution. Nearly every one of them was forced into prostitution. We should be embarrassed how we speak of this woman without evidence. Think too that what we often hear about her in sermons contradicts the actions of the Lord in this passage (and our profession). Women can sin in ways not connected to sex. Maybe she was a serial thief. Now think of this: we love the story of the centurion without insulting him; we love the story about the widow's son without degrading her; but we have insulted this woman for specifics that are not mentioned in the text. Enough said.

No, I can't stop there. In the next paragraph in this passage (7:39–43), a Pharisee named Simon points some judgmental fingers at both Jesus and the woman. Our assignment of this woman to the world of prostitution makes us more like Simon than Jesus. Now I'm done, let's move on.

(There are other accounts like this one in the Gospels [Mark 14:3–9 and Matthew 26:6–13, but also John 12:1–8] and there are important similarities between them, and differences too.)

The woman recognizes Jesus for who he is just as the Roman centurion did. She pours out expensive aromatics on his feet as she weeps over the joy of finding the holistic redeemer she has longed for. The Pharisee was offended by Jesus' acceptance of that kind of contact with that kind of woman, and he obviously doubted Jesus was the prophet others thought he was (7:36–39). Ever alert to a teaching moment, Jesus instructs Simon the Pharisee by giving a short story about two men with radically different debts being released from the debt. Who will love the forgiver more, he asks Simon, who must answer with the obvious: the one forgiven the most (7:40–43).

KISSING IN LUKE:
Luke 7:38, 45; 15:20; 22:48

Jesus turns the scene onto Simon by looking at the woman with the eyes of forgiveness. *You,* he says to him, *gave me no water, no kiss of fellowship, and no oil for my dusty, dirty feet, but she has washed my feet with the water of tears of gratitude, she kissed my feet, and she poured perfume all over my feet.*

There is at least some biting irony now expressed. Her many sins were forgiven, and she now has great love for me. Simon, what did he say? All we hear is crickets in the silence of a stunning moment of holistic redemption. The woman is forgiven while the stereotyped righteous man is put to shame. Instead of thumping our chests over not being like Simon, we should see instead the abundance of God's holistic redemption in Jesus who now sees a face of glory in that woman. She returns home redeemed, liberated from her sin into a new start in life. Just what Jesus' job description had on it.

The "other guests" have a question: "Who is this who even forgives sins?" (7:49). Exactly! He is the Messiah of holistic redemption, redeeming all sorts.

Questions for Reflection and Application

1. So far, what has Luke told us about who Jesus is?

2. How does Jesus redeem both slave and centurion?

3. Look at the passages about the prophets raising dead boys (1 Kings 17:17–24 and 2 Kings 4:32–37). How do those stories compare with Jesus and the widow's son in Nain?

4. What do the prophetic words in the Dead Sea Scrolls and the prophets like Isaiah tell us about Jesus and John?

5. Why do you think people commonly assume the sinful woman was a sexual sinner? How are similar assumptions used against women in the church today?

RESPONSES TO REDEMPTION

Luke 8:1–21

*1 After this, Jesus traveled about from one town and village to an-
other, proclaiming the good news of the kingdom of God. The Twelve
were with him, 2 and also some women who had been cured of evil
spirits and diseases: Mary (called Magdalene) from whom seven
demons had come out; 3 Joanna the wife of Chuza, the manager of
Herod's household; Susanna; and many others. These women were
helping to support them out of their own means.*

*4 While a large crowd was gathering and people were coming to
Jesus from town after town, he told this parable: 5 "A farmer went
out to sow his seed. As he was scattering the seed, some fell along
the path; it was trampled on, and the birds ate it up. 6 Some fell on
rocky ground, and when it came up, the plants withered because
they had no moisture. 7 Other seed fell among thorns, which grew
up with it and choked the plants. 8 Still other seed fell on good soil. It
came up and yielded a crop, a hundred times more than was sown."*

*When he said this, he called out, "Whoever has ears to hear,
let them hear."*

*9 His disciples asked him what this parable meant. 10 He said,
"The knowledge of the secrets of the kingdom of God has been given
to you, but to others I speak in parables, so that,*

" 'though seeing, they may not see;
though hearing, they may not understand.'

11 *"This is the meaning of the parable: The seed is the word of*
God. 12 *Those along the path are the ones who hear, and then the*
devil comes and takes away the word from their hearts, so that they
may not believe and be saved. 13 *Those on the rocky ground are the*
ones who receive the word with joy when they hear it, but they have
no root. They believe for a while, but in the time of testing they fall
away. 14 *The seed that fell among thorns stands for those who hear,*
but as they go on their way they are choked by life's worries, riches
and pleasures, and they do not mature. 15 *But the seed on good soil*
stands for those with a noble and good heart, who hear the word,
retain it, and by persevering produce a crop.

16 *"No one lights a lamp and hides it in a clay jar or puts it*
under a bed. Instead, they put it on a stand, so that those who come
in can see the light. 17 *For there is nothing hidden that will not be*
disclosed, and nothing concealed that will not be known or brought
out into the open. 18 *Therefore consider carefully how you listen.*
Whoever has will be given more; whoever does not have, even what
they think they have will be taken from them."

19 *Now Jesus' mother and brothers came to see him, but they*
were not able to get near him because of the crowd. 20 *Someone told*
him, "Your mother and brothers are standing outside, wanting to
see you."

21 *He replied, "My mother and brothers are those who hear*
God's word and put it into practice."

Some more faces of redemption appear suddenly in the opening paragraph of this Luke 8 passage, and here we meet a special theme in this Gospel. Luke likes to tell redemptive stories about women. Think about those whom we've met already: Elizabeth, Mary, Anna, Simon (Peter's) mother-in-law, the widow from Nain, the "sinful" woman, and now we meet some women who were healed by Jesus. Perhaps they were part of the unnamed in 4:40–41 or 5:15: "Mary (called Magdalene),[1] from whom seven demons had come out; Joanna the wife of Chuza [some think this is Junia in Romans 16:7], the manager of Herod's household; and many others. These women were helping to support them out of their own means" (8:3). A common assumption is that the women were supporters, not co-missioners, but the text is not so obvious. It can be read as Jesus and the twelve with him *and some women* were all involved in the mission, with the women also supporting the ministry from their funds. I agree with Scott Spencer who sees in the women "cooperative, collaborative partnership with Jesus and his male confidants" (Spencer, *Luke*, 202).

As women of means these patrons supported Jesus and his followers in their village-by-village kingdom mission (8:1). There is a world of suggestion in these names. They had experienced holistic redemption through Jesus, they were drawn into his circle, and they voluntarily, against the majority, and perhaps at risk joined the kingdom mission of Jesus. They were all set free to minister because of the support of these women. Questions arise and Jesus responds by telling short stories we call "parables."

What's a Parable?

Parables were favorites of Jewish teachers, as fables and short stories were favorites in the ancient world. Parables are imaginative analogies, uber-short-stories, designed to offer an alternative worldview. That is, Jesus tells a little story with a character or two or three and the attentive listener enters through her imagination to envision that short story occurring. Here's Eugene Peterson's take on Jesus' parables:

> Jesus told stories. As it turns out, he was a very good storyteller. His stories, as good stories always do, penetrate our imaginations and take on lives of their own in us. We find ourselves, often without even being aware of it, inhabiting the world of the story. Now Jesus has us where he wants us, understanding life from *his* point of view, seeing ourselves, God, and one another from the inside, from inside the kingdom of God (*As Kingfishers Catch Fire*, 249).

And, in entering into such a narrative space, Jesus often surprises the reader with some little detail that is designed to shift that person's worldview. Jesus' parables invite us to "imagine a world like this," and the world he wants us to imagine is the kingdom of God.

How to Interpret a Parable?

To interpret a parable of Jesus we need to read the story carefully in a quest to *determine the central analogy Jesus is making.* The short story is "laid next to" (that's a literal translation of "parable" in Greek) something about a kingdom worldview, so the quest is to figure out what connects the story to the kingdom. We cannot stop until we can frame the central analogy to a simple sentence, and we need always be ready to adjust our sentence as we enter deeper into the short story. The simple sentence, however, is never a substitute for getting lost in the story itself. The simple sentence gives us a light to see where the path leads in that storied world Jesus creates.

It is important as well to stick to the first century Jewish world of Jesus to make sense of the parable. We should not think in this passage of farming in Iowa or Nebraska. As well, we can keep our eyes on the Gospel of Luke's themes and bigger context for helping us see what Jesus teaches here. And remember that reading a parable is more than an exercise in detecting a purpose. These parables are meant to transform the hearers and, now that they are written out, the readers (like you and me).

One warning: avoid getting cute and finding hidden treasures that distract us from the central analogy. The rocky soil is not something specific, like the Sadducees. We can imagine seed falling on rocky soil where seeds can't take root. That gives us plenty of space for our imaginations to kick in.

The Parable of the Sower Explained

In this parable (8:4–15), we encounter a sower, some seeds, and some soils. So we can call it The Parable of the Sower tossing seeds into various soils. Each matters. One farmer, many seeds, a farmer scattering seeds as we might do with grass seed, and four separate landings: the path, some rocky ground (lots of that in Galilee), thorns, and good soil. Only one soil is approved.

Now some basics in the central analogy: Jesus explicitly explains to his disciples, who are sent out to expand the mission, that the "seed is the word of God" (8:11). So, that means the kingdom message. The first three soils are not fertile for differing reasons, each representing the kinds of responses he and the disciples have and will continue to experience in their gospel mission work. The good soil is explained: "those with a noble and good heart," or an "excellent [beautiful] and good heart," who "hear the word, retain it, and by persevering produce a crop" (8:15).

Imagine a world in which there are various responses when the kingdom is preached. Some reject it, but the ones who respond properly to Jesus accept the word and surrender into a transformed life.

Responses Expanded

The various responses to Jesus form the heart of our passage. So much so that Jesus says these Yes or No responses are part of God's entire plan. Jesus used parables to teach for precisely this reason: believers perceive them, even if they have to ask him for help, while unbelievers reject them and him (8:10). His parables, this text tells us, dull the senses of the unbeliever. As Levine and Witherington phrase it, they "befuddle hearers" (Levine-Witherington, *Luke*, 234).

As if Jesus wants to give us some practice, he next provides a few short riddle-like lines about *responding to the kingdom mission of Jesus and his followers*: lamps are not put in clay jars or under beds but on a stand so light suffuses the entire room; nothing hidden will remain hidden; and the one who has responded properly will be blessed with more blessings from God; and those who don't respond will be diminished in their capacities to respond to the goodness of God's kingdom (8:16–18).

He's not done. The various responses come home to roost. "Jesus' mother and brothers" want to see him but there are so many surrounding Jesus they can't get to him. So someone says that to Jesus and he pushes back by transferring biological language to spiritual language: his spiritual "mother and brothers are those who hear God's word," and, echoing the end of the parable of the sower (8:15), "put it into practice" (8:21). Even in his own family there could be rocky or thorny soil.

Here's what may well be underpinning all this: if you have the kingdom message and if you are the Messiah, and you are preaching this to the people of Galilee, they ought to be flocking to Jesus. Except they weren't. Which is why this theme of response rises high on the hills of Galilee.

Questions for Reflection and Application

1. What might it shift for our understanding of ministry to see these women as involved disciples, traveling with Jesus?

2. What can parables do for our imaginations?

3. How can we be wise and careful in interpreting parables?

4. What is the central analogy of the parable of the sower, in one sentence?

5. How do the various people around Jesus respond to him? How do you see the people around you today responding to Jesus and his message?

FOR FURTHER READING

Eugene Peterson, *As Kingfishers Catch Fire: A Conversation on the Ways of God Formed by the Words of God* (New York: WaterBrook, 2017).

FOUR MORE FACES OF REDEMPTION

Luke 8:22–56

22 One day Jesus said to his disciples, "Let us go over to the other
side of the lake." So they got into a boat and set out. 23 As they
sailed, he fell asleep. A squall came down on the lake, so that the
boat was being swamped, and they were in great danger.

24 The disciples went and woke him, saying, "Master, Master,
we're going to drown!"

He got up and rebuked the wind and the raging waters; the storm subsided, and all was calm.

25 "Where is your faith?" he asked his disciples.

In fear and amazement they asked one another, "Who is this? He commands even the winds and the water, and they obey him."

26 They sailed to the region of the Gerasenes, which is across
the lake from Galilee. 27 When Jesus stepped ashore, he was met
by a demon-possessed man from the town. For a long time this man
had not worn clothes or lived in a house, but had lived in the tombs.
28 When he saw Jesus, he cried out and fell at his feet, shouting
at the top of his voice, "What do you want with me, Jesus, Son of
the Most High God? I beg you, don't torture me!" 29 For Jesus had
commanded the impure spirit to come out of the man. Many times
it had seized him, and though he was chained hand and foot and

kept under guard, he had broken his chains and had been driven
by the demon into solitary places.

30 Jesus asked him, "What is your name?"

"Legion," he replied, because many demons had gone into him.

31 And they begged Jesus repeatedly not to order them to go into
the Abyss.

32 A large herd of pigs was feeding there on the hillside. The
demons begged Jesus to let them go into the pigs, and he gave them
permission. 33 When the demons came out of the man, they went
into the pigs, and the herd rushed down the steep bank into the lake
and was drowned.

34 When those tending the pigs saw what had happened, they
ran off and reported this in the town and countryside, 35 and the
people went out to see what had happened. When they came to
Jesus, they found the man from whom the demons had gone out,
sitting at Jesus' feet, dressed and in his right mind; and they were
afraid. 36 Those who had seen it told the people how the demon-
possessed man had been cured. 37 Then all the people of the region
of the Gerasenes asked Jesus to leave them, because they were overcome with fear. So he got into the boat and left.

38 The man from whom the demons had gone out begged to go
with him, but Jesus sent him away, saying, 39 "Return home and
tell how much God has done for you." So the man went away and
told all over town how much Jesus had done for him.

40 Now when Jesus returned, a crowd welcomed him, for they
were all expecting him. 41 Then a man named Jairus, a synagogue
leader, came and fell at Jesus' feet, pleading with him to come to
his house 42 because his only daughter, a girl of about twelve, was
dying.

As Jesus was on his way, the crowds almost crushed him.

43 And a woman was there who had been subject to bleeding for
twelve years, but no one could heal her. 44 She came up behind him
and touched the edge of his cloak, and immediately her bleeding
stopped.

45 "Who touched me?" Jesus asked.

When they all denied it, Peter said, "Master, the people are crowding and pressing against you."

46 But Jesus said, "Someone touched me; I know that power has gone out from me."

47 Then the woman, seeing that she could not go unnoticed, came trembling and fell at his feet. In the presence of all the people, she told why she had touched him and how she had been instantly
healed. 48 Then he said to her, "Daughter, your faith has healed
you. Go in peace."

49 While Jesus was still speaking, someone came from the house of Jairus, the synagogue leader. "Your daughter is dead," he said. "Don't bother the teacher anymore."

50 Hearing this, Jesus said to Jairus, "Don't be afraid; just believe, and she will be healed."

51 When he arrived at the house of Jairus, he did not let anyone go in with him except Peter, John and James, and the child's father
and mother. 52 Meanwhile, all the people were wailing and mourning for her. "Stop wailing," Jesus said. "She is not dead but asleep."

53 They laughed at him, knowing that she was dead. 54 But
he took her by the hand and said, "My child, get up!" 55 Her spirit
returned, and at once she stood up. Then Jesus told them to give her
something to eat. 56 Her parents were astonished, but he ordered
them not to tell anyone what had happened.

We gradually are growing accustomed to Luke's holistic understanding of redemption. For him redemption, which is often translated with "salvation," includes at least the following kinds of redemption:

1. healing a man's hand (6:9)
2. forgiveness leading to social restoration (1:77; 7:50)
3. exorcism (8:36)

4. a condition of excessive bleeding (8:48)
5. resurrection (8:50)
6. leprosy (17:19)
7. social pariah or lost (19:9, 10)
8. from a crucifixion (23:37, 39)

In addition to these specific senses of redemption, at times Luke uses this term in a general sense, in which case it is holistic in implications (8:12; 9:24; 13:23; 23:35), and also in a national sense (1:69, 71). So, let us keep in mind that for Jesus' mission, redemption is holistic: spiritual, personal, social, physical, and national.

In our passage Jesus redeems or saves or liberates four more "faces": the disciples from being drowned, a demonized man from evil spirits, a synagogue leader's daughter from death, and a woman from a condition of excessive menstrual flow. Perhaps we need this reminder: heaven will not be for the soul-saved but for the whole-saved. The holistic spectrum of salvation prompts us to pursue redemption in all dimensions of life, and it permits us to see acts of compassion and justice and peace as the working of God and not just results of our own efforts. Furthermore, the Gospel of Luke reveals such redemption as the work of God through Jesus Christ.

Redeemed from Drowning

Jesus orders his apprentices, which include the women of 8:1–3, to sail across the Sea of Galilee to the eastern shore, during which trip Jesus falls asleep like Jonah (1:5), a "squall came down on the lake," the boat was in danger of capsizing, and the disciples were wetting themselves in fear (8:22–23). So they disrupt their master's sleep, Jesus awakens and "rebuked the wind and the raging waters" and lo and behold!

the "storm subsided, and all was calm" (8:24). Just like God (Psalms 89:9; 107:29).

Which leads Jesus to a question that blankets an accusation: "Where is your faith?" (8:25). The question discomforted them. Had they had faith in that situation they would have neither needed to wake up Jesus nor would they have fallen into the fear of drowning because God can save from nature's power. For me this raises the question of why God doesn't always do this, and the reason is not because people don't pray or trust in God. There is no satisfying answer to this.

Before they can answer Jesus' good question, they ask another, which is the preeminent question of all four Gospels, namely, "Who is this? He commands even the winds and the water, and they obey him" (8:25). The face of the redeemed can at times express serious wondering. The answer is implicit, but we can't go wrong starting with this answer: Jesus is the Lord over all creation.

Redeemed from Demons

On the eastern shore of the Sea, Jesus encounters a demonized man. So dire is the man's condition that he himself resides among tombs, reminding us that the devil's mission is death. He also had acquired through the demons extraordinary strength (8:29). Because Jesus has ordered the "impure spirit" to exit the man, the man petitions Jesus, addressing him as "Jesus, Son of the Most High God," not to torture him (8:27–28).

Jesus commands the man to give his name. The man answers "Legion," which means "many" and indicates that the man was influenced by many demons, who now gain the platform and plead with Jesus not to send them into the "abyss" (the place of the dead; notice 1 Peter 3:19; Revelation 20:1–2). The next part of the story is even more well-known.

Jesus, now in gentile territory on the east coast of the Sea, permits the demons to enter into (gentile-territory) pigs who haul it down a slope into the Sea where they drown, and so put the demons into the watery chaos. If this strikes you as odd, you are in the majority.

The farmers report the event to "the town and countryside" and of course some wander out to gawk and snoop. They find Jesus and the man "dressed and in his right mind" (Luke 8:35). Holistic redemption includes exorcisms and return to mental health, but such a powerful act by Jesus overwhelms the locals with fear, so much so that they plead with Jesus to go away.

Which he does. What a sad commentary.

The redeemed man wants Jesus to stay but Jesus, instead of remaining, orders him to become a witness of "how much God has done for you"—exactly what the man then does (8:38–39). Or does he? Luke says he "told all over town how much *Jesus* had done for him" (8:39). The face of this redeemed man is glad.

Redeemed from Excessive Bleeding

The next section in our passage has two episodes with two faces. Since the story of the woman with an unceasing, that is twelve years, menstrual flow finishes first, we begin with her and what could be seen as her kind of disability (8:42b–48).

Many have said (and preached) that menstruation makes a woman unclean, which it does; they then say such a person is quarantined at home, which is not true; then they say she makes others unclean, which is more or less true, but something first century Jews didn't get hung up about. Uncleanness had to do with participating in the temple, not participating in normal life. And the poor of Galilee had no option but to continue working. Notice too that no one is bent out of shape about this woman touching Jesus.

Luke's entire focus is on her desperate need of healing. The simple act of touching Jesus' fringes healed her; her discomfort ended, and her joy returned. The NIV's "healed her" is better translated "saved her" as the Greek term is *sōzō* (to save, to redeem, to liberate). NIV readers could miss holistic salvation, and may not even connect healing with salvation, which Luke does over and over. As one person has observed, Luke describes the "man with a flow of power" who heals the woman with a flow of blood (see Levine-Witherington, *Luke*, 241). The face of this redeemed woman is relieved.

Redeemed from Death

Nothing is more holistic in redemption than being raised to life after death! Jairus, the "synagogue leader," and we don't know the location but perhaps Jesus is back in Capernaum, has a twelve-year-old daughter who "was dying" (8:40). Then Jesus encounters the bleeding woman and redeems her. As Jesus was speaking, someone from Jairus's home informs him that his daughter has died, and he can suspend his push to get Jesus to come to his home. They all are about to experience the height of holistic redemption.

Jesus: "just believe, and she will be" saved/redeemed (NIV: "healed"; 8:50), Jesus tells the messengers. He now backs up his word by going to the home with "Peter, John and James," encounters grieving people to whom Jesus says "Stop wailing. She is not dead but asleep" (8:52). He takes the dead twelve-year-old's hand, orders her to "get up" and she "stood up." The wailers are ignored, and Jesus speaks only to her "astonished" parents, and he tells them "mum's the word on this." The faces of the young girl and her parents were astonished.

The demand for Jesus is growing so in our next passage we will discover that Jesus sends the twelve apostles out to expand the kingdom mission at work in power and glory.

Questions for Reflection and Application

1. How are Luke's stories so far expanding your understanding of the term "salvation"?

2. What is your reaction to the question of why God doesn't always save people from nature's power, and the claim that there is no satisfying answer to this?

3. What is your view of demon possession, and what do you think is the significance of Jesus' exorcisms in the Gospels?

4. How does "salvation" blend with physical healing in Luke's Gospel?

5. How do you talk about your own "salvation"? What story do you tell about Jesus' work in your life and your response to him?

AGENTS OF REDEMPTION

Luke 9:1–17

1 When Jesus had called the Twelve together, he gave them power
and authority to drive out all demons and to cure diseases, 2 and he
sent them out to proclaim the kingdom of God and to heal the sick.
3 He told them: "Take nothing for the journey—no staff, no bag, no
bread, no money, no extra shirt. 4 Whatever house you enter, stay
there until you leave that town. 5 If people do not welcome you,
leave their town and shake the dust off your feet as a testimony
against them." 6 So they set out and went from village to village,
proclaiming the good news and healing people everywhere.

7 Now Herod the tetrarch heard about all that was going on.
And he was perplexed because some were saying that John had
been raised from the dead, 8 others that Elijah had appeared, and
still others that one of the prophets of long ago had come back to life.
9 But Herod said, "I beheaded John. Who, then, is this I hear such
things about?" And he tried to see him.

10 When the apostles returned, they reported to Jesus what they
had done. Then he took them with him and they withdrew by themselves to a town called Bethsaida, 11 but the crowds learned about it
and followed him. He welcomed them and spoke to them about the
kingdom of God, and healed those who needed healing.

12 Late in the afternoon the Twelve came to him and said,
"Send the crowd away so they can go to the surrounding villages
and countryside and find food and lodging, because we are in a
remote place here."
13 He replied, "You give them something to eat."
They answered, "We have only five loaves of bread and two
fish—unless we go and buy food for all this crowd." 14 (About five
thousand men were there.) But he said to his disciples, "Have them
sit down in groups of about fifty each." 15 The disciples did so, and
everyone sat down. 16 Taking the five loaves and the two fish and
looking up to heaven, he gave thanks and broke them. Then he
gave them to the disciples to distribute to the people. 17 They all ate
and were satisfied, and the disciples picked up twelve basketfuls of
broken pieces that were left over.

The tendency today is to build a bigger church with a bigger platform, and then to convert that platform into conferences that expand that church's ideas to other churches. And the next thing we know, we've got an association or even a new denomination, and then we have centralized powers and structures and institutions that eventually become harder than dinosaur fossils. What's fossilized today is "the bigger, the better."

Jesus commissioned his agents to form small groups. Luke 9 is Luke's first sending out of agents of redemption, twelve of them, and in Luke 10 we will read about an expanded group of agents, some seventy of them. In reading our passage we can easily see that their mission was, like Jesus', holistic redemption.

Agents of Power

Jesus "gave" the twelve apostles "power and authority," which means capacity that has been authorized by Jesus, "to drive out all demons and to cure diseases" and "to heal the sick" (9:1, 2). Look back over Luke chapters four through eight to observe that exorcisms and healings are integral to kingdom redemption (4:31–37, 38–44; 5:12–16, 17–26; 7:1–10, 11–17, 21; 8:22–25, 26–39, 40–56). The apostles do not go rogue. They expand the reach of Jesus' own kingdom mission to more than what he can do by himself.

The apostles had neither capacity nor the wherewithal to authorize themselves. Only the one *doing holistic redemption* had the power to authorize them. The apostles then were agents through whom Jesus' own power was at work. After a cure they couldn't say, "Look what I have done!" Instead, they had to admit, "This is not me but the power of God at work through me."

Agents of Preaching

In addition to the exorcisms and the healings, Jesus empowered them to "proclaim the kingdom of God" (9:2). There are five elements in what Jesus means by kingdom:

A king (God, Jesus)
A rule (by way of both redemption and governing/lordship)
A people (Israel, the church)
A law (Moses, Jesus' own teachings of that law)
A territory (the land)

As we read through the Gospel of Luke, we will encounter each of these often. God is the true king, and he has sent Jesus as the Son of God, as Messiah, and both of those categories evoke kingship. King Jesus "rules" first by redeeming holistically and then ruling the redeemed as Lord. Those redeemed are the people of the king, who gives them his teachings or law (6:17–49), and spreads them out throughout the land (Galilee, Judea, and even beyond as he has already crossed the Sea into the gentile territories). Put simply, the twelve apostles were sent to declare that God's kingdom is launched through Jesus, and those who want to dwell in that kingdom are to repent and follow Jesus with them.

A word to consider: the word "kingdom," whether spoken in Aramaic (Jesus' native language) or Greek (the language of the New Testament), evoked "empire" for anyone who lived in the Roman empire at that time. I consider "empire" the most evocative and accurate translation, not least because it reminds us that the Land of Jesus was under Roman control at the time. For him to have chosen that term for his mission raised more than eyebrows among those in power.

Jesus preached the kingdom (4:14–30), his agents preach the kingdom; what Jesus preached is what they were to preach. Their calling was to extend what Jesus was doing: nothing more, nothing less.

Noticeably, Jesus wanted his apostles to trust in God to provide, who provides not with manna-from-heaven but with open hearts and hands and homes of those who responded positively to the kingdom (9:3–6). Hospitality became the habit of kingdom people. Which means only some were sent and far more stayed home and became agents of redemption through hospitality.

Some people would reject the agents entirely (9:5) while others were curious about the goings on. Herod Antipas overhears "what was going on" (9:7) and then heard a variety of answers in his circles of who was at work: perhaps John the Baptist raised from the dead, perhaps Elijah returned, or perhaps a prophet raised from the dead (9:7–8). He knew the first guy was dead because he had him decapitated but somehow Luke knew Herod wanted to "see" Jesus (9:9). He will, but not until the trial scenes near the end of the Gospel of Luke.

Agents of Distribution

Luke drops that little curiosity about Herod's curiosity and tells us the twelve returned and gave reports to Jesus about the power of God at work through them. Jesus perceives their need for a retreat, so they choose Bethsaida, a village under Herod Philip, but the crowds choose to accompany them (9:10–11a). Jesus welcomes the crowd and does more holistic redemption (9:11b).

In this location out of the way of the busyness of Capernaum, the disciples make a proposal: it's late in the day and the people are hungry so send them into the villages to get food (9:12). Jesus' response surprised them for he instructs the agents of redemption with an order: "You give them something to eat" (9:13). They respond that they have a mere pittance of food ("five loaves" and "two fish"). Except that it was about to be enough! Luke wants us to know the disparity between need and resources by telling us there were 5,000 men, which means lots more than 5,000 because women and children were not included in the number.

You know the story. Jesus has his agents divide them into groups of fifty, and then Jesus blesses the bread and fish (sounds like the Eucharist). Let's pause over this word "blesses" because the NIV has only "gave thanks" and that's not quite enough. Yes, we all know blessing someone can be as blank as ministers asked to say a word of blessing at events like, as Frederick Buechner once wrote, "Rotarian wienie roasts." No, when it comes to the Bible's sense of blessing, as Buechner himself says of blessing someone, "you irreversibly convey into my life not just something of the beneficent power and vitality of who you are, but something also of the life-giving power of God" (Buechner, *Beyond Words*, 47, 48). So, having blessed the bread and fish into abundance by the power of God, Jesus feeds the entire mass of people with "twelve basketfuls" left over, one basket for each apostle. Jesus' agents of redemption become agents of abundant distribution.

In each of these episodes God is at work through Jesus whose power is granted to the apostles who themselves become agents of Jesus' holistic redemption. The task of a disciple is not to do one's own thing but to extend the thing of Jesus!

Questions for Reflection and Application

1. How and why did Jesus authorize the apostles to go out?

2. What does "kingdom" mean to Jesus?

3. What is the significance of translating "kingdom" as "empire"?

4. How does the meaning of "blessing" go beyond "gave thanks"?

5. In what ways are you working "to extend the thing of Jesus" rather than doing your own thing?

FOR FURTHER READING

Frederick Buechner, *Beyond Words: Daily Readings in the ABC's of Faith* (San Francisco: Harper SanFrancisco, 2004).

TWO OF REDEMPTION'S MAJOR MOMENTS

Luke 9:18–36

18 *Once when Jesus was praying in private and his disciples were*
with him, he asked them, "Who do the crowds say I am?"
19 *They replied, "Some say John the Baptist; others say Elijah;*
and still others, that one of the prophets of long ago has come back
to life."
20 *"But what about you?" he asked. "Who do you say I am?"*
Peter answered, "God's Messiah."
21 *Jesus strictly warned them not to tell this to anyone.* 22 *And*
he said, "The Son of Man must suffer many things and be rejected
by the elders, the chief priests and the teachers of the law, and he
must be killed and on the third day be raised to life."
23 *Then he said to them all: "Whoever wants to be my disciple*
must deny themselves and take up their cross daily and follow me.
24 *For whoever wants to save their life will lose it, but whoever loses*
their life for me will save it. 25 *What good is it for someone to gain*
the whole world, and yet lose or forfeit their very self? 26 *Whoever is*
ashamed of me and my words, the Son of Man will be ashamed of
them when he comes in his glory and in the glory of the Father and
of the holy angels.

*27 "Truly I tell you, some who are standing here will not taste
death before they see the kingdom of God."*

*28 About eight days after Jesus said this, he took Peter, John
and James with him and went up onto a mountain to pray. 29 As
he was praying, the appearance of his face changed, and his clothes
became as bright as a flash of lightning. 30 Two men, Moses and
Elijah, appeared in glorious splendor, talking with Jesus. 31 They
spoke about his departure, which he was about to bring to fulfillment at Jerusalem. 32 Peter and his companions were very sleepy,
but when they became fully awake, they saw his glory and the
two men standing with him. 33 As the men were leaving Jesus,
Peter said to him, "Master, it is good for us to be here. Let us put
up three shelters—one for you, one for Moses and one for Elijah."
(He did not know what he was saying.) 34 While he was speaking,
a cloud appeared and covered them, and they were afraid as they
entered the cloud. 35 A voice came from the cloud, saying, "This
is my Son, whom I have chosen; listen to him." 36 When the voice
had spoken, they found that Jesus was alone. The disciples kept
this to themselves and did not tell anyone at that time what they
had seen.*

To begin a conversation in class I have often asked students, "What are the top ten events in the life of Jesus?" (No sayings of Jesus are allowed.) That question leads to good discussions, and sometimes to creative answers (groans deleted). The big events disclose new insights into the identity of Jesus. Two of those events are in our passage: the confession by Peter and the transfiguration. Each reveals more about who Jesus is, and both answer the question the disciples asked in the boat: "Who is this?" (8:25). As we see in this passage, the answer to that very question determines the shape of what it means to follow Jesus to this very day. Notice the progression below.

Jesus Is Messiah

In a private time of prayer Jesus asks a rather innocent question about public opinion about who he is. Their answers echo what Herod was hearing (9:7–9): "John the Baptist . . . Elijah . . . one of the prophets" (9:19). A sharp turn, a hopping of lanes, a rise in temperature follow, revealing that Jesus' question was far from innocent: "But what about you? Who do you say I am?" (9:20). Peter's answer is "God's Messiah." Messiah means "the anointed one," and that points us at the act of anointing someone to be king.

Christians have learned, as they should, to read the Old Testament as anticipating the Messiah. But the term Messiah is not only rare in the Old Testament and also rare in Jewish sources outside the Old Testament, but there was more than one *theory* about what the Messiah would accomplish. Some anticipated a warrior, liberating Messiah (cf. Isaiah 45:1), some anticipated more of a royal Messiah, others anticipated a prophet better than the prophets, while the community of the Dead Sea Scrolls anticipated two Messiahs, one royal and one priestly. What was undeniable was this: Jewish folks expected the Messiah to bring liberation for Israel, justice, peace, and a world put to rights.

Jesus Defines Messiah Anew

Peter confesses Jesus as Messiah. Jesus accepts the label but suddenly and shockingly redefines what will happen to this Messiah, but wait for it. Instead of referring to himself as Messiah, Jesus changes registers, takes us back to Daniel 7's famous glorious, kingly figure, namely, the "Son of Man." But his new version of the Son of Man, as part of God's plan of holistic redemption, "must suffer many things" and must experience denunciation by Jerusalem's leading authorities, and he "must be killed" but "on the third day" he will be "raised to life" (9:22).

Jesus redefines Messiah to the Son of Man who must suffer. But his suffering will be turned inside out with a resurrection. The Gospels show the disciples didn't get it.

Jesus Defines Discipleship Anew

So far in Luke's biography of Jesus a disciple is someone who hears the call of Jesus, becomes an agent of redemption, and practices his teachings. A major connection is made more explicit now. Who Jesus is—the suffering Messiah who will be raised—becomes the paradigm for the disciple in her daily life. A disciple is one whose everyday life is like Jesus' life. If he suffers, she will suffer; if he is raised, she will be raised. Discipleship is the flipside of the identity of Jesus. It is marked, not by self-interest or a "what's in it for me?" disposition. No, it is shaped by self-denial for the sake of Jesus. So vital is the identity of Jesus for discipleship that Messiah people will be judged by the Son of Man *in accordance with their conformity to the Way of the Messiah* (9:23–27). Self-denial is not the higher Christian life; it is that life.

Jesus Is the Son of God

Jesus' last words in this discipleship instruction make a prediction that "some who are standing here" (the disciples) "will not taste death before they see the kingdom of God" (9:27). Matthew's version is slightly different: ". . . not taste death before they see *the Son of Man coming in his kingdom*" (16:28). Before they die? Did the kingdom come by the end of the first century? Was Jesus mistaken? It is best to read this statement in light of what follows. The transfiguration not only anticipates the kingdom of God; the kingdom of God invades earth in the transfiguration. This is beyond what the Irish call "thin places." Here the thin membrane separating God from humans has been pierced by the Light.

The transfiguration occurs before only three disciples, one of whom brings it up in a letter (2 Peter 1:16–18). While praying, Jesus began to glow, an inside-out manifestation of his essential divine glory (Luke 9:29). Two major figures, the law-giver Moses, who also shone (Exodus 34:29–35), and the prophet Elijah, appear "in glorious splendor" conversing with Jesus. They spoke of Jesus' "exodus" (NIV: "departure") in Jerusalem, which means these two major figures know the "must" of Jesus' suffering will be death in Jerusalem. The three, obtusely worn out from climbing, are asleep but awaken to the glory around them. Peter suggests building a tent so the mountaintop experience can last longer. Luke adds that "he did not know what he was saying." Luke's right.

As I have said above, major events reveal the identity of Jesus. The Father speaks of the Son to the three disciples and, as he said of Jesus at his baptism, announces that "This is my [royal] Son, whom I have chosen." No sooner than the voice was heard the entire scene is gone and "Jesus was alone" (9:35). So overwhelming was the event, so revealing, and so utterly mystifying for them that the three told no one what they had seen–until Peter did in a letter (2 Peter 1:15–18).

Who Jesus is determines who we are to be. What Jesus did determines discipleship's central themes. He is Messiah, which means we are to be allegiant to king Jesus. He is a suffering Messiah, which means self-denial. He is a glory-filled and glory-destined Son of Man kind of Messiah, which means beyond our cross-bearing comes an eternal glory. All because of who Jesus is.

Questions for Reflection and Application

1. What were the range of expectations for the Jewish Messiah?

2. How does Jesus turn such expectations upside down?

3. What does "disciple" mean in Luke?

4. How do the ideas of Messiah, discipleship, and transfiguration weave together in this section?

5. How does coming to understanding Jesus more impact your allegiance to him?

REDEMPTION'S AGENTS STUMBLE

Luke 9:37–50

[37] The next day, when they came down from the mountain, a large crowd met him. [38] A man in the crowd called out, "Teacher, I beg you to look at my son, for he is my only child. [39] A spirit seizes him and he suddenly screams; it throws him into convulsions so that he foams at the mouth. It scarcely ever leaves him and is destroying him. [40] I begged your disciples to drive it out, but they could not."

[41] "You unbelieving and perverse generation," Jesus replied, "how long shall I stay with you and put up with you? Bring your son here."

[42] Even while the boy was coming, the demon threw him to the ground in a convulsion. But Jesus rebuked the impure spirit, healed the boy and gave him back to his father. [43] And they were all amazed at the greatness of God.

While everyone was marveling at all that Jesus did, he said to his disciples,

[44] "Listen carefully to what I am about to tell you: The Son of Man is going to be delivered into the hands of men." [45] But they did not understand what this meant. It was hidden from them, so that they did not grasp it, and they were afraid to ask him about it.

[46] *An argument started among the disciples as to which of them would be the greatest.* [47] *Jesus, knowing their thoughts, took a little child and had him stand beside him.* [48] *Then he said to them, "Whoever welcomes this little child in my name welcomes me; and whoever welcomes me welcomes the one who sent me. For it is the one who is least among you all who is the greatest."*

[49] *"Master," said John, "we saw someone driving out demons in your name and we tried to stop him, because he is not one of us."*

[50] *"Do not stop him," Jesus said, "for whoever is not against you is for you."*

Jesus has called some disciples; he has taught them; he has permitted them to accompany him as his ministry explodes with power; he has accepted their confession as Messiah; he has explained the dark and light of future days; and he has revealed that he is full of God's glory. They've had beyond enough experience. Down from the mountain things go fast. Yet, the disciples stumble in today's passage in three ways as we learn that holistic redemption takes a lifetime, and more (!).

They at Times Lack Faith

When a desperate father pleads with Jesus to redeem his son from demonic control, he informs Jesus that the disciples were unable to exorcise this stubborn demon (9:37–40). Jesus erupts into strong words: "You unbelieving and perverse generation" (9:41). He's about had it: "How long shall I . . . put up with you?" You could put an exclamation point through the question mark.

They failed to trust. The boy and his father suffered longer. Jesus healed the son, revealing what trust looks like. Holistic redemption includes liberation from demons, and no doubt the father was shouting from rooftops and the boy thrilled to be healed. Luke, however, does not offer a glib solution to the problem. He does not say "you gotta have faith." He knows this world is racked by sin and Satan and systemic injustices, and he knows that not all are healed and not all prayers are answered as we want, but he still presses the disciples to trust God for the powers to liberate.

They at Times Desire Greatness

I'm less bothered by the inability of the disciples to tap into God's power to redeem a boy from demons than I am, and this comes next in Luke, by their inexcusable worldly desire to be great. Jesus for a second time prophesies his death to disciples who don't understand (9:44).

Afraid to ask him for a clearer prediction, they turn from something profoundly significant in the "life of Jesus," his impending death, to face off against one another in a feat of comparison as to who is the "greatest" (9:45). Jesus embodies his self-denying Son-of-Man way of life by having a child stand next to him in order to teach all over again what true discipleship means: "it is the one who is least among you all who is the greatest" (9:46–48). Humility shatters the desire for greatness, but disciples grow into a full embrace of what discipleship means.

They Fail at Exclusiveness

They've failed at exorcism; they've failed in desiring the glory and status of greatness; now they fail by wanting an exclusive club. John, the son of Zebedee, observed some "maverick minister" (Spencer, *Luke,* 251) exorcising demons in Jesus' name, something the disciples had just failed to accomplish. John's beef about the man is as insensitive as it can be for a victim of demonic attacks, that is, John's words are trauma *in*sensitive. John's gripe is "he is not one of us," which makes him appear sectarian and elitist. Jesus blows John's attitude up with the anti-elitist "whoever is not against you is for you" (9:50). Many there are who would prefer that Jesus had not said this, but he did, and it is ours to embrace it. Wherever there is liberation, there is God's holistic redemption. As my father might have said, "Deal with it."

I have experienced this—yea, I have been part of it myself—among evangelicals where they think they, or we, are the only believers. I've experienced this among Catholics and among Lutherans and among the Churches of Christ and among Eastern Orthodox. To each Jesus has a word: "whoever is not against you is for you." God is bigger than any of us can know. Deal with it.

Questions for Reflection and Application

1. Why do you think the disciples didn't succeed in driving out the evil spirit?

2. How do the disciples fail to understand Jesus in these stories?

3. How did the disciples fail to understand their own mission in these stories?

4. How would you characterize Jesus' reactions to his disciples' failures?

5. Have you ever wanted to see your subsection of Christianity as the "right" one, the exclusive one? What might Jesus say to you about this?

REDEMPTION CHALLENGES DISCIPLES

Luke 9:51–62

*51 As the time approached for him to be taken up to heaven, Jesus
resolutely set out for Jerusalem. 52 And he sent messengers on
ahead, who went into a Samaritan village to get things ready for
him; 53 but the people there did not welcome him, because he was
heading for Jerusalem. 54 When the disciples James and John saw
this, they asked, "Lord, do you want us to call fire down from heav-
en to destroy them?" 55 But Jesus turned and rebuked them. 56 Then
he and his disciples went to another village.*

*57 As they were walking along the road, a man said to him, "I
will follow you wherever you go."*

*58 Jesus replied, "Foxes have dens and birds have nests, but the
Son of Man has no place to lay his head."*

59 He said to another man, "Follow me."

But he replied, "Lord, first let me go and bury my father."

*60 Jesus said to him, "Let the dead bury their own dead, but
you go and proclaim the kingdom of God."*

*61 Still another said, "I will follow you, Lord; but first let me go
back and say goodbye to my family."*

62 Jesus replied, "No one who puts a hand to the plow and looks back is fit for service in the kingdom of God."

It is not the things Jesus said that I *don't* understand that bother me. It's the words I do understand that bother me. A saying like this has been falsely attributed to Mark Twain so it often goes under his name.[1] What Twain didn't say fits our passage completely. The disciples of Jesus have been clearly taught that to follow Jesus means to follow the path that leads to the cross. That path is walked daily, and in our passage holistic redemption challenges those who find off ramps on the Way of Jesus.

The Missional Intent of Jesus

Luke's opening line to this passage informs us that Jesus "resolutely set out for Jerusalem" (9:51), and as Christian readers that sounds ominous. Jesus intends to confront the powers of Jerusalem with the kingdom mission. The NIV's decision in "taken up *to heaven*"—to make it sound like it was exclusively about his assumption to heaven (Acts 1:9)—narrows the expression too much, and the word "heaven" is not in the original text at all. The term means "taken up" or "lifted up," but it could refer (as it does in the Gospel of John) to his crucifixion, or it could also include his resurrection and ascension. I prefer the NRSV's "taken up" as it leaves us wondering what it might mean, which the text does!

His mission is to get to Jerusalem with his kingdom mission, and that involves more than going to heaven. That wider mission is made clear because he "sent messengers" into "a Samaritan village to get things ready for him" (9:52). That is, they were the advance crew telling people Jesus and his kingdom powers were coming, but the response was not welcoming.

The Response to Jesus

Some Samaritan village did not "welcome" him because they perceived his mission was Jerusalem, which stereotypically did not get along well with Samaria (9:53). As Levine and Witherington say so well, they had "rival Temples, rival priesthoods, rival claims to be heirs of the patriarchs, and rival messianic views" (Levine-Witherington, *Luke*, 268). The Samaritans' perception of Jesus' intent to head to Jerusalem does not dissuade the "disciples James and John," who instead of grieving over their response prefer that Jesus wreak havoc on the place. Something on the order of "nuke 'em til they glow" (9:54; cf. 6:27 and 2 Kings 1:9–12). Jesus once again has to rebuke his own closest followers (9:55).

So the journey continues through Samaria. A word about Luke's organization. One might get the impression in reading 9:51–56 that Jesus is headed directly to Jerusalem, but he doesn't get there until 19:28. Most dub this section from 9:51 to 19:27 "The Travel Narrative." If one reads the whole of it through the notes sounded in 9:51–56 (and 10:38 confirms that kind of reading), one has one kind of reading; if one thinks Luke adds sayings and events from other periods in the ministry of Jesus to the journey, one has a different reading. The second option seems more likely.

The Challenge from Jesus

The missional intent of Jesus requires commitment from his followers because, as he has already taught them, following him means daily self-denial (9:23). Whether people are volunteering to follow Jesus or whether he is calling people to follow him, the challenges are real so he wants them to join him only if they realize what they will experience.

Walter Brueggemann once preached a sermon that opened with these solemn words that evoke the sanctity of these words of Jesus:

> There is nothing ordinary about the key claims of biblical faith. Indeed, there is almost nothing about biblical faith that can be understood according to our usual analytical, scientific, objective, or commonsense control of life. The Bible is, rather, organized around the explosive moments when the holiness of God touches down in our midst and changes everything. Such touchdown moments are not sweet and romantic. They are not pious and religious. Rather, they are moments of threat and risk, when our worlds are shattered and everything is changed (Brueggemann, *Collected Sermons*, 65).

Following him can mean a form of volunteer homelessness (9:57–58). Following him can mean suspending family requirements. The Way of Jesus challenges tradition and social hierarchies because his followers are now committed to God's empire (9:59–60). Following Jesus can suspend even social courtesies, courtesies previously granted to Elisha (1 Kings 19:19–21), because kingdom time is now, and commitment is total (9:61–62).

I have used the term "can" because Jesus' words are terse and edgy, and they are not required of everyone. Rather, they illustrate in hyperbolic form the challenge of commitment. Each person will discover in following Jesus what resists their commitment, and at that point a decision needs to be made. When I am speaking or teaching on topics and texts like this I often say, "Someone needs to quote Bonhoeffer here." I'll be that someone, and lay before us some his most challenging words from *Discipleship*:

> Costly grace is the gospel which must be sought again and again, the gift which has to be asked for, the door at which one has to knock. It is costly, because it calls to discipleship; it is grace because it calls us to follow Jesus Christ. It is costly, because it costs people their lives; it is grace, because it thereby makes them live. It is costly, because it condemns sin; it is grace, because it justifies the sinner. Above all, grace is costly, because it was costly to God, because it costs God the life of God's Son "you were bought with a price" and because nothing can be cheap to us which is costly to God.

Only the believers obey—that is said to the obedient person inside the believer. Only the obedient believe—that is said to believers in their obeying. If the first statement remains alone, the believer is prey to cheap grace, that is, damnation. If the second statement remains alone, the believers are prey to their works, that is, damnation.

> Whenever Christ calls us, his call leads us to death.
> But how should disciples know what their cross is?
> They will receive it when they begin to follow the suffering Lord. They will recognize their cross in communion with Jesus.
> Discipleship in essence never consists in a decision for this or that specific action; it is always a decision for or against Jesus Christ.
> (*Discipleship*, 67, 87, 89, 202).

Bonhoeffer's edgy words mimic the edginess of Jesus.

Questions for Reflection and Application

1. How does Luke begin to show the challenges of discipleship in this section?

2. What is the significance of the narrative shifting here with the geographical movement?

3. What is your reaction to the Brueggemann quote?

4. What is your reaction to the Bonhoeffer quote?

5. In following Jesus, what has challenged you most?

FOR FURTHER READING

Dietrich Bonhoeffer, *Discipleship* (Dietrich Bonhoeffer Works 4; Minneapolis: Fortress, 2001).

Walter Brueggemann, *The Collected Sermons of Walter Brueggemann* (Louisville: Westminster John Knox, 2011).

REDEMPTION'S AGENTS EXPAND

Luke 10:1–24

[1] *After this the Lord appointed seventy-two others and sent them two by two ahead of him to every town and place where he was about to go.*

[2] *He told them, "The harvest is plentiful, but the workers are few. Ask the Lord of the harvest, therefore, to send out workers into his harvest field.* [3] *Go! I am sending you out like lambs among wolves.* [4] *Do not take a purse or bag or sandals; and do not greet anyone on the road.*

[5] *When you enter a house, first say, 'Peace to this house.'* [6] *If someone who promotes peace is there, your peace will rest on them; if not, it will return to you.* [7] *Stay there, eating and drinking whatever they give you, for the worker deserves his wages. Do not move around from house to house.*

[8] *When you enter a town and are welcomed, eat what is offered to you.* [9] *Heal the sick who are there and tell them, 'The kingdom of God has come near to you.'* [10] *But when you enter a town and are not welcomed, go into its streets and say,* [11] *'Even the dust of your town we wipe from our feet as a warning to you. Yet be sure of this: The kingdom of God has come near.'* [12] *I tell you, it will be more bearable on that day for Sodom than for that town.*

*[13] Woe to you, Chorazin! Woe to you, Bethsaida! For if the
miracles that were performed in you had been performed in Tyre
and Sidon, they would have repented long ago, sitting in sackcloth
and ashes. [14] But it will be more bearable for Tyre and Sidon at the
judgment than for you. [15] And you, Capernaum, will you be lifted
to the heavens? No, you will go down to Hades.*

*[16] Whoever listens to you listens to me; whoever rejects you
rejects me; but whoever rejects me rejects him who sent me."*

*[17] The seventy-two returned with joy and said, "Lord, even the
demons submit to us in your name." [18] He replied, "I saw Satan
fall like lightning from heaven. [19] I have given you authority to
trample on snakes and scorpions and to overcome all the power of
the enemy; nothing will harm you. [20] However, do not rejoice that
the spirits submit to you, but rejoice that your names are written
in heaven."*

*[21] At that time Jesus, full of joy through the Holy Spirit, said,
"I praise you, Father, Lord of heaven and earth, because you have
hidden these things from the wise and learned, and revealed them
to little children. Yes, Father, for this is what you were pleased to do.*

*[22] "All things have been committed to me by my Father. No one
knows who the Son is except the Father, and no one knows who
the Father is except the Son and those to whom the Son chooses to
reveal him."*

*[23] Then he turned to his disciples and said privately, "Blessed
are the eyes that see what you see. [24] For I tell you that many prophets and kings wanted to see what you see but did not see it, and to
hear what you hear but did not hear it."*

The Jesus movement in Galilee was not big even if at times thousands gathered to see him or hear him or watch him—or get fed by him. Jesus' purpose was not to attract a crowd, count the numbers, assess growth, and then chart the future. His approach gathered radically committed followers who would also spread redemption. In chapter nine Jesus sent out the Twelve (9:1–6). The Twelve become the Seventy-two (or Seventy; cf. Genesis 10:2–31) missioners in chapter ten (10:1).

Notice, too, that the mission instructions of chapter nine were briefer than those in chapter ten (cf. 9:1–6 with 10:1–24). In chapter nine the mission was about power, evangelism, provisions, and instructions on negative responses. In chapter ten the topics increase to ten mission instructions. Each of us is a missioner of Jesus in whatever calling each of us has. Ours is to discern in these instructions how we might adapt them to our context. As Jesus' own instructions developed from chapter nine to ten, so ours can develop too. I count ten instructions for the seventy-two missioners, and I will make brief comments for each.

Missioners Prepare for Jesus

Jesus expanded the missioners from twelve to seventy-two, but this did not make them their own agents. They were sent out two-by-two, which is better for safety and mission support. There is no reason to assume the only ones sent were males. Look back to Luke 8:1–3 and then read Romans 16 and notice the women on mission. Their mission was to go "where he was about to go" (10:1). That is, their task was to get a place ready for Jesus. Missioners can be seduced by success into thinking it is about themselves, about their abilities, gifts, platforms, brands, and intelligence. It is not. Missioners prepare the ground for seeds Jesus will drop into the soil. We introduce people to Jesus, get them started, and then usher them into reading the Gospels to listen to Jesus, to watch Jesus, and to become apprentices of Jesus.

Missioners Pray

We don't know how many villages the missioners entered. What we do know is the need was greater than the number of missioners. Jesus observes that they are "few" (10:2) so part of their task is to pray that God will raise up "workers," that is, more missioners who can work in *God's* "harvest field." Note again: it is not their harvest field, their parish, their church, their team, their tribe. It's God's. Those who pray for more missioners share the mission instead of assigning roles to subordinates, sycophants, and servants.

Missioners Are Vulnerable

The powers of this world are at work so Jesus likens them to "lambs" surrounded by "wolves" (10:3). Lambs have not a chance against wolves. The image is drastic: they will be wounded and can lose their life. In the Gospels, false prophets are wolves (Matthew 7:15) and so are false pastors (John 10:12). The apostle Paul knew of the same kinds of wolves (Acts 20:29). Sometimes church people can be the wolves.

I know of very few pastors who did not experience being a lamb-among-wolves during the Covid pandemic season.

Missioners Are on Mission

So concentrated are the missioners on their mission, instead of doing labor to provide, they are to trust God to provide food and clothing, and so urgent is that mission they are not to pause for the customary time-consuming greetings of folks on the path (10:4). Knowing one's mission permits one to establish boundaries, discipline one's time, and concentrate one's efforts.

Missioners Are Accepted

The missioners and their message about Jesus will be received at times (10:5–9), but not always (10:10–15). Here we focus on the former and then turn to the latter. Hospitality or inhospitality embody a person's response. The message they bring is, like the angels at the birth of Jesus, "peace" (10:5; cf. 2:13 and 1:79; 2:29; 7:50; 8:48; 19:38, 42; 24:36), or kingdom redemption, and transcends warm inner feelings. Those who receive the peace message of Jesus are called "children of peace" (NIV: "someone who promotes peace"; 10:6), and God's peace saturates such a home. Such peace promotes hospitality and provision for the missioners and avoids social climbing to the nicest villa in the village (10:7). (An early Christian text reveals that some did not follow these instructions of Jesus so they had to make a rule of how long persons could stay (*Didache* 11–13).[1]

Recall their mission was to prepare for Jesus (10:1) as it expanded the very mission of Jesus. Since Jesus healed, they are to heal also (10:9), but this healing is not magic nor is it showing off divine powers. Rather, as with the mission of the twelve (9:2), the kingdom of God breaks into this world with holistic redemption (10:9).

Missioners Are Rejected

One never knows how people will respond to Jesus' mission and message about the kingdom of God. Experienced missioners know the dark side of rejection. Jesus' instruction about rejection manifests the eternal gravity of the kingdom. As hospitality embodies welcome, so Jesus teaches the missioners to embody rejection with a prophet-like symbolic action: they were to wipe off the dust from their feet

(10:10), and then warn them that what happened to Sodom and Gomorrah could happen to them (10:11–12). He heightens the gravity of the response to the kingdom: it will be "more bearable" for those ancient cities than for the village that rejects Jesus. Jesus turns to three villages, all on the north side of the Sea of Galilee and utters severe warnings for their rejections (10:13–15). To be sure, these words are uncomfortable for many, but perhaps our comfort needs unsettling by rethinking the gravity of Jesus' kingdom offer.

Missioners Are Agents of Jesus

As long as we are gospeling Jesus to others, as long as we behave in a manner consistent with Jesus, and as long as we don't let it fill our chest with pride, we can redirect rejection in knowing that response to us is response to Jesus, and response to Jesus is response to the Father who sent him (10:16). In extending the kingdom we become agents of God in this world, which itself expresses all over again the seriousness of the kingdom mission. Your self-esteem can be lifted in remembering that God is at work through us for the redemption of others, and that means *you matter immensely to God*.

Missioners Are Surprised

Having witnessed Jesus' many mighty miracles (chapters 4–9), we may be as surprised at the seventy-two as they were at the powers at work through them (10:17). We hear their surprise in one English word: "even." In chapter nine we read that Jesus "gave them power and authority to drive out demons and to cure diseases" (9:1), and that kingdom power was extended to the seventy-two. But they were joyfully surprised at the results of their mission work. "Even the demons submit to us in your name," they reported to Jesus (10:17). You may know that experience of being surprised at what God has done in, with, and through you. Here the missioners are themselves witnesses to God's redemption, and so they admit the powers were not theirs because they know they couldn't do such mighty works.

They see exorcisms, but Jesus sees deeper, so he explains their little exorcisms in cosmic terms. What they were experiencing was actually the fall of Satan to the power of Jesus (10:18). They see small, he sees big, so he ushers them into the holistic redemption of the kingdom of God: they'll do all kinds of miracles because he has given them such "authority" (10:19; cf. Isaiah 11:8). Scott Spencer says this poetically: they will "declaw *wolves,* defang *snakes,* and de-tail *scorpions*" (Spencer, *Luke,* 274; his italics). Their temptation will be to gloat in their powers, and Jesus diverts attention from that ministry to the bedrock reality that their "names are written in heaven" (10:20). They are surprised because they see successful ministry, and Jesus sees the invasion of God's kingdom on earth.

Missioners Are "in the Know"

In fact, as redeemed "little children" they are "in the know" about God's mysterious kingdom (10:21). With an eye glance at the religious authorities of his day, Jesus says they, not the "wise and learned," have come to know the redemption in Jesus. Jesus is the conduit and agent of this redemptive knowledge (10:22). Which means that those who know him know the Father.

Missioners Are Blessed

Again, as long as we don't let this carry us onto the high spaces of arrogance, knowing God by knowing Jesus means we are God-"blessed" (10:23). It means more than happy or fortunate. What the "prophets and kings wanted to see" and "to hear" is what those who trust in Jesus have seen and heard (10:24). Jesus has opened up a new chapter in God's work in this world, and those who know him know the fullness of God's revelation in the kingdom's holistic redemption.

Questions for Reflection and Application

1. What do you think of the idea that some of the sent seventy-two were women?

2. Have you ever felt like a lamb wounded by wolves in the church?

3. When as a missioner have you been accepted, and when have you been rejected? How does it help you temper those experiences to remember that the acceptance or rejection were really of Jesus, not of you?

4. How did Jesus' view of the disciples' ministry success differ from their own?

5. What might it mean for you to be a missioner of Jesus in your context?

REDEMPTION'S CALLING

Luke 10:25–37

25 On one occasion an expert in the law stood up to test Jesus. "Teacher," he asked, "what must I do to inherit eternal life?"

26 "What is written in the Law?" he replied. "How do you read it?"

27 He answered, "'Love the Lord your God with all your heart and with all your soul and with all your strength and with all your mind'; and, 'Love your neighbor as yourself.'"

28 "You have answered correctly," Jesus replied. "Do this and you will live."

29 But he wanted to justify himself, so he asked Jesus, "And who is my neighbor?"

30 In reply Jesus said: "A man was going down from Jerusalem
to Jericho, when he was attacked by robbers. They stripped him of
his clothes, beat him and went away, leaving him half dead. 31 A
priest happened to be going down the same road, and when he saw
the man, he passed by on the other side. 32 So too, a Levite, when he
came to the place and saw him, passed by on the other side. 33 But
a Samaritan, as he traveled, came where the man was; and when
he saw him, he took pity on him. 34 He went to him and bandaged

his wounds, pouring on oil and wine. Then he put the man on his own donkey, brought him to an inn and took care of him. [35] *The next day he took out two denarii and gave them to the innkeeper. 'Look after him,' he said, 'and when I return, I will reimburse you for any extra expense you may have.'*

[36] *"Which of these three do you think was a neighbor to the man who fell into the hands of robbers?"*

[37] *The expert in the law replied, "The one who had mercy on him."*

Jesus told him, "Go and do likewise."

One of the Bible's most profound questions appears in our passage: "Who is my neighbor?" Jesus asks that same question in a slightly different form at the end of the passage: "Which of these three do you think was a neighbor to the man who fell into the hands of robbers?" Those questions have an answer that reveals redemption's calling for each of us, and the answer is wrapped up in a parable (see remarks at Luke 8:1–21). Because of our mistaken stereotyping of characters in this passage, I will concentrate on correcting our readings.

Stereotype 1

Stereotypes are useful except they aren't, and many use stereotypes to read this passage in a way that wounds more than it redeems. In Luke's Gospel a person designated as an "expert in the law" tends to be negative, and you can look up some references for proof (7:30; 11:45, 46, 52; 14:3). Such persons had deep concerns with the influence of Jesus, of course, but the problem is that too many Christians move from this text into thinking all rabbis are like this and then all Jews are like this, and before long we are staring into the face of our own anti-Semitism.

The lawyer here has a serious question: What do I need to do to enter the kingdom? (10:25). Jesus, in true rabbi-like fashion, answers the question by asking a question. The lawyer answers Jesus with the heart of what I call the Jesus Creed—love God, love your neighbor as yourself, both from the law of Moses (Deuteronomy 6:5–9; Leviticus 19:18). Jesus then tells him to "do this and you will live" into the kingdom (Luke 10:28).

The lawyer now acts out a stereotype. Wanting "to justify himself," he asks, "Who is my neighbor?" (10:29), which surely means "Who is actually not my neighbor?" (Levine-Witherington, *Luke,* 290). To shame the man out of his arrogance Jesus tells his most well-known, hospitable—and social-justice-naming parable.

Stereotype 2

In the parable three more stereotypes come to the surface: a (1) priest and a (2) Levite are depicted as Jewish religious leaders who are heartless followers of a law not even mentioned in this text. Namely, they excused their lack of compassion because they wanted to follow laws of purity. Yes, Numbers 19:11–13 teaches about defiling oneself by touching a corpse, and this is especially true for priests (Leviticus 21:1–4). But, as I have myself, think again about it: the disabled man was not dead (Luke 10:30 has "half dead"), and the priest and Levite were not headed toward Jerusalem and the temple, where purity obtains, but away from the temple, where defilement was not so serious an issue. Jesus' audience was stunned by the lack of compassion of the priest and the Levite.

Stereotype 3

A third stereotype is the Samaritan. In very common listings the Bible speaks of priests, Levites, and Israelites (Ezra 10:5; Nehemiah 11:3). So common is that listing that the first two lead one to expect something about the third, an Israelite, but there's the surprise. Jesus hops lanes and speaks of a Samaritan (see Levine, *Short Stories*, 102–103).

We ache to find analogies in our world for this amazing parable of Jesus and we tend to grab something close to home: someone who is marginalized or oppressed. But both miss the point. A Samaritan in the first century was the ethnic, shunned, religious enemy (Matthew 10:5; John 4:9). Not only is the Samaritan the enemy, but Samaritans had just rejected the missioners of Jesus (Luke 9:51–56). The apostles thought the Samaritans deserved Sodom and Gomorrah's judgment! They thought of revenge; Jesus thought of love. Luke put this parable in this location to show how Jesus himself responded to Samaritans, and how the apostles should have responded.

(One more point: when we call the Samaritan the "good" Samaritan we suggest, or at least some suggest, the other Samaritans were not good. Which is ethnic profiling. Again, Levine-Witherington, *Luke*, 291.)

The Point

Jesus could not have been bolder: to expose the lack of compassion by two proponents of God's will and by a group of missioners who had revenge on their minds, Jesus reveals true compassion in the compassion of an enemy and so shames those who lack compassion. Instead of our pointing long fingers at the priest and Levite we are the ones, like the missioners, who need to be exposed for our lack of compassion on those in need, including those Samaritans who rejected Jesus. Perhaps we need to pause right now to ask ourselves "Am I likewise doing?"

Redemption's calling.

Questions for Reflection and Application

1. In what ways can this story be misinterpreted to move toward anti-Semitism?

2. How does Jesus challenge expectations by bringing in a Samaritan?

3. How does this parable show the difference between Jesus' response to Samaritans versus the disciples' response to them?

4. Have you ever considered what this parable taught the disciples, more than what it taught the original question-asker?

5. Where in your life might you need to develop more compassion that takes action?

FOR FURTHER READING

I have learned much from Amy-Jill Levine, *Short Stories by Jesus: The Enigmatic Parables of a Controversial Rabbi* (New York: HarperOne, 2014), 77–115. Her study leads me to want to revise some lines in my chapter on this passage in *The Jesus Creed*, 51–59, esp. 52–53.

REDEMPTION'S ONE THING

Luke 10:38–42

[38] *As Jesus and his disciples were on their way, he came to a village where a woman named Martha opened her home to him.* [39] *She had a sister called Mary, who sat at the Lord's feet listening to what he said.* [40] *But Martha was distracted by all the preparations that had to be made. She came to him and asked, "Lord, don't you care that my sister has left me to do the work by myself? Tell her to help me!"*

[41] *"Martha, Martha," the Lord answered, "you are worried and upset about many things,* [42] *but few things are needed—or indeed only one. Mary has chosen what is better, and it will not be taken away from her."*

Martha and Mary are two close friends and patrons of Jesus, like the women of 8:1–3, and they have a brother named Lazarus (cf. John 11:1–44; 12:1–11). The story is told in a way that exposes Martha's distraction and Mary's concentration. Yet, the first thing we need to notice is Martha's hospitality, what that implies for accepting not just Jesus but his Father (9:46–48; 10:16), and what hospitality implies for

Martha's (and Mary's) association with Jesus. Truth be told, what it implies is doing exactly what the Samaritan just did in the passage before this one! One might be led to think that Mary's lack of interest in hospitality tosses some shade on her behaviors, and some in the first century would have said so. Many women in the early church were known for their hospitality (Acts 12:12; 16:13–15, 40; Romans 16:3–5; 1 Corinthians 16:19; Colossians 4:15).

We should not be one bit surprised by Jesus' interaction with women. It is all too common to hear people speak of Jesus as the liberator of women when his relations with women never call forth criticisms by his fellow Jews. No, Jewish men and Jewish women converse all the time. Jesus isn't doing something other first century Jewish teachers would not have done—teach a woman. What stands out in our passage is not *that* Jesus talked with or taught women but that Jesus *valued Mary's behavior more than Martha's.* What Martha is doing is good, and she surely had a "legitimate lament" (Spencer, *Luke,* 288): in offering hospitality she's a deacon (the Greek term here is *diakonia,* translatable as ministry or service). Luke tells us her service is spinning her around in circles (NIV has "distracted"; 10:40). However distracted, she properly addresses Jesus in Luke's favorite title: "Lord."

In turning to Mary, Jesus does not denigrate Martha's ministry but instead he ranks what's most important in that moment: Mary's tranquil listening and attending to Jesus, sitting in the posture (perhaps) of a student (Acts 22:3), and thus listening to the "word" of Jesus (NIV has "what he said"; 10:39), contrasts with Martha's getting lost in the weeds of hospitality. Mary's one thing, which is "good" (not "better" as in NIV at 10:42) should not be overly dissected or romanticized: her heart, mind, and imagination were lost in the face and words of her Lord Jesus.

Redemption's one thing is Jesus, hospitality can wait.

Questions for Reflection and Application

1. What are some of the ways you have heard this story taught and applied before?

2. What is significant about Martha's hospitality?

3. How is Jesus' behavior surprising and significant in this story?

4. When can good acts like service and hospitality get in our way and distract us from truly focusing on Jesus?

5. What causes you to feel distracted from Jesus in your daily life?

REDEMPTION PRAYING

Luke 11:1–13

1 One day Jesus was praying in a certain place. When he finished,
one of his disciples said to him, "Lord, teach us to pray, just as John
taught his disciples."

2 He said to them, "When you pray, say:
" 'Father,
hallowed be your name,
your kingdom come.
3 Give us each day our daily bread.
4 Forgive us our sins,
for we also forgive everyone who sins against us.
And lead us not into temptation. ' "

5 Then Jesus said to them, "Suppose you have a friend, and
you go to him at midnight and say, 'Friend, lend me three loaves of
bread; 6 a friend of mine on a journey has come to me, and I have
no food to offer him.' 7 And suppose the one inside answers, 'Don't
bother me. The door is already locked, and my children and I are in
bed. I can't get up and give you anything.' 8 I tell you, even though

he will not get up and give you the bread because of friendship, yet
because of your shameless audacity he will surely get up and give
you as much as you need.

9 *"So I say to you: Ask and it will be given to you; seek and you*
will find; knock and the door will be opened to you. 10 *For every-*
one who asks receives; the one who seeks finds; and to the one who
knocks, the door will be opened.

11 *"Which of you fathers, if your son asks for a fish, will give*
him a snake instead? 12 *Or if he asks for an egg, will give him a*
scorpion? 13 *If you then, though you are evil, know how to give good*
gifts to your children, how much more will your Father in heaven
give the Holy Spirit to those who ask him!"

Prayer's #1 problem is that the Bible promises more answers to our prayers than we get. If this isn't your problem, please skip to the next passage. But that problem is a problem, and we can confess it with candor. Just name the prayers you wanted most to come true that have not been answered as you wanted. We indwell a world ripped apart with gun violence, with racism, with sexism, with pastoral abuses, with parental neglect, with economic disparities, and with life's inequities. Have not millions prayed for the ending of each? Over and over? The problem is not simply that we don't get what we want or that we don't get what is entirely consistent with God's kingdom. The problem is that we are promised too much, or at least that's the way we read the Bible's promises.

Luke has gathered into a tight bundle three separate teachings of Jesus about prayer. The first, called the Lord's Prayer or the Our Father, deals explicitly with the big themes of holistic redemption, and that redemption shapes the next two teachings about prayer in Luke's bundle.

Praying with a Pattern

One of Jesus' disciples asks Jesus to "teach us to pray, just as John taught his disciples" (11:1). If John's group had a prayer that distinguished them, the disciples thought Jesus' own group should have one. Jesus' response can be under-noticed. His response is not, as in the NIV, "When you pray" but "When*ever* you pray" (11:2). The distinction earns comment: Jesus gives to the disciples a prayer to memorize and recite every time they pray. That's a reasonable, if literal, translation. What Jesus gives here is thus a *pattern* for disciples when they pray. Reciting this prayer rewires our brains to pray like this prayer whenever we pray. The earliest churches recited this prayer (*Didache* 8).[1]

The pattern has two major parts, a God part and an Others part:

> Address God as Father, which is not unique to Jesus, but it is his distinct emphasis.

1. Begin with ***God***, by asking God to establish the kingdom (or Empire) of his holistic redemption
2. Turn then to ***Others***, by asking God for daily provisions for others and yourself, by asking God to forgive others and yourself, and by asking God to preserve others and yourself from the final ordeal in history

As Jesus shaped all ethics into loving God and loving others, so he teaches his followers that love for God means praying for God's kingdom and love for others requires praying for provisions, forgiveness, and preservation.

Reciting the Our Father over and over and over, as many churches do and as many of us do, opens us to being formed into its patterns for prayer.

Praying with Confidence in God's Generosity

The second lesson on prayer in this passage hangs on the translation of one term perhaps more than any passage in the New Testament. The Greek word that interprets the whole scene in 11:8 is *anaideia* (NIV: "shameless audacity") and it occurs but once in the entire New Testament. This term points to something negative: shamelessness, either because one is ignorant of what is honorable or because one is willing to cross boundaries into the world of shame in order to get what one wants.

On top of a difficult word the passage is a bit tricky because words like "his" shift from the Knocker to the Resident Friend, and I provide my own translation here because it will help clarify who is saying/doing what.

> Which of you [Knocker] will have a friend and will journey to him [Resident Friend] in the middle of the night and say to him, [Knocker]: "Friend, lend me three breads [6] since my friend came to me from the path and I don't have something that I may present to him."
>
> [7] That person inside [Resident Friend], responding, said, "Don't present labor for me. Already the door has been closed and my children are with me in the bed. I am unable, arising, to give [anything] to you."
>
> [8] I say this to you: "Even if he [Resident Friend] will not, arising, give [breads] to him [Knocker] because he is his [Resident's] friend, yet because of his [Knocker's] impudence,[2] being raised, he will give to him whatever he requires."

As you can see, everything does hinge on that one term. Again, the term points out something negative, a man knocking at a door who is audacious, rude, shameless, and impudent, but willing to do what it takes to provide for his family.

Here is the crux. How does rudeness fit with our prayers? *It doesn't.* The logic is called "from lesser to greater." If a less-than-excited sleeping human responds to a friend's rudeness with generosity, how much more will God, who is never asleep and never unresponsive, respond to disciples, who are not rude before God, when they ask God for provisions. The parable then encourages us to come to God with confidence because God is good and generous, so unlike humans. This passage does not promise too much.

Praying with Expectation

Now to back up. Today's passage begins with Jesus giving his disciples a prayer that forms disciples into those who pray for God's holistic redemption, and the short parable about the Knocker and his Friend leads us to see a God who is good and therefore generous. Because God is good and generous, Jesus instructs disciples to turn to God and "ask" and "seek" and "knock," which has led to a million acronym lessons: A.S.K. Fair enough. We do need to approach God with our requests.

But this short passage in 11:9–13 is about far more than *what we do* (ask). It is about *what God is like.* We can come to God with our petitions for redemption in all its dimensions *because God is generous.* That is,

> If we ask, "it will be given."
> If we seek, we "will find."
> And, if we knock, "the door will be opened.

And does a human father give a slimy snake or a disgusting scorpion to his son if the son asks for a fish or an egg? Of course not. And once again the logic is from lesser to greater: if human fathers give "good gifts," what will the "Father in heaven give" to us if we ask? The "Holy Spirit."

I'm thinking "Holy Spirit" surprised many. But, if we begin with the themes of the Our Father, which were holistic redemption (kingdom, provisions, forgiveness, and preservation from the ordeal), we can see that the Holy Spirit sums them all up.

And the Father generously grants the Spirit to all who ask.

Questions for Reflection and Application

1. How does Luke's bundling of these teachings on prayer help us better flesh out Jesus' ideas of prayer?

2. How does the Lord's Prayer/Our Father function as a prayer pattern?

3. What can the parable of the Knocker teach us about prayer?

4. What can this section teach us about what God is like?

5. How do you want to change or deepen your approach to prayer?

REDEMPTION'S OPPOSITIONS

Luke 11:14–54

14 Jesus was driving out a demon that was mute. When the de-
mon left, the man who had been mute spoke, and the crowd was
amazed. 15 But some of them said, "By Beelzebul, the prince of
demons, he is driving out demons." 16 Others tested him by asking
for a sign from heaven.

17 Jesus knew their thoughts and said to them: "Any kingdom
divided against itself will be ruined, and a house divided against
itself will fall. 18 If Satan is divided against himself, how can his
kingdom stand? I say this because you claim that I drive out de-
mons by Beelzebul. 19 Now if I drive out demons by Beelzebul, by
whom do your followers drive them out? So then, they will be your
judges. 20 But if I drive out demons by the finger of God, then the
kingdom of God has come upon you.

21 "When a strong man, fully armed, guards his own house,
his possessions are safe. 22 But when someone stronger attacks and
overpowers him, he takes away the armor in which the man trusted
and divides up his plunder.

23 "Whoever is not with me is against me, and whoever does
not gather with me scatters.

*24 "When an impure spirit comes out of a person, it goes through
arid places seeking rest and does not find it. Then it says, 'I will
return to the house I left.' 25 When it arrives, it finds the house swept
clean and put in order. 26 Then it goes and takes seven other spirits
more wicked than itself, and they go in and live there. And the final
condition of that person is worse than the first."*

*27 As Jesus was saying these things, a woman in the crowd
called out, "Blessed is the mother who gave you birth and nursed
you." 28 He replied, "Blessed rather are those who hear the word of
God and obey it."*

*29 As the crowds increased, Jesus said, "This is a wicked generation. It asks for a sign, but none will be given it except the sign of
Jonah. 30 For as Jonah was a sign to the Ninevites, so also will the
Son of Man be to this generation. 31 The Queen of the South will
rise at the judgment with the people of this generation and condemn
them, for she came from the ends of the earth to listen to Solomon's
wisdom; and now something greater than Solomon is here. 32 The
men of Nineveh will stand up at the judgment with this generation
and condemn it, for they repented at the preaching of Jonah; and
now something greater than Jonah is here.*

*33 "No one lights a lamp and puts it in a place where it will
be hidden, or under a bowl. Instead they put it on its stand, so
that those who come in may see the light. 34 Your eye is the lamp
of your body. When your eyes are healthy, your whole body also
is full of light. But when they are unhealthy, your body also is
full of darkness. 35 See to it, then, that the light within you is not
darkness. 36 Therefore, if your whole body is full of light, and no
part of it dark, it will be just as full of light as when a lamp shines
its light on you."*

*37 When Jesus had finished speaking, a Pharisee invited him
to eat with him; so he went in and reclined at the table. 38 But the
Pharisee was surprised when he noticed that Jesus did not first
wash before the meal.*

[39] *Then the Lord said to him, "Now then, you Pharisees clean*
the outside of the cup and dish, but inside you are full of greed and
wickedness. [40] *You foolish people! Did not the one who made the*
outside make the inside also? [41] *But now as for what is inside you—*
be generous to the poor, and everything will be clean for you.

[42] *"Woe to you Pharisees, because you give God a tenth of your*
mint, rue and all other kinds of garden herbs, but you neglect justice
and the love of God. You should have practiced the latter without
leaving the former undone.

[43] *"Woe to you Pharisees, because you love the most important*
seats in the synagogues and respectful greetings in the marketplaces.

[44] *"Woe to you, because you are like unmarked graves, which*
people walk over without knowing it."

[45] *One of the experts in the law answered him, "Teacher, when*
you say these things, you insult us also."

[46] *Jesus replied, "And you experts in the law, woe to you, be-*
cause you load people down with burdens they can hardly carry,
and you yourselves will not lift one finger to help them.

[47] *"Woe to you, because you build tombs for the prophets, and*
it was your ancestors who killed them. [48] *So you testify that you ap-*
prove of what your ancestors did; they killed the prophets, and you
build their tombs. [49] *Because of this, God in his wisdom said, 'I will*
send them prophets and apostles, some of whom they will kill and
others they will persecute.' [50] *Therefore this generation will be held*
responsible for the blood of all the prophets that has been shed since
the beginning of the world, [51] *from the blood of Abel to the blood of*
Zechariah, who was killed between the altar and the sanctuary.
Yes, I tell you, this generation will be held responsible for it all.

[52] *"Woe to you experts in the law, because you have taken*
away the key to knowledge. You yourselves have not entered, and
you have hindered those who were entering."

[53] *When Jesus went outside, the Pharisees and the teachers of*
the law began to oppose him fiercely and to besiege him with ques-
tions, [54] *waiting to catch him in something he might say.*

Today's passage of some forty verses gathers together *Jesus' responses* to those who oppose the launching of God's kingdom. The connections between some of these passages, which I have separated in the translation above, don't always stand up with clarity. But if you scan down to the last few verses you will perceive where this long passage is headed: opposition and rejection.

Responding to Cosmic Opposition

Jesus launched the kingdom, and the exorcisms of demons and impure spirits dramatically display the kingdom's holistic redemption. Jesus as the agent of God's holistic redemption threatens the systemic powers of the cosmos. Satan's system is about un-redemption and death and enslaving humans. Satan and the demons recognize Jesus for who he is, and they go to battle against him. Jesus draws swords to liberate humans from the clutches of the demons.

To observe Jesus liberate a person from a demon requires the observer to make sense of what was seen. "Some of them" think Jesus' power is actually the power of "Beelzebul," a term that means "lord" (*ba'al* in the Old Testament) of the "high places." So, they accuse Jesus of alliance with Baal, the Canaanite god.[1]

Jesus deconstructs their accusation by saying (1) if I am in alliance with the "prince of demons" (11:15), then (2) a major demon is at war with minor demons, and (3) thus, the evil kingdom is divided against itself (11:17–18). He then asks them by whom "do your followers" exorcise? The question is not clear and the NIV's "your followers" is not the only possible translation. It can be translated more literally as "your sons," which leads to the question: Who are these sons? I suggest they are those exorcists already mentioned at 9:49, who were in fact exorcising in the name of Jesus.

Which is why Jesus then explains the power at work behind his name: "If I drive out demons by the finger of God, then the kingdom of God has come upon you" (11:20). The "finger of God" points us to the powers of Aaron (Exodus 8:18), or to the revelation to Moses (Deuteronomy 9:10), or most likely to the "Spirit of God" in Matthew 12:28. Exorcisms are not only a sign of the kingdom, not only evidence of the kingdom, but they *are* the kingdom because exorcisms are spiritual redemption of a person. Jesus, then, is the "someone stronger" who plunders the "strong man's" house (Luke 11:21–22).

Jesus' response then comes down to one claim: either one is "with me" or one is "against me," or one who gathers people into the kingdom with Jesus or drives them away (11:23).

Again, in response to those who accuse him of alliance with the lord of demons, Jesus explains how Satan's evil system works: liberation from a demon can lead at times to other demons taking up space in a person's life, and "the final condition of that person is worse than the first [condition]" (11:26). We suggest that exorcisms not followed up with the inhabitation of the Spirit of God can make a person vulnerable to greater demonic attack.

Out of nowhere a woman blurts out a blessing on Jesus' mother, which Jesus flips into a greater blessing on those who respond positively to Jesus and his kingdom (11:27–28).

Responding to "This Generation's" Opposition

More often than not, the kingdom mission did not succeed, as we define succeed. Jesus was opposed by those who witnessed his exorcisms and, in fact, he looks at growing "crowds" and perceives a "wicked generation" (11:29). Jesus encountered systemic rejection, he named it, and he warned those who rejected him.

Jonah was himself a "sign to the Ninevites" as Jesus, the "Son of Man" is to his generation. Connecting himself to Jonah means Jesus sees himself as one who utters the warnings of judgment but who also offers forgiveness to the repentant. Jesus now compares the "Queen of the South" (cf. 1 Kings 10:1–10) and the Ninevites to Jesus' contemporaries, with the former two groups given a more favorable rating. He intensifies the negative verdict with a self-claim: "something greater than Jonah is here" (11:32).

Responding to Two Responses

To get his audience to think afresh about the two responses to the kingdom, Jesus plays with the human eye: light or darkness. Lamps are for lighting a space and, somehow, the eye is like a light for the body. He suggests eyes permit light to pass into the human body (an ancient theory of vision, actually). If one has "healthy" eyes, the "whole body" becomes "full of light," but if one has "unhealthy" eyes the body is "full of darkness." Jesus wants his hearers to be open to the light that dispels the darknesses of demons and death in this generation (11:33–36).

Responding to the Pharisees' Opposition

A Pharisee's response to Jesus was an invitation to recline at the table with Jesus, which suggests a formal conversation about who Jesus is (11:37). The Pharisee, thinking of Jesus as both informed and observant of the Torah, was offended that Jesus did not first wash his hands. A ritual ablution of one's hands was a marker of commitment to doing the whole will of God for the Pharisee. Which gave Jesus an opportunity to turn the formal conversation into a prophetic sermon against the way of the Pharisees.

Reminder: this section is a fierce intra-Jewish critique, not a universal denunciation of law observance or all Jews, or even all Pharisees. Furthering this point, there's nothing in these words of Jesus that I have not witnessed in Christians. Which means these accusing words are not peculiar to Pharisees or Jews but are endemic to religious people. So, let's commit to mutual, not tribal, growth in righteousness. Pick your preferred Christian poison: perhaps you will start with the very recent "The Rise and Fall of Mars Hill" podcast at Christianity Today, or you will back up to some classics, like Samuel Butler's *The Way of All Flesh*, Upton Sinclair's *Elmer Gantry*, or Mark Twain's *Huckleberry Finn*.

First, Jesus was not against the law of Moses. He obeyed the law. But Jesus certainly at times disagreed with the interpretations of the law by the Pharisees. In particular, he was irritated often by the culture the Pharisees created. Second, the word translated "Woe" for many suggests something like "A curse be on you" or even "God will damn you to hell." The term in Greek is *ouai*, which is almost transliterated into "Woe," but it is not a damning word. Instead, it is a warning, and perhaps the best equivalent is "Oy!" It is a way of saying, "Be warned, guys." Third, Jesus warns them about greed (cf. 16:14) and an imbalanced commitment to the external act unaccompanied by an inner reality that flows out into generosity (11:39–41), to rigorous tithing unaccompanied by "justice and the love of God" (11:42), to a desire for celebrity status (11:43), and to their tragic contamination of all sorts of people because of their pastoral neglect (11:44). These are particularly terse words for an afternoon table talk at the Pharisees' home!

"One of the experts in the law" informs Jesus that his words offend not only the Pharisees, but also Torah-lawyers (11:45). The Torah-lawyer probably thinks his sort are a bit higher on the status scale.

Jesus turns to his next page of notes to utter some Oys! to the Torah-lawyers (11:46–52). An equal opportunity critic, he is. They are pastorally uncaring (11:46) and they become complicit in the murder of the prophets when they build and decorate tombs for the martyred prophets (11:47–51). Jesus warns them of the coming destruction of Jerusalem (66–73 AD). Finally, he offers a final Oy! to the Torah-lawyers for their abusive hoarding of knowledge, of their failure to respond properly to it, and of their obscuring that knowledge to those who need it. He uses "entered" here as an image of entering or not entering the kingdom (11:52).

The Pharisees' response grows fiercer in their opposition (11:53–54).

If we think the Bible promises at times too much for our prayers, we may also be guilty of promising too much positive response to the kingdom mission today.

Questions for Reflection and Application

1. How do exorcisms function as kingdom work?

2. What are the parallels between Jesus and Jonah?

3. What is the difference between seeing the conflict with Jesus and the Pharisees as an intra-Jewish critique versus an anti-Jewish argument?

4. How would you summarize Jesus' responses to those who oppose him?

5. What would you like to adopt from Jesus' example of responding to opposition to live out in your life?

FOR FURTHER READING

The Rise and Fall of Mars Hill: https://www.christianitytoday.com/ct/podcasts/rise-and-fall-of-mars-hill/

REDEMPTION AND LESSONS IN DISCIPLESHIP

Luke 12:1–34

1 Meanwhile, when a crowd of many thousands had gathered, so that they were trampling on one another, Jesus began to speak first to his disciples, saying: "Be on your guard against the yeast of the Pharisees, which is hypocrisy. 2 There is nothing concealed that will not be disclosed, or hidden that will not be made known. 3 What you have said in the dark will be heard in the daylight, and what you have whispered in the ear in the inner rooms will be proclaimed from the roofs.

4 "I tell you, my friends, do not be afraid of those who kill the body and after that can do no more. 5 But I will show you whom you should fear: Fear him who, after your body has been killed, has authority to throw you into hell. Yes, I tell you, fear him. 6 Are not five sparrows sold for two pennies? Yet not one of them is forgotten by God. 7 Indeed, the very hairs of your head are all numbered. Don't be afraid; you are worth more than many sparrows.

8 "I tell you, whoever publicly acknowledges me before others, the Son of Man will also acknowledge before the angels of God. 9 But whoever disowns me before others will be disowned before the angels of God. 10 And everyone who speaks a word against the Son

of Man will be forgiven, but anyone who blasphemes against the
Holy Spirit will not be forgiven.

11 "When you are brought before synagogues, rulers and
authorities, do not worry about how you will defend yourselves or
what you will say, 12 for the Holy Spirit will teach you at that time
what you should say."

13 Someone in the crowd said to him, "Teacher, tell my brother
to divide the inheritance with me."

14 Jesus replied, "Man, who appointed me a judge or an arbiter
between you?" 15 Then he said to them, "Watch out! Be on your
guard against all kinds of greed; life does not consist in an abundance of possessions."

16 And he told them this parable: "The ground of a certain rich
man yielded an abundant harvest. 17 He thought to himself, 'What
shall I do? I have no place to store my crops.'

18 "Then he said, 'This is what I'll do. I will tear down my
barns and build bigger ones, and there I will store my surplus
grain. 19 And I'll say to myself, "You have plenty of grain laid up for
many years. Take life easy; eat, drink and be merry." '

20 "But God said to him, 'You fool! This very night your life will
be demanded from you. Then who will get what you have prepared
for yourself?'

21 "This is how it will be with whoever stores up things for themselves but is not rich toward God."

22 Then Jesus said to his disciples: "Therefore I tell you, do not
worry about your life, what you will eat; or about your body, what
you will wear. 23 For life is more than food, and the body more than
clothes. 24 Consider the ravens: They do not sow or reap, they have
no storeroom or barn; yet God feeds them. And how much more
valuable you are than birds! 25 Who of you by worrying can add a
single hour to your life? 26 Since you cannot do this very little thing,
why do you worry about the rest?

27 "Consider how the wild flowers grow. They do not labor or
spin. Yet I tell you, not even Solomon in all his splendor was dressed

like one of these. 28 *If that is how God clothes the grass of the field,*
which is here today, and tomorrow is thrown into the fire, how
much more will he clothe you—you of little faith! 29 *And do not set*
your heart on what you will eat or drink; do not worry about it.
30 *For the pagan world runs after all such things, and your Father*
knows that you need them. 31 *But seek his kingdom, and these things*
will be given to you as well.

32 *"Do not be afraid, little flock, for your Father has been*
pleased to give you the kingdom. 33 *Sell your possessions and give*
to the poor. Provide purses for yourselves that will not wear out, a
treasure in heaven that will never fail, where no thief comes near
and no moth destroys. 34 *For where your treasure is, there your*
heart will be also.

If you were asked to teach a young adult or an adult group about the basic virtues of the Christian life, what would be your top five virtues? In Christian history theologians adjusted the classical philosophical virtues of prudence, justice, temperance, and fortitude. The church also developed seven capital virtues matched by seven deadly sins: chastity, temperance, charity, diligence, kindness, patience, and humility, and then the deadlies are pride, greed, wrath, envy, lust, gluttony, and sloth.

Three observations: first, it doesn't take much effort for us to find something like these virtues in Jesus' teachings and behavior. Second, we have never participated in a church that used these classic virtues as the basics of Christian practice. Theoretically and with some measure of success, a virtue is a habit that, if intentionally practiced over time, forms a person into virtuous character. Now a third observation: Protestants, especially of the evangelical sort, have never been able to embrace the Christian virtue tradition because—let the truth be told—the Roman Catholics have. Jesus does not teach that tradition, but his teachings do overlap significantly, and nothing in that tradition contradicts what Jesus teaches his disciples.

In our passage, four of Jesus' virtues come to the surface.

Transparency

Having just sternly warned the Pharisees and Torah-lawyers (11:37–54), and though surrounded by a "crowd of many thousands," Jesus somehow warned only his disciples of the Pharisees' sourdough starter, that is, "hypocrisy" (12:1). To this warning Jesus reveals that God will unmask our privacies and secrecies in the final judgment (12:2–3).

Hypocrisy deserves careful definition. First, hypocrisy involves conscious pretense about our external appearance and our internal reality. Second, hypocrisy involves a desire for public recognition. Third, hypocrisy involves finding faults with others, and fourth, it leads others into a false life. All this can be found in the chapter of chapters about hypocrisy, Matthew 23 (Matthew's version of Luke 11:37–54). A hypocrite is not just someone who pretends to greater piety than she has, but it is someone who sits in judgment on others and leads others astray. False teaching and even heresy are at the heart of the term hypocrisy.

Jesus teaches the virtue of transparency. That is, be who you are, be honest about yourself, avoid curating your public image, and cease dragging people into your own corrupted teachings and behaviors.

Courage

Without using the word courage, Jesus teaches his disciples they are to witness to Jesus in word and act, even if it means facing persecution (12:4–12). This is a Christian version of the virtue of courage, one that flips manliness and military courage on its head and turns it into obedience of God. Instead of being scared of humans who can put someone to death, they were to fear God alone. Jesus calls his followers to "acknowledge" him, the Son of Man, publicly because divine approval comes to those who acknowledge him (and vice versa).

An ever-debated verse occurs at 12:10, in which Jesus says whoever "speaks" against himself is forgivable but whoever "blasphemes" the Holy Spirit is unforgivable. Blasphemy refers to degrading God or upgrading oneself to the level of God (and so degrading God). We have one important difference between words against Jesus and words against the Spirit: *speaking against* (Jesus) is a lesser form of degrading than *blaspheming* (Holy Spirit). Criticizing Jesus in his earthly existence is not as severe a sin as rejecting the redemptive work of God, manifest through the Spirit. Granted, this is a very fine distinction that often may have no difference.

In context, Jesus calls his disciples to a courageous witness in the face of opposition and threats to their life, and they stiff arm the opposition with public confession of their allegiance to Jesus in the power of the Spirit (12:11–12).

Priorities

Long ago I learned a word for something important to Jesus: mammonolatry. The word *mammon* is the Aramaic word for things, for possessions. At the end of a word, "olatry" means worship of. In other words, greed, one of the deadly sins. One can look online at ads to see the unalterable capacity of possessions to tempt us into a life of acquisition.

Here's the best definition of mammonaltry I've ever seen:

> This sin may be defined as the spirit of grasping greed and acquisitiveness, the insatiable longing for more of material possessions and a consequent lack of contentment and absence of trust in God our Father who has promised to supply all needful things to His children (Martin, 82).

If that's the best definition, a character embodying such a sin is described here by Jesus in his parable about the "rich man" who wanted bigger and bigger barns in which to hoard his abundance—all so he could retire early and live decades on permanent vacation (Luke 12:16–21).

The man's priorities were riches in this life, or "an abundance of possessions" (12:15), and Jesus' priority is to become "rich toward God" (12:21). Greed stiffens a person's hands because it so (seemingly) satisfies a person's heart until it freezes it into heartless ice. Our first priority is God—life with God, life before God, life for others for the sake of God.

Trust

Chapter twelve's teachings gather what Jesus said on various occasions. How do we know this? Luke 12:1 finds a parallel at Matthew 16:6, 12; Luke 12:2–12 at Matthew 10:26–33; Luke 12:13–21 has no parallel; and 12:22–34 has a parallel at Matthew 6:25–33. Luke told us at 1:1–4 that he had done his homework to find out about Jesus from eyewitnesses, and he has put the material together in his own way. I say this all because the most likely original context for our next passage (12:22–34) is instructions to missioners about learning to trust God for day-to-day provisions. So, we need to be alert both to contextual but also insensitive readings.

These words are not directed at the homeless or the starving; they are addressed to those who have the option of trusting God to provide through others. Notice what is said in 12:33, which can only be said to those who have more than enough.

The fourth virtue for the disciples of Jesus is trust, one that undergirds each of the seven cardinal virtues of the Christian tradition. Barbara Brown Taylor, describing her granddaughter, once said, "There is no fear in those sea-blue eyes. She sleeps and eats and sighs when she is full. Her world is as wide as her mother's arms, and as safe. That is all she knows" (Taylor, *The Preaching Life,* 95). Jesus wants his followers to form that kind of life in God's providing arms. Jesus' mode of instruction is illustration: from the "ravens" who don't need to farm because God feeds them; from humans who are unable to add "a single hour" to life; from the decorative flowers in the grasses of a field that don't lift a finger to sew fabrics into clothing (12:28).

So, the disciples are not to fix their desires on food and clothing. Pagans, like those living in Tiberias (visible from Capernaum and the region of Jesus' ministry), get fixated on such things (cf. 7:25), but the disciples are to learn to trust God (10:4, 10).

How do they learn by habit and practice to trust God? By seeking the kingdom that God has given them (12:31–32), by selling their possessions and giving to the poor, and in so doing to fashion "purses" that never go threadbare, purses that signify an incorruptible "treasure in heaven" (12:33). His finishing pull of the thread connects one's personal treasure, whether it is possessions or being "rich toward God," to where one's "heart" is (12:34).

Four virtues–transparency, courage, priorities, and trust–that are in the heart of kingdom living.

Questions for Reflection and Application

1. What would you list as the top five virtues for Christian living?

2. How do Jesus' four virtues compare to the classical and Christian lists of virtues? How do they compare to your list?

3. What is hypocrisy, and how does transparency overcome it?

4. How does it impact your understanding of Jesus' teachings on worrying about possessions to see them as directed toward missioners/apostles?

5. So far, what has Luke told us about who Jesus is?

FOR FURTHER READING

Ralph P. Martin, *Worship in the Early Church* (Grand Rapids: Wm. B. Eerdmans, 1975).

Barbara Brown Taylor, *The Preaching Life* (Lanham, Maryland: Cowley, 1993).

REDEMPTION'S JUDGMENT

Luke 12:35–59

35 *"Be dressed ready for service and keep your lamps burning,* 36 *like*
servants waiting for their master to return from a wedding banquet,
so that when he comes and knocks they can immediately open the
door for him. 37 *It will be good for those servants whose master finds*
them watching when he comes. Truly I tell you, he will dress himself
to serve, will have them recline at the table and will come and wait
on them. 38 *It will be good for those servants whose master finds*
them ready, even if he comes in the middle of the night or toward
daybreak. 39 *But understand this: If the owner of the house had*
known at what hour the thief was coming, he would not have let his
house be broken into. 40 *You also must be ready, because the Son of*
Man will come at an hour when you do not expect him."

41 *Peter asked, "Lord, are you telling this parable to us, or to*
everyone?"

42 *The Lord answered, "Who then is the faithful and wise man-*
ager, whom the master puts in charge of his servants to give them
their food allowance at the proper time? 43 *It will be good for that*
servant whom the master finds doing so when he returns. 44 *Truly*
I tell you, he will put him in charge of all his possessions. 45 *But*

suppose the servant says to himself, 'My master is taking a long
time in coming,' and he then begins to beat the other servants, both
men and women, and to eat and drink and get drunk. 46 The master of that servant will come on a day when he does not expect him
and at an hour he is not aware of. He will cut him to pieces and
assign him a place with the unbelievers.

47 "The servant who knows the master's will and does not get
ready or does not do what the master wants will be beaten with
many blows. 48 But the one who does not know and does things
deserving punishment will be beaten with few blows. From everyone
who has been given much, much will be demanded; and from the
one who has been entrusted with much, much more will be asked.

49 "I have come to bring fire on the earth, and how I wish it
were already kindled! 50 But I have a baptism to undergo, and what
constraint I am under until it is completed! 51 Do you think I came
to bring peace on earth? No, I tell you, but division. 52 From now
on there will be five in one family divided against each other, three
against two and two against three. 53 They will be divided, father
against son and son against father, mother against daughter and
daughter against mother, mother-in-law against daughter-in-law
and daughter-in-law against mother-in-law."

54 He said to the crowd: "When you see a cloud rising in the
west, immediately you say, 'It's going to rain,' and it does. 55 And
when the south wind blows, you say, 'It's going to be hot,' and it
is. 56 Hypocrites! You know how to interpret the appearance of the
earth and the sky. How is it that you don't know how to interpret
this present time?

57 "Why don't you judge for yourselves what is right? 58 As
you are going with your adversary to the magistrate, try hard to
be reconciled on the way, or your adversary may drag you off to
the judge, and the judge turn you over to the officer, and the officer
throw you into prison. 59 I tell you, you will not get out until you
have paid the last penny."

At times Jesus used what some have called "difficult words," and by difficult they do not mean "hard to understand" so much as "difficult to live." Whatever we call such words, Jesus can cut through our pretenses and comfort us with a sword that lands with a piercing crack followed by a loud thud. Our passage today is one of them. We need to get right to it.

In themes, our passage begins with A then moves to B then turns back to A. The A theme prepares disciples for the grand finalé of history (12:35–48), B inserts the theme of the inherent divisiveness of Jesus (12:49–43), and then back to the A theme, being prepared (12:44–59). I'll begin with B to keep the A theme together.

Jesus Divides

Many have a Romantic theory of Jesus. That he's all tolerance and kindness and graciousness and even courteousness and politeness, even sweetness. Such persons must not be reading our Gospels. At times Jesus draws and flashes a sword, and a Jesus without a flashing sword is not Jesus.

It must have taken about a week before Jesus began to experience stiff opposition to his claims about the kingdom: that he was the agent of God's kingdom, that its message of holistic redemption required a holistic response of trust and allegiance, and that what people decided about him and his kingdom mattered. Eternally. It didn't even take a week.

Jesus experienced opposition after his inaugural sermon in Nazareth. Heated opposition, so much they wanted to toss him off the cliff. It didn't take long then for Jesus to discern that he was tossing balls of "fire" on the land (12:49; "land" is better than the NIV's "earth") or advocating some kind of "baptism" (12:50) and creating "division" and not offering date-sweet packages of "peace" (12:51). Families, he tells his disciples, will split over me (12:52–53). Jesus legitimated that division by appealing to works from the prophet Micah (Micah 7:6).

The preaching of Jesus cracked families and communities and synagogues. Jesus was dead serious. He put Jerusalem, its leaders, and the Land, and its leaders, in the dock. If they didn't respond to his warnings, Rome would burn the city to the ground. Rome's vindictiveness made Jesus' words believable.

Jesus Warns Because He Divides

You may have wondered why I didn't say something in that previous paragraph about the Second Coming at the end of history. I didn't because today's passage is not about the Second Coming at the end of history but about the imminent catastrophe that occurred in 66–73 AD (Wright, *Jesus and the Victory of God*, 320–368). I know that may give you pause so give me a chance to explain.

Jesus' own words, first, in parabolic or metaphorical language, speak about "lamps burning" and "servants" (actually "slaves") and their "master" and people being "ready" when the master returns, which he connects to the kind of surprise one encounters with a night-time thief (12:35–39). Then, second, he interprets that entire set of images as words about himself, that is, about when "the Son of Man will come" (12:40).

Many think of this as the future (to us) Second Coming, but that is quite unlikely. Here's why: in Luke 9, just before the transfiguration, what did Jesus say? He said, "some who are standing here will not taste death before they see the kingdom of God" (9:27). That's no more than 30–50 years from when he spoke it. (Not nearly 2,000.) Now flip in your Bible over to Luke 17 where Jesus connects the arrival of that imminent kingdom with the coming of the Son of Man. There Jesus says the kingdom is actually "in your midst" right then and there (17:21) and then he predicts the imminent coming of the Son of Man (17:22–37). Then we skip over to Luke 21, where Jesus tells his closest living disciples they will experience stiff opposition, betrayal in families (remember, he said this too in our passage), he predicted Jerusalem's demise, and then said this, which echoes what he said in 9:27: "this generation will certainly not pass away until all these things [I have just predicted in 21:7–28] have happened" (21:32). That's a lot to think about in such a short description, but these are the basic reasons why we think Jesus wants his standing-next-to-him followers to be ready for the coming destruction of Jerusalem, which is described as a coming of the Son of Man in judgment.

Peter wants to know if this stuff is for him and the circle around Jesus or for those outside his circle (12:41). Jesus, instead of answering the question, turns to the theme of being prepared for those days (12:42–48). Those who are ready will experience redemption; those who are not ready will be consumed in the destruction. Which is why Luke has a brief interruption about the divisiveness of Jesus' message (see above). He wept over what would happen to his beloved city, Jerusalem (19:41–44), which Josephus described as one hideous story after another (Josephus, *Jewish War*).

Then Jesus reproaches the crowd, giving Peter a bit of a reprieve. He tells them they have the skill to interpret the coming weather but not the skill to discern the times of coming judgment, which is why he urges his listeners to be ready for what looms on their own horizon. It's about like saying, "You Americans will never see 2050."

What About Us?

Thanks for asking. Sticking these warnings about readiness back into the first century and assigning them only to the disciples of Jesus at that time doesn't satisfy. Here's the best way to think about this: *What Jesus said about his day, namely, that God's judgment was looming, was as true for them as it is for us. What he said about the imminent destruction of Jerusalem foreshadows all of God's judgments in history.* We, too, must be ready for the day on which God will judge. But it is too easy to think entirely in terms of some magnificent Grand Finalé than it is of the judgment of God in our own time. Alan Jacobs says the great Day of Judgment is actually a "summary court in perpetual session" (Jacobs, *Shaming the Devil,* 64). Exactly. It's not only at the End but is happening Now.

We have a big question: Are you and I ready to be put in the dock of God's judgment for faithfulness to the Way of Jesus and for the final reckoning?

Questions for Reflection and Application

1. Have you ever held a "romantic" theory of Jesus, seeing him as polite and sweet? How has your view of Jesus changed as you read the Gospels more?

2. In what ways does Jesus bring division?

3. What do you think of the argument that Jesus here is not speaking of the Second Coming at the end of time but about the destruction of Jerusalem?

4. How can we be prepared for the end that Jesus warns his disciples is coming?

5. What do you think God's judgement in our time might look like?

FOR FURTHER READING

Alan Jacobs, *Shaming the Devil: Essays in Truthtelling* (Grand Rapids: Wm. B. Eerdmans, 2004).

Josephus, *Jewish War*, can be read in an older translation at: https://www.gutenberg.org/files/2850/2850-h/2850-h.htm

N.T. Wright, *Jesus and the Victory of God* (Minneapolis: Fortress, 1996). For a less academic approach by Wright, see his *The Challenge of Jesus* (rev. ed.; Downers Grove: IVP Books, 2015), chapters two and three.

PANORAMA OF REDEMPTION

Luke 13:1–35

*1 Now there were some present at that time who told Jesus about
the Galileans whose blood Pilate had mixed with their sacrifices.
2 Jesus answered, "Do you think that these Galileans were worse
sinners than all the other Galileans because they suffered this way?
3 I tell you, no! But unless you repent, you too will all perish. 4 Or
those eighteen who died when the tower in Siloam fell on them—
do you think they were more guilty than all the others living in
Jerusalem? 5 I tell you, no! But unless you repent, you too will all
perish."*

*6 Then he told this parable: "A man had a fig tree growing in
his vineyard, and he went to look for fruit on it but did not find
any. 7 So he said to the man who took care of the vineyard, 'For
three years now I've been coming to look for fruit on this fig tree and
haven't found any. Cut it down! Why should it use up the soil?'*

*8 " 'Sir,' the man replied, 'leave it alone for one more year, and
I'll dig around it and fertilize it. 9 If it bears fruit next year, fine! If
not, then cut it down.' "*

*10 On a Sabbath Jesus was teaching in one of the synagogues,
11 and a woman was there who had been crippled by a spirit for
eighteen years. She was bent over and could not straighten up at*

all. [12] When Jesus saw her, he called her forward and said to her,
"Woman, you are set free from your infirmity." [13] Then he put his
hands on her, and immediately she straightened up and praised God.

[14] Indignant because Jesus had healed on the Sabbath, the synagogue leader said to the people, "There are six days for work. So
come and be healed on those days, not on the Sabbath."

[15] The Lord answered him, "You hypocrites! Doesn't each of
you on the Sabbath untie your ox or donkey from the stall and lead
it out to give it water? [16] Then should not this woman, a daughter of
Abraham, whom Satan has kept bound for eighteen long years, be
set free on the Sabbath day from what bound her?"

[17] When he said this, all his opponents were humiliated, but
the people were delighted with all the wonderful things he was
doing.

[18] Then Jesus asked, "What is the kingdom of God like? What
shall I compare it to? [19] It is like a mustard seed, which a man took
and planted in his garden. It grew and became a tree, and the birds
perched in its branches."

[20] Again he asked, "What shall I compare the kingdom of God
to? [21] It is like yeast that a woman took and mixed into about sixty
pounds of flour until it worked all through the dough."

[22] Then Jesus went through the towns and villages, teaching as
he made his way to Jerusalem. [23] Someone asked him, "Lord, are
only a few people going to be saved?"

He said to them,

[24] "Make every effort to enter through the narrow door, because
many, I tell you, will try to enter and will not be able to. [25] Once
the owner of the house gets up and closes the door, you will stand
outside knocking and pleading, 'Sir, open the door for us.'

"But he will answer, 'I don't know you or where you come
from.'

[26] "Then you will say, 'We ate and drank with you, and you
taught in our streets.'

27 "But he will reply, 'I don't know you or where you come from.
Away from me, all you evildoers!'
28 "There will be weeping there, and gnashing of teeth, when
you see Abraham, Isaac and Jacob and all the prophets in the king-
dom of God, but you yourselves thrown out. 29 People will come
from east and west and north and south, and will take their places
at the feast in the kingdom of God. 30 Indeed there are those who are
last who will be first, and first who will be last."
31 At that time some Pharisees came to Jesus and said to him,
"Leave this place and go somewhere else. Herod wants to kill you."
32 He replied, "Go tell that fox, 'I will keep on driving out de-
mons and healing people today and tomorrow, and on the third
day I will reach my goal.' 33 In any case, I must press on today and
tomorrow and the next day—for surely no prophet can die outside
Jerusalem!
34 "Jerusalem, Jerusalem, you who kill the prophets and stone
those sent to you, how often I have longed to gather your children
together, as a hen gathers her chicks under her wings, and you were
not willing. 35 Look, your house is left to you desolate. I tell you, you
will not see me again until you say, 'Blessed is he who comes in the
name of the Lord.'"

Redemption, like the human body, is complicated. There are layers under layers, and no two layers are alike. Among many of us redemption is simplistic and simple (and greatly underestimated). Some think it is about feeling guilty, recognizing one's sinfulness, asking God for forgiveness in Jesus, receiving that grace, and that's it.

One would be hard-pressed to find anything so simple about redemption in the Gospel of Luke. The stories about Jesus, who really does know more about redemption than any one in history, reveal one layer of redemption after another.

No two people are alike; no two situations are the same; and redemption takes on as many shapes and colors and sounds as a deep gorge does as the sun passes through it. Luke's thirteenth chapter is a panorama of redemption.

Requirement for Redemption

A story circulated, ramped up in the several passings, among Galileans that Pilate had some of them murdered when they went to Jerusalem to sacrifice in the temple. There was the suggestion, one that enters into the minds of the majority of humans at times and not just first century Judeans, that the Galileans' sins caused their demise. Jesus, adding to the Galileans' story the tragic death of some eighteen upon whom the Tower of Siloam fell, knocks their argument—that death is deserved for some more than others—into outer space by saying the sole and necessary requirement *for all humans* is to repent (Luke 13:1–5).

To use words of Phil Collins, "you can't hurry love" or repentance. It cannot be coerced or forced or else one violates another person. Repentance has to come from within, and one has to give humans the freedom to perceive enough of their own condition to repent freely. Which is why Jesus tells the little parable of waiting an extra year for a fig tree to produce fruit (13:6–9).

In his biography about Jesus, Luke emphasizes repentance: John preached it (3:3, 8), Jesus said his mission was to summon people to repentance (5:32), the ideal redemption story is the repentant prodigal son (15:7, 10), and after his resurrection he explains the mission of the disciples as calling others to repentance (24:47). Also, toss in the Zacchaeus story as the perfect illustration of repentance (19:1–10). To repent is to sense one's failure to do what God wants, to admit one's wrong, to ask God for the graces of forgiveness, and to turn one's life around into a new way of life. Repentance is more than sorrow, even if it includes sorrow. It's a candid recognition of what we have done to others and made of ourselves, what we have done to ourselves and to others, what we have done to God. A biographer of George Orwell once said this of the famous author's own self-realization of his complicity in the injustices of British imperialism and domination in India: "The role and the uniform had taken him over and he hated what he had become" (Bowker, *Inside George Orwell*, 87). Repenters recognize what and who they have become. Repentance can be translated effectively as "conversion" as long as one understands that either term points to an ongoing, growing reality in a genuine follower of Jesus.

Power of Redemption

Over and over we encounter redemption as *holistic*: spiritual, emotional, physical, psychological, individual, communal, vocational, social, governmental, and financial. A disabled woman is described as "bent over and could not straighten up at all" (13:11). Jesus tells her she is now liberated from her eighteen-year—yes, the number eighteen again (see 13:4)—physical condition. No surprise, her back straightens up and she could suddenly meet eye to eye with her peers as she praised God for her redemption (13:12–13). Physical healing is kingdom redemption.

No surprise for many, too, that a "synagogue leader" was galled that Jesus had healed the woman in the middle of a Sabbath service and suggested to Jesus that a more observant form of physical redemption would take place Sunday through Friday (13:14). We have a habit of stereotyping this leader, aggravated as it is by our *not knowing* that the famous Jewish source of legal rulings, the Mishnah, has this line: "And any matter of doubt as to danger to life overrides the prohibitions of the Sabbath" (*m. Yoma* 8:6). So, perhaps it is not because Jesus did this on the Sabbath *per se* but because the woman's life was not in jeopardy and still he healed on a Sabbath, and perhaps also because he did so in the service and drew attention to the kingdom's redemptive powers when he could have waited until after the service.

Jesus tosses down the hypocrite card, and exclaims that, since they have no issue with caring for farm animals on the Sabbath, why should they not want this "daughter of Abraham" to be liberated from Satan's grip (13:15–16)? Life in jeopardy or not, Jesus knew the woman deserved redemption at that moment.

Noticeably, those who were represented by the leader's questioning of Jesus were "shamed" or "humiliated," which means their social status was put in jeopardy by the power of God at work in Jesus (and not in them) (13:17). The "whole crowd" (NIV: "people") was thrilled at what Jesus had done.

Result of Redemption

Luke now includes two shortest-of-the-short stories of Jesus, the parable of the mustard seed and of yeast (13:18–21), both of which are comparable in some way to the kingdom of God and its holistic redemption. I'd like to jump straight to the point: these two parables are not about growth of the kingdom but about the shocking difference between small beginnings and massive implications. As a tiny mustard seed becomes a "tree," and use of hyperbole or exaggeration fits the story perfectly, and as yeast penetrates into the entire batch of dough, so what seems so small at that time—the low numbers of true followers of Jesus—will become a massive community over time. Google it: there are nearly 3 billion people connected to Christianity in the world today. How many were there at the time Jesus told these parables?

Numbers of Redemption

So few were the numbers that someone asked Jesus that very question: "Lord, are only a few people going to be saved?" (13:22). Jesus' response would not a modern, fast-talking, invitation-counting evangelist satisfy. For many, their church's megachurch size proves their church is the best and they are right in the middle of God's plan for the world. Jesus' words right here contradict that conviction and teach us that the measure of redemption is not quantity but devotion to Jesus, something often only noticed over time by those with eyes to see and ears to hear the presence of God's Spirit.

Luke's version of Jesus' response (13:24) is not as clear as Matthew's version (Matthew 7:13–14), where "many" poses against "few." Luke only has the "many" will-not-make-it part. The implication, however, is as Matthew reports it. Some of those many, Jesus informs his listeners, will protest their non-inclusion in the *olam ha-ba*, the Age to Come, which in our Gospels appears mostly as the kingdom of God. Jesus will on Judgment Day dismiss the protesters as "evildoers" despite their claims (Luke 13:25–27). Jesus' words are stiff warnings because he continues by informing them that on the day of judgment they will be excluded while some "people" all the way "from east and west and north and south" will enter the kingdom (13:28–29). The implication is clear: some of his Jewish contemporaries, who claim to be God's eternally covenanted people, will be excluded from the kingdom because they have not done the will of God. He says this with his famous "first will be last" saying (13:30). I hasten to add, that the shoe is now on the other foot: many presumptuous Christians would be making the same claims and will be the first surprised by some closed doors.

So, what's the solution? It's not going to church or even believing all the proper Christian doctrines. No, the solution is the kind of repentance that leads to transformation into a person who does God's will, namely, who loves God and loves others. As Jesus told the lawyer in the Samaritan parable, the "go and do likewise" person attended the wounded because he loved God and loved others (10:25–37). #wegottalistentoJesus

Sorrows of Redemption

Repentance is required, holistic redemption is on offer, the numbers who are committed to Jesus (then or now) are not great, and this caused (and causes) Jesus great sorrow (13:31–35). Herod, some Pharisees informed Jesus, was out for Jesus' life (13:31). Jesus' response is a prophetic judgment: "Go tell that fox" that I'm headed for Jerusalem, regardless of these little tidbits and hints of problems lurking for me, because there my mission will meet its goal: death (13:32–33). This theme of death-in-Jerusalem has lurked, if sometimes more often in the far background, since 9:51 where Jesus "resolutely set out for Jerusalem."

Luke zippered his biography of Jesus tightly with stories of rejection, but the biggest cause of sorrow for Jesus was how recalcitrant the City of Jerusalem and its dominant leaders were. From Mount Olivet, just to the east of the City, one could have scanned the whole city. When Jesus looked it over, as he surely often did, he knew its tragic fate: it would be sacked by Rome (66–73 AD).

Part of the destruction's explanation for Jesus, for Luke, and for early Christians (but not for Josephus or the rabbis) was their rejection of Jesus as Messiah. Jesus longed for it to fall under his kingdom mission, but it was "not willing" (13:34). So he predicts its demise: "your house is left desolate" and the next time it will see Jesus will be when the Son of Man's judgment visits (cf. 12:35–48).

We need to close up shop for this passage, but before we can turn out the lights, we need to remind ourselves again of the complicated layers of redemption: it includes repentance, holistic redemption, at times a very small number of receptive listeners, and it includes negative consequences for those who turn away from what God wants for God's people. It's not a simplistic gospel plan but a thick description of redemption's many layers.

Questions for Reflection and Application

1. How does this section define repentance?

2. Why did Jesus' healing on the Sabbath lead to conflict?

3. How do the two small parables serve to illustrate a point about small things becoming large?

4. What causes Jesus' sorrow?

5. Why do you think the nature of repentance and redemption keep small the number of people who choose to take Jesus up on his kingdom offer?

FOR FURTHER READING

Gordon Bowker, *Inside George Orwell: A Biography* (New York: Palgrave Macmillan, 2003).

Phil Collins, "You Can't Hurry Love," *Virgin Records* (2014). [format not known]

REDEMPTION AND PRETENSION

Luke 14:1–24

[1] One Sabbath, when Jesus went to eat in the house of a prominent Pharisee, he was being carefully watched. [2] There in front of him was a man suffering from abnormal swelling of his body. [3] Jesus asked the Pharisees and experts in the law, "Is it lawful to heal on the Sabbath or not?" [4] But they remained silent. So taking hold of the man, he healed him and sent him on his way.

[5] Then he asked them, "If one of you has a child or an ox that falls into a well on the Sabbath day, will you not immediately pull it out?" [6] And they had nothing to say.

[7] When he noticed how the guests picked the places of honor at the table, he told them this parable: [8] "When someone invites you to a wedding feast, do not take the place of honor, for a person more distinguished than you may have been invited. [9] If so, the host who invited both of you will come and say to you, 'Give this person your seat.' Then, humiliated, you will have to take the least important place. [10] But when you are invited, take the lowest place, so that when your host comes, he will say to you, 'Friend, move up to a better place.' Then you will be honored in the presence of all the other guests. [11] For all those who exalt themselves will be humbled, and those who humble themselves will be exalted."

12 *Then Jesus said to his host, "When you give a luncheon or*
dinner, do not invite your friends, your brothers or sisters, your
relatives, or your rich neighbors; if you do, they may invite you
back and so you will be repaid. 13 *But when you give a banquet,*
invite the poor, the crippled, the lame, the blind, 14 *and you will be*
blessed. Although they cannot repay you, you will be repaid at the
resurrection of the righteous."

15 *When one of those at the table with him heard this, he said*
to Jesus, "Blessed is the one who will eat at the feast in the kingdom
of God."

16 *Jesus replied: "A certain man was preparing a great banquet*
and invited many guests. 17 *At the time of the banquet he sent his*
servant to tell those who had been invited, 'Come, for everything is
now ready.'

18 *"But they all alike began to make excuses. The first said, 'I*
have just bought a field, and I must go and see it. Please excuse me.'

19 *"Another said, 'I have just bought five yoke of oxen, and I'm*
on my way to try them out. Please excuse me.'

20 *"Still another said, 'I just got married, so I can't come.'*

21 *"The servant came back and reported this to his master.*
Then the owner of the house became angry and ordered his servant,
'Go out quickly into the streets and alleys of the town and bring in
the poor, the crippled, the blind and the lame.'

22 *" 'Sir,' the servant said, 'what you ordered has been done,*
but there is still room.'

23 *"Then the master told his servant, 'Go out to the roads and*
country lanes and compel them to come in, so that my house will be
full. 24 *I tell you, not one of those who were invited will get a taste*
of my banquet.' "

Christian teachers and preachers go to battle more with those who are closest than with those who are remote. Baptists argue with Anglicans who argue with non-denominationalists because, truth be told, they too often compete for the same people. To be sure, some raise Reepicheep's rapier over theological topics—baptism of infants, women pastors and preachers, the rapture—but even those battles that seem theological are driven by protective fences around their own tribe.

So let me make this important point: among the various group options facing Galileans who were giving Jesus their ear, groups like the Essenes and Zealots, the group closest to Jesus and his followers were the Pharisees. Both had a similar audience—ordinary Jewish folks—and a similar biblical foundation, yet they were at odds on some issues. At the heart of their difference were the centrality of Jesus, the significance of his idea of the kingdom, his approachableness to the otherwise marginalized, and especially his own way of "observing" the law of Moses. The Pharisees had one way, which included a strong interpretive tradition, and Jesus had another way. They were close but too close is a good way of saying it. Scott Spencer gets this right when he observes this is an "in-house debate" not a conflict between "hardcore enemies" (Spencer, *Luke*, 366).

The entire passage poses Jesus challenging the pretentiousness of those who considered themselves persons of high status and superior to others. Since all of this passage appears to occur at a leading Pharisees' house, the entire passage strikes a careful reader as a challenge to the status claims of some leading Pharisee.

Heal Whenever

It doesn't take much thinking to recall when following some rule was more important to someone than doing something compassionate or loving. Our family has spent three years listening to stories of church leaders protecting the reputation of an institution at the expense of caring for someone wounded by a pastor or a leader at the church.

We read a story in the previous chapter (13:10–17) where I sought to soften the tension between Jesus and a synagogue leader by suggesting Jesus may have interrupted a synagogue service. No such service occurs in our passage (14:1–6), which means the tension in the event in chapter thirteen may also have been over what is permissible on the Sabbath day itself. At a leading Pharisee's home Jesus encounters a disabled man with edema, or fluid retention, most likely in the legs (14:2). Since he was being observed carefully, which gives many readers a sense that there's a set up in action, Jesus turns to those who claim careful observance to query them on the appropriateness of healing the man on a Sabbath (14:3).

Silence after a question, we have all learned and this group of experts knew, often staves off a heated argument. It also surrenders the platform. In their silence, Jesus heals the man (14:4), which leads to another common discussion he must have had with the ones claiming special levels of observance. Jesus asks them the question: Would you not rescue a son (NIV has "child") or an "ox" if it fell into a cistern on the Sabbath? A "yes" means he can heal; a "no" shames them for a lack of compassion. We are back to the Samaritan story again (10:25–37).

Acts of mercy rule. One can heal whenever one finds someone in need.

Flip Status

We need to read the parable in Luke 14:7–14 as comedy. In an honor-shame culture, as first century Galilee and Judea were, one protected and lived out one's status. As in someone thinking they should never be seen in public without one's clerical collar or without makeup or in one's only-in-the-house clothes. In the first century one's status was embodied by where one sat at a banquet, and this meal has the appearance of an evening symposium with Jesus as the guest speaker. The higher one's honor the closer one sat to the host; the lower one's honor the farther one sat away from the host. A meal put people in their place by a recognized pecking order.

"Glory," the American novelist Gore Vidal once said, "is a drug more addictive than any other" (627). Susan Neiman adds insight to Vidal when she says, "Two passions, for glory and for luxury, are the source of all our ills; we are wicked because of the one and miserable because of the other" (Neiman, *Why Grow Up?,* 45). Let us not then suppose that the status issue at work in our passage can be dismissed as little more than one's society's preferences. Driving the desire for glory and honor and status can become reckless and abusive.

Jesus gives a fun exercise for his disciples to ponder, perhaps drawn out of Proverbs 25:6–7 (also see Matthew 23:6). When they get invited to a banquet, they are to take the lowest seats because, if they take a closer-than-their-status spot, they will likely get bumped down, which was shaming to their status. So, he says, take distant seats so you can get bumped up closer. In getting bumped up, their chests can swell with pride. What a hoot!

He flips the status game on its head with a second brief story. When you host a banquet, don't invite your family, friends, and rich connections. Instead, send out invitations to the "poor, the crippled, the lame, the blind" (Luke 14:13). If the former group could invite you to their parties, which is called reciprocal benevolence, the latter can do no such thing. Don't invite to get invited; invite to expand grace and generosity. Another what a hoot!

Jesus' *nimshal*, or explanation (both at 14:11 and 14:14), pertains to discipleship: self-exaltation is against the way of Jesus; self-abasement is the way of Jesus; leveling the playing field by inviting all is the way of Jesus. Which, again, is not about self-esteem or about one's worthiness before God. His eye is on the elitists of his world. Jesus wants followers who are not trying to expand their brand and market themselves but who want to serve others. Since these comedic parables are windows into a kingdom reality, the flipping of the script, like the beatitudes (6:20–26), points listeners to God's evaluation of humans in the final kingdom.

Invite Everyone

Serving others is the way of Jesus in yet another parable (14:15–24). A man hosts a "great banquet" and invites "many guests" but, when the time for the banquet arrived, "they all alike began to make excuses" for not coming. (Surely a comedic exaggeration.) When the slave (NIV has "servant") returned with all the bad news, the master of the house "became angry" because their non-arrival shamed him. So, the man orders his slave to invite "the poor, the crippled, the blind and the lame" (14:21). Even then there was "still room" for more. He ordered the slave to go "out to the roads and country lanes" and find anyone who will come. Again, the social context is about status, about the wealthy vs. the poor. With that as the social context, this parable creates an imagined world in which the poor are shown the compassion of provision.

But Jesus is throwing shade on those of high status, perhaps some Pharisees, but especially anyone who considered himself an elite or superior to others and neglectful of those in need. He does so in parables that are comedic to the ordinary Galilean and challenging, if not offensive, to those who occupied social honor. Pretentiousness has no part in the kingdom of God. Jesus is the One and Only with High Status at the High Table. Everyone else is a sister or a brother.

Questions for Reflection and Application

1. Why did Jesus and the Pharisees have some disagreements, even though their beliefs were ideologically similar?

2. How does Jesus illustrate that compassion is more important than rules?

3. How can an understanding of honor-shame culture impact our interpretation of parables such as these about banquets?

4. What does Jesus teach about wealth, glory, and riches in these stories?

5. How might Jesus be calling you to set aside your status in order to do kingdom work?

FOR FURTHER READING

Susan Neiman, *Why Grow Up? Subversive Thoughts for an Infantile Age* (rev. ed.; New York: Farrar, Straus and Giroux, 2016).

Gore Vidal, "The Memories of the Glorious Bird and an Earlier Self," in P. Lopate, *The Art of the Personal Essay* (New York: Anchor Doubleday, 1994), pp. 623–638.

REDEMPTION NURTURES DISCIPLESHIP

Luke 14:25–35

25 Large crowds were traveling with Jesus, and turning to them he
said: 26 "If anyone comes to me and does not hate father and moth-
er, wife and children, brothers and sisters—yes, even their own
life—such a person cannot be my disciple. 27 And whoever does not
carry their cross and follow me cannot be my disciple.

28 "Suppose one of you wants to build a tower. Won't you first
sit down and estimate the cost to see if you have enough money to
complete it? 29 For if you lay the foundation and are not able to fin-
ish it, everyone who sees it will ridicule you, 30 saying, 'This person
began to build and wasn't able to finish.'

31 "Or suppose a king is about to go to war against another
king. Won't he first sit down and consider whether he is able with
ten thousand men to oppose the one coming against him with twen-
ty thousand? 32 If he is not able, he will send a delegation while the
other is still a long way off and will ask for terms of peace. 33 In the
same way, those of you who do not give up everything you have
cannot be my disciples.

34 "Salt is good, but if it loses its saltiness, how can it be made
salty again? 35 It is fit neither for the soil nor for the manure pile; it
is thrown out.

"Whoever has ears to hear, let them hear."

A follower of Jesus is someone who follows Jesus. Sounds a bit trite, perhaps, but we use "follower of Jesus" so glibly that we can stun some people when they hear the "who follows Jesus" bit. Jesus did not make "Christians" as we understand it in our institutionalized Christianity and church-dom world. He made disciples, that is, persons who turned from one way of life to follow him, wherever that following would take them. In our passage Jesus gives three basics of a follower of Jesus, and his words come off in the context as a "recruitment speech" (Levine-Witherington, *Luke*, 400). The "compel them to come in" of the previous passage (14:13, 21) may well have generated the need for these three basics of following Jesus.

Following Means Cross

Jesus cut his audience from "large" to probably few by turning to the adoring crowd with two of his most famous, and least comfortable, sayings. (1) A follower was to "hate" one's family and one's self (see #2), which in his world was a powerful "either you're for me or you're against me" kind of saying (14:26). Honoring one's parents and family can work together with this saying's hyperbolic sounds (cf. 2:51 and 18:20). (2) One must shoulder one's own cross to be a genuine follower of Jesus, and one's cross implies a willingness to live one's life in such allegiance to the Crucified One that one may also be a martyr (14:27). Such commitment is what Jesus means by hating one's own life in 14:26, but it does not mean suffering for the sake of suffering (Levine-Witherington, *Luke*, 401). It means experiencing what comes our way because we follow Jesus.

A claim on redemption without discipleship is what Bonhoeffer called "cheap grace." So I quote him again:

> Cheap grace is grace without discipleship, grace without the cross, grace without the living, incarnate Jesus Christ (Bonhoeffer, *Discipleship*, 44).

> Costly grace is the gospel which must be sought again and again, the gift which has to be asked for, the door at which one has to knock. It is costly, because it calls to discipleship; it is grace because it calls us to follow Jesus Christ. It is costly, because it costs people their lives; it is grace, because it thereby makes them live. It is costly, because it condemns sin; it is grace, because it justifies the sinner. Above all, grace is costly, because it was costly to God, because it costs God the life of God's Son "you were bought with a price" and because nothing can be cheap to us which is costly to God (Bonhoeffer, *Discipleship*, 45).

The sternness of Bonhoeffer matches the either-or-ness of Jesus' own words. As we sit with them, their clarity beckons us forward onto the path with Jesus with a more rigorous commitment to him.

Following Means Converting Our Possessions

An "as old as humans" principle, "Don't start what you don't have resources to finish," finds its way into Jesus' parabolic use of a tower builder and a warring king. Builders need funds for supplies and warring kings need soldiers. Without them their plans fail. Jesus turns those images into a surprising shift. One expects him to say "you need consider that it will cost your life," as in 14:26–27, but instead he narrows it to one of life's symbolic expressions in his third basic instruction for followers: (3) the NIV has "give up everything" but the Greek text can be better translated "say farewell to your possessions" or "give up *all your things*" (as at 12:33). These are not suggestions. The words are strong: if you don't do this "you cannot be my disciples" (14:33).

We in the wealthy western world prefer the generalization of the NIV because it permits us to live more comfortably with our possessions. There's a reason for Jesus saying it the way he did. As then, so now: possessions embody our discipleship. That is, how many we have, how important they are, how much attention they consume, how much nurturing we do of them as Gollum did with his ring, and what we do with them. Barbara Brown Taylor's words speak to me:

> As far as Jesus is concerned, money is like nuclear power. It may be able to do a lot of good in the world, but only within strongly built and carefully regulated corridors. Most of us do not know how to handle it. We get contaminated by its power, and we contaminate others by wielding it carelessly ourselves—by wanting it too desperately or using it too manipulatively or believing in it too fiercely or defending it too cruelly (Taylor, *The Preaching Life*, 130).

Of course there's hyperbole present (in Taylor and Jesus). Jesus loved hyperbole. But hyperbole only works if it exaggerates what needs to be said, and what Jesus said was that our possessions need to be converted too. Some will be tossed aside, some given away, and what remains repurposed for the kingdom of God.

Following Means "Salt"

These three basics—turning from family to Jesus, shouldering one's cross, and saying good-bye to our possessions—when not present in those around Jesus turn the salt of discipleship into the insipidness of nominal faith. Salt is good until it isn't, and it isn't good when it "loses its saltiness" or its ability to do what it can do for "soil" or a "manure pile" (14:34–35). That happens when salt is contaminated with dirt and grime, at which time it is tossed out the window onto alley ways where it becomes road grit.

Followers of Jesus, very simply put, are those who follow Jesus daily. Half-day followers pollute discipleship. You may think me tottering along as some oldster by what I'm about to say but, while I have a platform like these wonderful Bible studies, I'll say what I think. The biggest challenge—then and now—to following Jesus was and is the World—its System and its Ways that make us fit into the World. The World's Ways are both more invisible than we can see and far more powerful in us and on us than we know. The heart of the World's System today is the Self, unadulterated, unhindered, unchecked. Following Jesus consistently turns from the World, what C.S. Lewis once called the desire to be accepted in the "Inner Ring" (*Weight of Glory*). In place of the Inner Ring, Jesus frames the whole of life by the World's Biggest Enemy: the Cross.

Questions for Reflection and Application

1. What is the difference between a common understanding of "Christian" in the Western world today and a Lukan understanding of "disciple" or "follower of Jesus"?

2. What does shouldering one's cross have to do with allegiance to Jesus?

3. How does the translation "say farewell to your possessions" affect your understanding of the call to discipleship?

4. What is the difference between being "salty" and having "nominal faith"?

5. What aspects of the World's Systems and Ways most try to draw you away from discipleship?

FOR FURTHER READING

Dietrich Bonhoeffer, *Discipleship* (DBW 4; Minneapolis: Fortress, 2001). Formerly titled *The Cost of Discipleship*.

C.S. Lewis, *The Weight of Glory and Other Addresses* (San Francisco: HarperSanFrancisco, 1980), pp. 141–157. His essay stimulated the last paragraph.

Barbara Brown Taylor, *The Preaching Life* (Lanham, Maryland: Cowley, 1993).

REDEMPTION COMES HOME

Luke 15:1–32

[1] Now the tax collectors and sinners were all gathering around to
hear Jesus. [2] But the Pharisees and the teachers of the law muttered,
"This man welcomes sinners and eats with them."
[3] Then Jesus told them this parable: [4] "Suppose one of you has a
hundred sheep and loses one of them. Doesn't he leave the ninety-nine
in the open country and go after the lost sheep until he finds it? [5] And
when he finds it, he joyfully puts it on his shoulders [6] and goes home.
Then he calls his friends and neighbors together and says, 'Rejoice
with me; I have found my lost sheep.' [7] I tell you that in the same way
there will be more rejoicing in heaven over one sinner who repents
than over ninety-nine righteous persons who do not need to repent.
[8] "Or suppose a woman has ten silver coins and loses one.
Doesn't she light a lamp, sweep the house and search carefully un-
til she finds it? [9] And when she finds it, she calls her friends and
neighbors together and says, 'Rejoice with me; I have found my lost
coin.' [10] In the same way, I tell you, there is rejoicing in the presence
of the angels of God over one sinner who repents."
[11] Jesus continued: "There was a man who had two sons. [12] The
younger one said to his father, 'Father, give me my share of the es-
tate.' So he divided his property between them. [13] Not long after that,
the younger son got together all he had, set off for a distant country

*and there squandered his wealth in wild living. 14 After he had spent
everything, there was a severe famine in that whole country, and he
began to be in need. 15 So he went and hired himself out to a citizen
of that country, who sent him to his fields to feed pigs. 16 He longed
to fill his stomach with the pods that the pigs were eating, but no one
gave him anything. 17 When he came to his senses, he said, 'How
many of my father's hired servants have food to spare, and here I
am starving to death! 18 I will set out and go back to my father and
say to him: Father, I have sinned against heaven and against you.
19 I am no longer worthy to be called your son; make me like one
of your hired servants.' 20 So he got up and went to his father. But
while he was still a long way off, his father saw him and was filled
with compassion for him; he ran to his son, threw his arms around
him and kissed him. 21 The son said to him, 'Father, I have sinned
against heaven and against you. I am no longer worthy to be called
your son.' 22 But the father said to his servants, 'Quick! Bring the
best robe and put it on him. Put a ring on his finger and sandals on
his feet. 23 Bring the fattened calf and kill it. Let's have a feast and
celebrate. 24 For this son of mine was dead and is alive again; he was
lost and is found.' So they began to celebrate.*

*25 Meanwhile, the older son was in the field. When he came near
the house, he heard music and dancing. 26 So he called one of the servants and asked him what was going on. 27 'Your brother has come,'
he replied, 'and your father has killed the fattened calf because he has
him back safe and sound.' 28 The older brother became angry and
refused to go in. So his father went out and pleaded with him. 29 But
he answered his father, 'Look! All these years I've been slaving for
you and never disobeyed your orders. Yet you never gave me even a
young goat so I could celebrate with my friends. 30 But when this son
of yours who has squandered your property with prostitutes comes
home, you kill the fattened calf for him!' 31 'My son,' the father said,
'you are always with me, and everything I have is yours. 32 But we
had to celebrate and be glad, because this brother of yours was dead
and is alive again; he was lost and is found.'"*

The Pharisees are back again, and they've got another issue with Jesus. He's cavalier in his table habits in dining with "sinners." What one ate and with whom one ate both mattered, and the "with whom" has always mattered for most societies. Eating with someone embodied acceptance if not also approval. As we have said already, Jesus and the Pharisees were rivals so expecting them not to make observations about Jesus is like asking a mama goose not to hiss when someone gets near a gosling. Most of the mama's hissing, like the Pharisees, is protective boundary marking.

This well-loved set of parables about what is lost and found requires two commitments by the reader to encounter its fullness. The first is what is usually ignored: 15:1–2 describes the setting, and in each of the three parables Jesus explains himself to the grumblers. The second is to read the parables from the inside and let that inside contain all your ideas. The inside is clear: Jesus eats with "tax collectors and sinners" because his Father responds in joy over every person who repents and comes home, and he welcomes, too, the grumblers themselves. In the history of interpreting these parables, especially the parable about the so-called "prodigal son," many have lost contact with the inside by speculating about what the coin stands for, what the ring stands for, or what the robe might signify, and even what the fattened calf signifies. They are incidental details in the story that fill out a parable about God's joy over repentant sinners.

The Context

Both "tax collectors" and "sinners" are stereotyped characters in the Gospel of Luke, the one signifying *collaboration with Rome* (by abandoning one's people) and *exploitation*, and the other a label tossed at those one considered *disobedient to the Torah (as interpreted by the label-tosser)*. As such, these two terms point out those who have abandoned covenant and family and nation and temple. Not everyone was scrupulous and not everyone cared, but some did and they're the ones pointing fingers in this opening verse. The problem Jesus pointed out was that the Pharisees and experts in the law thought Jesus' hanging out with such persons could compromise observance of the Torah (again, *as interpreted*). All three parables respond to this expressed concern.

Losing What Matters

In each parable—lost sheep, lost coin, lost son—something valuable is lost: a sheep, a coin, and a son. The sheep matters to the shepherd, that coin had value to the poor woman, and the father loved his lost son immensely. A categorical jump occurs from the first two parables to the third: sheep and coins matter but a human being is far more valuable. Jesus set up the grumblers by speaking of ordinary losses that matter only to show that a human, a son, matters far more. Which means he sees the tax collectors and sinners as children of a father who deserve to be home.

The Joy of Discovery

Each of the parables turns joy into a major theme. The shepherd summons "friends and neighbors" and calls them to "rejoice with me" (15:5–7), and the woman offers the same invitation (15:9). But in the lost son parable, joy turns into a massive feast of celebration that includes first a father's embrace, then clothing and a ring and sandals to evoke welcome, and then a feast of a fattened calf (15:20–24).

This joy morphs for the reader from a human (shepherd, woman, father) to God's own celebration. Twice we read about heaven's joy (15:7, 10) to remind us that the joy is God's.

Grumbling

The theme of joy shoots a barbed eye at the grumblers for their grumbling when they ought to be celebrating. One would have to be a very rigid person to think all Pharisees or teachers of the law despised tax collectors and sinners so much they would have not been thrilled to see such persons enter onto the path of redemption and moral reformation. Again, we need to see the sharpness of images for what they do, and we need to avoid thinking of them as a crystal glass on reality. Flannery O'Connor's images in the tradition of Southern grotesque take their cues from these stories of Jesus. Her characters are not real people but real people turned into characters.

Those who grumble over eating with sinners who are morally reforming deserve a kick in the shins, which Jesus gave. In the words of Matthew Croasmun and Miroslav Volf, "one common way to end up on the outside of Jesus' invitation was to refuse the irrelevance of qualifications for presence at the table" (*Hunger for Home*, 43–44). The irony is that we (often) sit in judgment on the Pharisees here because we think they are the ones unqualified!

Effort

Notice, too, the strenuous efforts of the shepherd who searches for his lost sheep "until he finds it" (15:4) and the lighting of a lamp and sweeping and search of the woman (15:8) along with the father who longs for his son's return, then spots his son though a long way off, and then running to his son (15:20). And the father's efforts to get his older grumbling son back into the home are noticeable too (15:28). The efforts of these humans are comparable to the intense desire of God the Father for his children to come home. There is utterly nothing un-Jewish or surprising to a Jewish audience that God would respond like this.

Fellowship

In each of the parables the celebration occurs with family and friends and neighbors. The lost son parable, too, describes such a fellowship of joy in the feast with friends, so many present that they slay a calf for a meal accompanied by music and dancing. Their joyous fellowship participates in the fellowship of the angels and archangels and the communion of the saints who take delight in earth's grand redemption stories.

Repentance

The first two parables do not raise repentance in their little stories, but each of them ends with that theme, reminding us to keep our eyes on the grumblers who are irritated over the tax collectors and sinners turning over a new leaf. But the lost son parable provides brilliant introspection about repentance: (1) the son chooses to leave home for the diaspora; (2) the son creates distance between himself, his father, and home as a sign of running away; (3) the son's patterns of behavior violate Jewish piety; (4) the son's suffering from a lack of food is a consequence of his reckless behaviors; (5) the son hits rock bottom when he feeds pigs and no one is there to help him; (6) the son "came to his senses" when he realizes, in his suffering, his own culpability for all he has done; (7) the son determines to return home and confess his sins to his loving father; (8) the son realizes being a "hired servant" in his father's home is better than his distant residence and his own status as a son; (9) the son returns home to a father's embrace. That list identifies elements of repentance: sinfulness, recognition of one's sinfulness before God, even shame for what one has done, determination to return, choosing to act in returning, and confession to the father for what he had done. Another example is Zacchaeus (19:1–10), the words of John the Baptist to his audience illustrate repentance, and another example can be seen in Peter (3:7–14; 5:1–11).

Such persons are lost and then found. Such persons are the source of God's joy and heaven's celebrations. Such persons are restored to family status as God's children.

Grumblers Welcome

We have traditionally stopped right there in our reading of this third parable, but we cannot. This is a parable, not just about the so-called prodigal, younger son, but the parable of two lost sons.

Luke really cares about the older, grumbling son. In the son's grumbling the father goes out to him (as he did to the younger son) where he gets an earful from his grumbling son over how he has been disrespected. He thinks he has deserved—notice the context of this parable again—a party for his observance and family commitments. Surprise to some, the father does not reject the son but reminds him that "you are always with me" and even more "everything I have is yours" (15:31). So he enjoins the older, grumbling son to turn from grumbling about the sinner-son to "celebrate and be glad" because the sinner-son was "lost" and is now "found." He was "dead and is alive again" (15:32). Jesus writes the grumblers of 15:1–2 into the older son in order to invite them to the table with the sinners.

I riff here on something said by Tim Keller: forgiveness may be enacted quickly but reconciliation between an abused or sinned-against person can take time because it requires truth-telling, repentance, and the restoration of trust, and trust is earned over time. Here are Keller's wise words:

> On the other hand, "I forgive you" does not mean "I trust you." Some people think they haven't reconciled until they can completely trust the person who did the wrong. That is not the case. Forgiveness means a willingness to try to reestablish trust, but that reestablishment is always a process. The speed and degree of this restoration entail the re-creation of trust, and that takes time, depending on the nature and severity of the offenses involved.
>
> Until a person shows evidence of true change, we should not trust him or her. To immediately give one's trust to a person with sinful habits could actually be enabling him to sin. Trust must be restored, and the speed at which this occurs depends on the behavior.

Where Was Your Head When You Read This Story?

This is what I think we nearly all do. We point our fingers at the older son and say in ourselves *I am not the older son.* But Jesus told this story because, more than we care to admit it, *we, too, are more like the older son than we care to admit.* Instead of pointing our fingers at the Pharisees and teachers of the law, let us not be like their finger pointing but be like the angels in heaven who rejoice over known sinners returning home to enjoy family fellowship.

Questions for Reflection and Application

1. What do these parables have to do with protective boundary marking?

2. Luke uses the labels "tax collectors and sinners," which can get familiar enough for readers to pass over. What do these stereotypes actually mean?

3. How do the themes of sorrowful losing and joyful discovering play out in each parable?

4. What role does "grumbling" play in both the story and story's audience?

5. How can these stories help you cultivate your own Christlike response to the "tax collectors and sinners" you know?

FOR FURTHER READING

Tim Keller, "Forgiveness and Reconciliation," https://lindawillows.com/2021/06/14/forgiveness-and-reconciliation-tim-keller-pursuing-truth-love-relationship/#:~:text=%2C%20Love%2C%20Relationship)-,SERVING%20EACH%20OTHER%20THROUGH%20FORGIVENESS%20AND%20RECONCILIATION%20by%20DR.,within%20a%20community%20of%20believers.

I have for years learned immensely from Klyne Snodgrass's interpretations of the parables of Jesus. See his massive book *Stories with Intent: A Comprehensive Guide to the Parables of Jesus* (2d ed.; Grand Rapids: Wm. B. Eerdmans, 2018), pp. 93–143.

REDEMPTION AND RICHES

Luke 16:1–31

1 Jesus told his disciples: "There was a rich man whose manager
was accused of wasting his possessions. 2 So he called him in and
asked him, 'What is this I hear about you? Give an account of your
management, because you cannot be manager any longer.'

3 "The manager said to himself, 'What shall I do now? My
master is taking away my job. I'm not strong enough to dig, and I'm
ashamed to beg—4 I know what I'll do so that, when I lose my job
here, people will welcome me into their houses.'

5 "So he called in each one of his master's debtors. He asked the
first, 'How much do you owe my master?'

6 " 'Nine hundred gallons of olive oil,' he replied.

"The manager told him, 'Take your bill, sit down quickly, and
make it four hundred and fifty.'

7 "Then he asked the second, 'And how much do you owe?'

" 'A thousand bushels of wheat,' he replied.

"He told him, 'Take your bill and make it eight hundred.'

8 "The master commended the dishonest manager because he
had acted shrewdly. For the people of this world are more shrewd in
dealing with their own kind than are the people of the light. 9 I tell

you, use worldly wealth to gain friends for yourselves, so that when
it is gone, you will be welcomed into eternal dwellings.

10 "Whoever can be trusted with very little can also be trusted with much, and whoever is dishonest with very little will also
be dishonest with much. 11 So if you have not been trustworthy
in handling worldly wealth, who will trust you with true riches?
12 And if you have not been trustworthy with someone else's property, who will give you property of your own?

13 "No one can serve two masters. Either you will hate the one
and love the other, or you will be devoted to the one and despise the
other. You cannot serve both God and money."

14 The Pharisees, who loved money, heard all this and were
sneering at Jesus. 15 He said to them, "You are the ones who justify
yourselves in the eyes of others, but God knows your hearts. What
people value highly is detestable in God's sight.

16 "The Law and the Prophets were proclaimed until John.
Since that time, the good news of the kingdom of God is being
preached, and everyone is forcing their way into it. 17 It is easier for
heaven and earth to disappear than for the least stroke of a pen to
drop out of the Law.

18 "Anyone who divorces his wife and marries another woman
commits adultery, and the man who marries a divorced woman
commits adultery.

19 "There was a rich man who was dressed in purple and fine
linen and lived in luxury every day. 20 At his gate was laid a beggar
named Lazarus, covered with sores 21 and longing to eat what fell
from the rich man's table. Even the dogs came and licked his sores.

22 "The time came when the beggar died and the angels carried
him to Abraham's side. The rich man also died and was buried. 23 In
Hades, where he was in torment, he looked up and saw Abraham
far away, with Lazarus by his side. 24 So he called to him, 'Father
Abraham, have pity on me and send Lazarus to dip the tip of his finger in water and cool my tongue, because I am in agony in this fire.'

[25] *"But Abraham replied, 'Son, remember that in your lifetime*
you received your good things, while Lazarus received bad things,
but now he is comforted here and you are in agony. [26] *And besides*
all this, between us and you a great chasm has been set in place, so
that those who want to go from here to you cannot, nor can anyone
cross over from there to us.'

[27] *"He answered, 'Then I beg you, father, send Lazarus to my*
family, [28] *for I have five brothers. Let him warn them, so that they*
will not also come to this place of torment.'

[29] *"Abraham replied, 'They have Moses and the Prophets; let*
them listen to them.'

[30] *" 'No, father Abraham,' he said, 'but if someone from the*
dead goes to them, they will repent.'

[31] *"He said to him, 'If they do not listen to Moses and the*
Prophets, they will not be convinced even if someone rises from the
dead.'"

Jesus often taught about the corrupting powers of riches, which not only reflected the pervading presence of poverty among Galileans but also the power of possessions to oppress the poor even more. In our chapter he tells two parables about rich people in order to teach his disciples how to live as kingdom people who can redeem possessions. Between these two parables Luke inserts three sayings of Jesus.

True Riches

The first parable (16:1–15), often called the parable of the shrewd manager or the unjust steward, presents a challenge, especially to readers not yet used to Jesus' parables. Our instinct is to equate God with the rich man and the rich man's manager with the disciples. That instinct veers us off the tracks into a ditch of serious mistakes. This parable is not an allegory in which the rich man is God but an analogy between one situation (a rich man and his manager shrewdly preparing for an earthly future) and another situation (kingdom disciples shrewdly preparing for an eternal future). The parable does not teach disciples to cheat. Rather, it uses cheating to raise morality from a worldly way of life with the rich man to a kingdom way with God. The logic is simple: if worldly managers use their noggins to ready themselves for a future, so kingdom people need to use their noggins even more for the future kingdom of God.

Plus, there's an urgency in the story. The manager has been accused of "wasting" the rich man's possessions (16:1). His time is short, and he plots how he will survive beyond his day of reckoning. He uses his position in the business to cancel or decrease indebtedness, and so makes friends of the debtors, who will somehow help him after he is fired. This urgency transfers to kingdom living like this: the time is now to make your decision about how you use possessions. Notice, too, that Jesus' word for money in the NIV is "worldly wealth." The term is *mammon*, which suggests that money has the power to corrupt kingdom people. Jesus wants his followers to use a worldly good, their resources that don't last into eternity, for the good of the kingdom.

Notice, too, that Jesus knows from the beginning of this story that he will be comparing the "people of this world" with the "people of the light" (16:8, 13). In that deep contrast is the secret to this parable: kingdom people are people of the light, and they are to decide now to live in this world shrewdly by investing, not in this world as the rich man and his manager did, but in the kingdom of God with "true riches" (16:11).

The Pharisees overhear this parable, and Luke adds that they "loved silver" (NIV: "who loved money") and so they "sneered at Jesus" (16:14). Jesus responds by saying that what worldly people exalt as most important (mammon), God considers an abomination (16:15). It is a dull listener who doesn't catch his vibe. Money, things, and possessions intoxicate our moral senses, dull our compassions, and freeze our feet in place.

Three Sayings of Jesus

With the Pharisees on the scene, Jesus explains how to read God's plan for history. First came the time period of the "Law and the prophets" (16:16). Second, that period ended with John the Baptist. Third, with Jesus comes the period of the kingdom, which is being gospeled. But don't let this fool you into thinking this puts the Law into the rearview mirror. The first is fulfilled or leads to the second, and the second is fulfilled or leads to the third, and thus the third is the fullness of the first and the second!

What surprises is "everyone is forcing their way into it" (16:17). The word "forcing" can be negative—using violence to get in—or positive—determination to enter the kingdom. Everything hinges on your choice and there is nothing that makes a choice obvious. Perhaps Scott Spencer is right: Jesus' preaching of the kingdom provokes everyone to knock down doors to get in (cf. 14:21; see Spencer, *Luke*, 409), but it should be observed that the close parallel in Matthew 11:12 suggests violence against the people of God. Perhaps we can decide that we aren't sure what this verse means.

To show Jesus' kingdom ethics do not erase but are rooted in the law of Moses, Jesus clarifies his stance on divorce, and his stance in Luke is stronger than his stance in Matthew 5:32 and 19:9. Divorce is wrong and marrying a divorced woman is wrong. That's what he says. But in Jesus' world the law is not rigid and inflexible. Law requires interpretation and involves adaptation to situation. Matthew's version gives an exception for sexual immorality, and Paul provides another in 1 Corinthians 7. So why did Jesus say it so strictly in Luke? To get the attention of the Pharisees and the disciples. Read Matthew 19:10–12 to see that he sure got the attention of the disciples! He wants disciples who do all they can to stay married, though that is not always possible or wise or safe.

True Compassion

The second parable (16:19–31) requires the reader (or listener) to connect with the right person to get the power of the parable. And powerful it is. Stay with me then as we go through it rather quickly. There is a rich man, who acquired over time the name "Dives," and the rich man lived in luxury while a beggar named Lazarus (which means "God help us") lived at the rich man's gate. So poor and emaciated was he that dogs licked his sores. Both men die. The "angels carried" Lazarus "to Abraham's side," while the rich man was buried and taken off to "Hades, where he was in torment." He begs "Father Abraham" to send Lazarus to him for a mere drip of water to comfort him. Abraham has utterly no compassion on the rich man, not only because during his life he showed no compassion on Lazarus but also because the chasm between them is too great to cross. So the rich man pleads with Abraham to send messengers to his family so they will not end up in Hades, which is a temporary place for the dead before the final judgment. Abraham's message is that they have the "Law and the prophets" and that should be enough for them. From Genesis to Revelation the Bible is against injustice and all for generosity. The rich man says if someone like Lazarus returned from the place of the dead who knew what Hades was like, they'd repent. Abraham remains fixed on one's life span and amps up the point: *even if someone rises from the dead* they would not respond.

Most of us—dare I say all of us?—identify ourselves as those who will be with poor Lazarus at Abraham's side. In identifying with him we miss the whole point of the parable. Jesus' intent rings clear: the parable is aimed at the rich man's lack of compassion as the Samaritan parable was aimed at those without compassion. The chapter is about the challenges of living as kingdom people with possessions, and his point in this parable is to get us to see ourselves in the rich man so we can learn to look for a Lazarus at our own gates. Read it again, identify with the rich man, and you will feel the challenge differently. If we don't respond to the poor and needy in our world we will end up with the rich man in Hades.

There is an introduction question for you and me: How wealthy are we? The answer can be found if we ask ourselves, Are we begging? How needy for food and sustenance and shelter are we? If we say *Not begging, not needy,* then we are the rich man, and we need to look for those at our gates. As Klyne Snodgrass states it, "What the parable attacks is . . . wealth that does not *see* poverty and suffering." And he says, "Lazarus is still at the gate" (Snodgrass, *Stories with Intent,* 433, 434).

Questions for Reflection and Application

1. What is "mammon," and how does it corrupt people?

2. How does interpreting the parable change when we equate the entire situation of the manager preparing with the situation of the disciples preparing, rather than equating God with the rich man and the manager with the disciples?

3. What does it mean that Jesus fulfils the Law?

4. How does the parable of the rich man and Lazarus impact you if you see yourself as the rich man?

5. What would increased compassion and decreased attachment to possessions change in your discipleship life?

FOR FURTHER READING

Klyne Snodgrass, *Stories with Intent: A Comprehensive Guide to the Parables of Jesus* (2d ed.; Grand Rapids: Wm. B. Eerdmans, 2018).

REDEMPTION'S DUTIES

Luke 17:1–19

1 Jesus said to his disciples: "Things that cause people to stumble are bound to come, but woe to anyone through whom they come. 2 It would be better for them to be thrown into the sea with a millstone tied around their neck than to cause one of these little ones to stumble. 3 So watch yourselves.

"If your brother or sister sins against you, rebuke them; and if they repent, forgive them. 4 Even if they sin against you seven times in a day and seven times come back to you saying 'I repent,' you must forgive them."

5 The apostles said to the Lord, "Increase our faith!"

6 He replied, "If you have faith as small as a mustard seed, you can say to this mulberry tree, 'Be uprooted and planted in the sea,' and it will obey you.

7 "Suppose one of you has a servant plowing or looking after the sheep. Will he say to the servant when he comes in from the field, 'Come along now and sit down to eat'? 8 Won't he rather say, 'Prepare my supper, get yourself ready and wait on me while I eat and drink; after that you may eat and drink'? 9 Will he thank the servant because he did what he was told to do? 10 So you also, when you have done everything you were told to do, should say, 'We are unworthy servants; we have only done our duty.' "

11 Now on his way to Jerusalem, Jesus traveled along the bor-
der between Samaria and Galilee. 12 As he was going into a village,
ten men who had leprosy met him. They stood at a distance 13 and
called out in a loud voice, "Jesus, Master, have pity on us!"

14 When he saw them, he said, "Go, show yourselves to the
priests." And as they went, they were cleansed.

15 One of them, when he saw he was healed, came back, prais-
ing God in a loud voice. 16 He threw himself at Jesus' feet and
thanked him—and he was a Samaritan.

17 Jesus asked, "Were not all ten cleansed? Where are the other
nine? 18 Has no one returned to give praise to God except this for-
eigner?" 19 Then he said to him, "Rise and go; your faith has made
you well."

Kingdom living affects every facet of life, from how our life impacts others in negative ways to the simplicities of expressing thanks for something. It takes several readings of all four Gospels to collect all the various ways the kingdom impacts our daily life, but this passage, in short order, teaches us five kingdom duties. They are more random than they are organized into some special order. They appear like someone's notes at the end of a long day of watching Jesus do kingdom work. He said this, and then he did this, and then we asked him something and he said this. Speaking of taking notes, the notetaking here continues from the previous chapters, so the notebook is getting full!

Avoid Being a Stumbling Block

The teaching not to cause someone to stumble has been weaponized in the church. Disagreements over something, whether small or great, are not the same as a source of stumbling. To cause to stumble means to do something contrary to Jesus' teachings that turns a person away from following Jesus.

I was on the phone recently with someone who had experienced deep betrayal by a pastor, and it was not the first time it had happened, and the words were these: "I will never trust a pastor again. In fact, I don't know if I can ever go to church again." Mind you, this person loved and still loves Jesus. This person has been *scandalized* by the church and by its leaders. To be scandalized points at a person's deep-seated and heart-felt incapacity to endure Christianity as a church or institution. Those scandalized, so I find, still love Jesus and in some degree affirm major teachings of the faith, but their experience of the church is so painful they want to go it alone—or with only some cherished, trusted friends.

Moral failures and power abuse and sexual abuse and spiritual abuse precipitate scandals. Pastors who do this damage are causing people to stumble. Jesus' words warn others of potential judgment for causing scandals, so he tells his disciples "watch yourselves" (17:1–3a).

Forgive

It was C.S. Lewis who said, "Everyone says forgiveness is a lovely idea, until they have something to forgive" (*Mere Christianity*, 89). Well maybe not everyone. Forgiveness is such a great vision for people until the one you are asked to forgive has wounded you deeply. Then you may well wonder if it is a moral good or not.

Forgiveness is a multi-layered complication. In forgiveness you release another person from something that person did to you, and that release empowers you no longer to be marked and even controlled or identified by that person's deed. Forgiveness as release promotes healing. Reconciliation, however, is not the same as forgiveness, though they are connected. Forgiveness is the first step, and sometimes the time gap between the two is considerable because reconciliation requires truth telling, admission of fault, genuine repentance, the request for forgiveness, the discernment of the admission as true or fake, the acceptance of that admission, the beginning and development of trusting that person again, and then eventual reconciliation and restoration of a relationship. But sometimes, as Jesus taught, sins are forgiven, and sometimes they are not forgiven (John 20:23).

Jesus teaches in our passage that forgiveness is so high on his list of virtues that we must be ready to forgive someone as many as seven times if they confess their faults seven times. His intent is not to gloss over the kinds of destructive sins that are deeply damaging—like childhood sexual abuse, serial adultery, or patterns of pastoral abuse—but to put to the fore the value of forgiveness in the kingdom (see 15:1–31).

Faith Is Simple

By "simple" I don't mean simplistic, and I surely don't want to suggest silly. The disciples want the kind of (supposed) great and grand faith Jesus has so they ask for more faith (17:5). Jesus' response is that faith, even as small as a mustard-seed amount of faith, can unleash miracles because it trusts in the omnipotent God.

By "simple" faith then we mean the kind of faith that looks at the promise of God and the God of promise and says, "I believe," and then it steps out to walk on. Simple faith is not reducible to an inner urging but is a settled pattern of trusting God because of who God is and what God has done in the past.

One may well wonder if this "uprooting" in our section (17:6) has to do with uprooting of the unrepentant sinner of

17:3 ("if they repent" implies also "if they don't repent"), and it might hint back to the "millstone" threat of 17:2 (Levine-Witherington, *Luke*, 467). Perhaps so.

Service

The Germans have a little line that I have often quoted to my students: *Willst den Dichter Du verstehen? Musst in Dichter's Lande gehen*. "If you want to understand a poet, you must go to that poet's land." Which we now must do: Jesus lived in a world of slavery. Though the NIV again uses "servant" instead of "slave," he assumes slavery in this little parable-like story. To understand him, we must enter into his world of slavery. A slave worked for a master and worked until the master said the work was done, and when dinner was done, the slave got to eat. It was the slave's job to do those tasks.

Jesus turns this around to depict his followers as God's slaves. His followers are called to follow him, and they cannot expect God to pat them on the back and thank them for their help. That is, they are not acquiring money for themselves but for their master. They have not earned any rewards but have only done what they were called to do. Humans with a tendency to think too highly of themselves can learn humility and their place in this world from this harsh set of images.

However, one must be prepared to listen to those who think images for God and discipleship like slavery are no longer acceptable for many. African Americans hear this language in ways most white people cannot even begin to comprehend. Slavery is the exploitation of a body for the sake of profit for the master. The early Christians "Christianized" slavery somewhat, but it would take centuries for the Christian church to comprehend the moral horror of slavery. This, too, must arise in our readings of today's passage.

Say Thanks

Jesus flips the script one more time (17:11–19). Ten "scaly-skinned persons" or "leprous men" on the border between Samaria and Galilee yell out from their distance for the mercy of healing and cleansing. He instructs the disabled men to head toward Jerusalem and show their cleansed bodies to the priests and so get re-socialized. In their decision to start walking—this illustrates simple faith—"They were cleansed" (17:14). Amy-Jill Levine calls into question the simplistic Christian theory that these lepers had to remain at a distance from all humans. She notes that the laws about distance pertained to the sacred tabernacle, not to places as far from the temple as Galilee or Samaria (Levine-Witherington, *Luke*, 470).

Only one returned to Jesus "praising God" for what Jesus had done for him (17:15). So he falls before Jesus and "thanked him." Luke adds (wryly, don't you think?), "he was a Samaritan" (17:16). We're back to the Samaritan who acted with compassion (10:25–37), and now it comes full circle to looking at a Samaritan who is shown compassion.

Jesus reprimands the ones who were not present for not giving thanks, tells the healed man his "faith" healed him (17:19), and in so doing instructs all of us that we need to learn to return to God with thanks for the gifts of God. Recently on a tour of Greece with students, Kris tripped on the second-to-last step coming down from the Acropolis, broke her wrist, had surgery when we returned, and about ten days after the surgery had the initial splint and bandages removed. The news from the X-ray was good, and when we got home, relaxed and relieved from the good news, she sat in her chair and simply said, "Thank you, Jesus." Amen!

It's a duty to say thanks for God's gifts.

A good and joyous duty.

Questions for Reflection and Application

1. So far, what has Luke told us about who Jesus is?

2. What is the difference between forgiveness and reconciliation?

3. How can simple faith and gratitude function together in our discipleship?

4. Do you think it is appropriate to continue to use "slavery" language in talking about God and discipleship? Why or why not?

5. Have you experienced another Christian, especially a Christian leader, causing you to stumble? What was that experience like for you?

FOR FURTHER READING

C.S. Lewis, *Mere Christianity* (New York: Macmillan, 1956).

REDEMPTION'S COMING JUDGMENT

Luke 17:20–37

[20] Once, on being asked by the Pharisees when the kingdom of God would come, Jesus replied, "The coming of the kingdom of God is not something that can be observed, [21] nor will people say, 'Here it is,' or 'There it is,' because the kingdom of God is in your midst."

[22] Then he said to his disciples, "The time is coming when you will long to see one of the days of the Son of Man, but you will not see it. [23] People will tell you, 'There he is!' or 'Here he is!' Do not go running off after them. [24] For the Son of Man in his day will be like the lightning, which flashes and lights up the sky from one end to the other. [25] But first he must suffer many things and be rejected by this generation.

[26] "Just as it was in the days of Noah, so also will it be in the days of the Son of Man. [27] People were eating, drinking, marrying and being given in marriage up to the day Noah entered the ark. Then the flood came and destroyed them all.

[28] "It was the same in the days of Lot. People were eating and drinking, buying and selling, planting and building. [29] But the day Lot left Sodom, fire and sulfur rained down from heaven and destroyed them all.

[30] "It will be just like this on the day the Son of Man is revealed.
[31] On that day no one who is on the housetop, with possessions inside, should go down to get them. Likewise, no one in the field should go back for anything. [32] Remember Lot's wife! [33] Whoever tries to keep their life will lose it, and whoever loses their life will preserve it. [34] I tell you, on that night two people will be in one bed; one will be taken and the other left. [35] Two women will be grinding grain together; one will be taken and the other left."

[37] "Where, Lord?" they asked.

He replied, "Where there is a dead body, there the vultures will gather."

What do these two Q&A sessions have to do with us? Because our brief comments will drive us back to the first century and more or less leave us there wondering, I want to start with a few guideposts. First, our speculations about when Jesus will return align us with those who asked similar questions of Jesus in his day, and he was none too gentle with their curiosities. Second, instead of getting tied into rapture and millennium and Israel questions, we need instead to spend more time pondering divine judgment on society's bent toward injustices. Third, what Jesus said to his generation (Pharisees and disciples) is a paradigm of what he says to us: readiness is about faithfulness to following Jesus and discernment of personal and systemic sinfulness. As Noah and Lot could be figures for Jesus, so the generation around Jesus can be a figure for our generation. Redemption does not arrive until the rubble of sin has been cleared away.

Q&A WITH THE PHARISEES

The Pharisees ask the *When* question: "When the kingdom of God would come" or when God's empire comes (17:20).

(For the meaning of "kingdom," see note on 9:1–17 at p. 142.) Jesus' answer flies in the face of too much Christian speculation. First, he says it will not come according to your charts, maps, and timetables—that is, it is not something one can calculate (NIV has "observed" as in watching signs for its appearing). Second, nor can humans determine where it will appear ("here" and "there"; 17:21). No, one can't calculate time or location because, in fact, the "kingdom of God is in your midst" (or among you).

This means either that Jesus is the kingdom, and he is standing in their midst, or it means that the powers of the kingdom have been launched in the ministry of Jesus, or both—and both seem just about right. The Pharisees surely noticed all the hubbub around Jesus—stories about his miracles, his clever teachings, and the power of his kingdom vision. *It's already here,* but surely they know there's more to it than that. His answer is a bit evasive. Yes, the kingdom is already present, but it is also not yet consummated. There's more to come, which is what he tells the disciples.

Q&A with the Disciples

The last Q&A in verse thirty-seven provides the important clue to what Jesus says to the disciples. The disciples want an answer to what Jesus had said to the Pharisees above about "Where?" Jesus answers that question in v. 37 with a double, grotesque image: "Where the body is, there also the eagles are gathered" (my translation). The NIV, seeing here a dead body, translates with "corpse" and, since many state inaccurately that eagles don't eat carrion or roadkill (they do), the NIV translates as the roadkill experts "vultures" instead of eagles. It is eagles that provide the clue. The eagle was the Roman symbol of military might in battle. Rome-as-eagle is one image, and some "body" the other, and that body is

Jerusalem, which was sacked by Rome some forty years later. Jesus here predicts Rome's victory over Jerusalem. That answer to "where?" is Jerusalem. This is the clue that will be used to read the Q&A with the disciples.

Jesus gives a fuller version of the Pharisees' question and his answer to them in vv. 22–35. Notice that the arrival of the "kingdom of God" and the "Son of Man" coming are equated in verses 22–24. What is coming is the days of the Son of Man, but don't get trapped in their game of "Here he is!" or "There he is!" (17:21, 23). Instead, Jesus will first be utterly rejected by "this generation" (17:25) and only then will the Son of Man make an astonishing appearance (17:24). The horizon for Jesus' words then are sometime not too far beyond his crucifixion.

He puts onto the table two "days": the days of Noah, the days of Lot. Both of which describe normal human activities being shocked by the sudden, surprising appearance of divine judgment (17:26–29). The "day of the Son Man" will be "just like this," Jesus predicts (17:30), but his emphasis is on the suddenness and the need for lightning-fast flight. Whatever one is doing must be interrupted, and the one who hesitates to save one's things or life will lose it all (17:33). He shifts to sleeping: "two people will be in one bed; one will be taken and the other left" (17:34). Then to daytime millstone grinding: "one will be taken and the other left" (17:35). It has become traditional for many to think of this as the rapture: the "one taken" is taken in the rapture. But there's nothing whatsoever in our verses about the rapture; it must be imposed on the texts to be seen. Instead, some will lose their lives and some will survive the horrors of the judgment on that day. It's a kind of 50/50 split that serves quite well as a serious warning.

That horror was the eagle, Rome. Josephus' descriptions of Roman brutality, as I mentioned at Luke 12:35–59, are unsurpassed in barbaric savagery. Jesus' words, graphic for sure, are softer: a body and eagles.

Questions for Reflection and Application

1. How do Jesus' answers to the people's questions here point us toward the need to ponder divine judgment on society's bent toward injustices?

2. How does Jesus answer the "when" question about the kingdom?

3. How does he answer the "where" question?

4. What role does the might of Rome figure into Jesus' answers?

5. What are your questions for God about when the kingdom will come? Does this section help answer those for you?

TWO REDEMPTION PARABLES

Luke 18:1–14

*1 Then Jesus told his disciples a parable to show them that they
should always pray and not give up. 2 He said: "In a certain town
there was a judge who neither feared God nor cared what people
thought. 3 And there was a widow in that town who kept coming to
him with the plea, 'Grant me justice against my adversary.'*

*4 "For some time he refused. But finally he said to himself, 'Even
though I don't fear God or care what people think, 5 yet because this
widow keeps bothering me, I will see that she gets justice, so that she
won't eventually come and attack me!' "*

*6 And the Lord said, "Listen to what the unjust judge says.
7 And will not God bring about justice for his chosen ones, who
cry out to him day and night? Will he keep putting them off? 8 I tell
you, he will see that they get justice, and quickly. However, when
the Son of Man comes, will he find faith on the earth?"*

*9 To some who were confident of their own righteousness and
looked down on everyone else, Jesus told this parable:*

*10 "Two men went up to the temple to pray, one a Pharisee
and the other a tax collector. 11 The Pharisee stood by himself and
prayed: 'God, I thank you that I am not like other people—robbers,*

evildoers, adulterers—or even like this tax collector. [12] *I fast twice a week and give a tenth of all I get.'*

[13] *"But the tax collector stood at a distance. He would not even look up to heaven, but beat his breast and said, 'God, have mercy on me, a sinner.'*

[14] *"I tell you that this man, rather than the other, went home justified before God. For all those who exalt themselves will be humbled, and those who humble themselves will be exalted."*

Two parables come together here to clarify elements of redemption for disciples: they pray, and they confess. As with all of Jesus' parables, we only learn to read them well by reading them with others who see things we may not see. Remember, we need to seek the central analogy of the parable, and then to let that central idea reshape and control our readings.

Pray Theologically

He thinks disciples "should always pray and not give up" (18:1). Jesus portrays two characters: an uncompassionate judge and a widow who has experienced injustice (18:2–3). Her persistence pushes the judge beyond his tolerance, so he explains the reason for his decision. First, her relentless petitions are making his life increasingly difficult, probably to get through all his cases, and second, she's ruining his reputation as a good judge (18:5). The NIV's "eventually come and attack me" turns the metaphor of "blackening one's eye" into a physical attack. That's most unlikely, not to ignore unrealistic and profoundly reckless. Instead, the judge's metaphor points to his reputation in the community being destroyed.

This is a parable that is often misread. Here's the point: If even unjust judges eventually do what is right to protect their honor, how much more will the good and utterly just God answer the prayers for justice and the coming of the kingdom for God's prayer warriors. This is what is important: God is ***not just like*** the unjust judge; God is far better. God, Jesus tells his disciples, "will see that they get justice" (18:8). So the parable is not about persistence but about a just, kind, good God who welcomes the petitions of the faithful.

Petitions, that is, about justice. In context, the petitions of God's "chosen ones" may well be about the coming of the kingdom of God, the arrival of the Son of Man in judgment on systemic injustices, and the need for faithful, patient trust in God.

But Jesus finishes off with a trip around the roundabout a couple times and out where he entered, with a look at the disciples: "Will [the Son of Man] find faith on the earth" when he comes? (18:8). The intent of the question is to probe the disciples into introspection.

Confess Honestly

The parable of the Pharisee and tax collector is another parable that hooks most readers and listeners into identifying with the right character but are too often acting like the wrong character, and once one realizes that is the wrong way to read it, one suddenly realizes Jesus has us in a corner. Bear with me because I read it that way for a long time.

Everyone seems to like this parable of the self-persuaded Pharisee, who thinks he's right with God and entitled to being heard because of his faithful observance and beyond the law of Moses (18:10–12). In fact, he looks down on "other people," labeling them as "robbers, evildoers, adulterers" (18:11). The tax collector stands at a distance to embody his own unworthiness (18:13) and pleaded with God for "mercy" because he knew he was a "sinner."

Here's the hook: *did you not look down on the Pharisee for his priggish self-righteousness?* If so, you are the Pharisee as caricaturized in this parable. Sorry, but that's the whole point of this parable. Yes, I am that Pharisee too. I look down on others.

Or did you immediately identify with a compromised character, one who had sold his connection to Israel in becoming an agent of Rome? That is, with the tax collector. My bets are that you identified with the second character (after all, he's approved) by acting the part of the first. #amiright

If so or if not, the point of this parable is that we need to learn to approach God on the basis of our unworthiness, on the basis of God's good graciousness, and not on the basis of our merits. Be honest, confess your sins, including your self-righteousness at times. "Christians," Klyne Snodgrass says, "are as easily guilty of self-satisfaction as the Pharisee" (*Stories with Intent*, 475).

Questions for Reflection and Application

1. How can reading parables through the lenses of people different from us help us understand them better?

2. How does Jesus contrast the unjust judge with the just God?

3. Do you identify with the Pharisee or the tax collector? How do you respond to this parable pointing out our likelihood of being the Pharisee?

4. What are your personal practices of prayer and confession?

5. How can you increase the theological bent of your prayers and the honesty of your confessions?

FOR FURTHER READING

Klyne Snodgrass, *Stories with Intent: A Comprehensive Guide to the Parables of Jesus* (2d ed.; Grand Rapids: Wm. B. Eerdmans, 2018).

REDEMPTION'S WIDENESS

Luke 18:15–19:10

15 People were also bringing babies to Jesus for him to place his hands on them. When the disciples saw this, they rebuked them. 16 But Jesus called the children to him and said, "Let the little children come to me, and do not hinder them, for the kingdom of God belongs to such as these. 17 Truly I tell you, anyone who will not receive the kingdom of God like a little child will never enter it."

18 A certain ruler asked him, "Good teacher, what must I do to inherit eternal life?"

19 "Why do you call me good?" Jesus answered. "No one is good—except God alone. 20 You know the commandments: 'You shall not commit adultery, you shall not murder, you shall not steal, you shall not give false testimony, honor your father and mother.'"

21 "All these I have kept since I was a boy," he said.

22 When Jesus heard this, he said to him, "You still lack one thing. Sell everything you have and give to the poor, and you will have treasure in heaven. Then come, follow me."

23 When he heard this, he became very sad, because he was very wealthy. 24 Jesus looked at him and said, "How hard it is for the rich to enter the kingdom of God! 25 Indeed, it is easier for a camel to go through the eye of a needle than for someone who is rich to enter the kingdom of God."

26 Those who heard this asked, "Who then can be saved?"

27 Jesus replied, "What is impossible with man is possible with God."

28 Peter said to him, "We have left all we had to follow you!"

29 "Truly I tell you," Jesus said to them, "no one who has left home or wife or brothers or sisters or parents or children for the sake of the kingdom of God 30 will fail to receive many times as much in this age, and in the age to come eternal life."

31 Jesus took the Twelve aside and told them, "We are going up to Jerusalem, and everything that is written by the prophets about the Son of Man will be fulfilled. 32 He will be delivered over to the Gentiles. They will mock him, insult him and spit on him; 33 they will flog him and kill him. On the third day he will rise again."

34 The disciples did not understand any of this. Its meaning was hidden from them, and they did not know what he was talking about.

35 As Jesus approached Jericho, a blind man was sitting by the roadside begging. 36 When he heard the crowd going by, he asked what was happening. 37 They told him, "Jesus of Nazareth is passing by."

38 He called out, "Jesus, Son of David, have mercy on me!"

39 Those who led the way rebuked him and told him to be quiet, but he shouted all the more, "Son of David, have mercy on me!"

40 Jesus stopped and ordered the man to be brought to him. When he came near, Jesus asked him, 41 "What do you want me to do for you?"

"Lord, I want to see," he replied.

42 Jesus said to him, "Receive your sight; your faith has healed you." 43 Immediately he received his sight and followed Jesus, praising God. When all the people saw it, they also praised God.

19:1 Jesus entered Jericho and was passing through. 2 A man was there by the name of Zacchaeus; he was a chief tax collector and was wealthy. [3] He wanted to see who Jesus was, but because he was short he could not see over the crowd. [4] So he ran ahead and climbed a sycamore-fig tree to see him, since Jesus was coming that way.

[5] When Jesus reached the spot, he looked up and said to him, "Zacchaeus, come down immediately. I must stay at your house today." [6] So he came down at once and welcomed him gladly.

[7] All the people saw this and began to mutter, "He has gone to be the guest of a sinner."

[8] But Zacchaeus stood up and said to the Lord, "Look, Lord! Here and now I give half of my possessions to the poor, and if I have cheated anybody out of anything, I will pay back four times the amount."

[9] Jesus said to him, "Today salvation has come to this house, because this man, too, is a son of Abraham. [10] For the Son of Man came to seek and to save the lost."

Most churches appear mono-cultural and mono-ethnic and mono-racial and mono-economic and mono-educational and even mono-minivans. We like people who are like us, look like us, earn what we earn, and live where we live. Not so the kingdom of God, and not so the final display of New Jerusalem. The author of Revelation catches a glimpse of eternity and describes it like this:

"After this I looked, and there before me was a great multitude that no one could count, from every nation, tribe, people and language, standing before the throne and before the Lamb" (Revelation 7:9).

The kingdom of God's reach is wider than our wide and deeper than our deep, and today's passage catches a glimpse of the wideness of God's mercy for his kingdom. Notice the various groups experiencing the kingdom's holistic redemption.

Babies

No one knows for sure why parents brought their babies to Jesus for a blessing, but I caught a snatch of why one time when Bishop Kallistos Ware spoke. Following his address, scores of Orthodox men and women, some with children, stood in line for a prayer or a blessing and a word of appreciation. In the same way, parents wanted Jesus to bless their babies so they would be connected with Jesus and his kingdom. The disciples were miffed by such requests of such a great man.

Press release: one more time we must identify with the disciples, not the small children. When we see ourselves in the disciples, we hear the words as Jesus intended them.

First, he invites the babies. Second, he makes the astounding claim that the kingdom "belongs to such as these," or "is *of* such," and "of" is less specific, and could mean composed of or for such persons or looks like such persons. He is speaking of physical children here. But third, Jesus then explains that *all people enter as children or they don't enter the kingdom* (18:17). Some think this is about the unworthiness of a child in that culture (Gonzalez, *Luke*, 214), but Jewish culture valued children as covenant kids. In Jesus' worldview, children illustrate who enters the kingdom. The kingdom of God, put starkly, is not designed for those who want to wield their power, appeal to their intelligence, use their appearance, bank on their observance, or exploit their riches. The kingdom is for those who are as (or more) dependent on God as children on a parent.

Rich

Even the rich have to learn how to be a child, as Jesus explains to a "ruler" or "leader." The rich man genuinely asks

Jesus what he can do so he will "inherit eternal life," and by this he gives the first century synonym for the kingdom of God (18:18). He addressed Jesus as "Good teacher," and for some reason—like many a teacher I know—Jesus picked on the leader's choice of terms. "Why do you call me good?" because only God is good (18:19). That little sidebar goes no further unless one assumes the words of Jesus take on divine authority as we move deeper into this passage. Jesus moves on to give the man instructions of what it takes to get into the kingdom of God (with the children).

Jesus quotes from the Ten Words, or the Decalogue/Ten Commandments, but not in order (from Exodus 20:13–16, 12, or Deuteronomy 5:17–20, 16). Protestant Christians have always been annoyed by the man's response, as if he's claiming merit before God. But he's not. He was a life-long observant and when he failed to observe a command, he offered sacrifices of atonement, and he was forgiven (the obedience and forgiveness system of Judaism). So, he claims he's done these since he was a youngster (NIV: "boy").

Jesus does not reprimand the man for false claims or for self-righteousness, though many read those into the text. Jesus simply says, "You still lack one thing" (18:22), and here Jesus goes full-on Jesus: "Sell everything you have" (yowzers; as at 12:33 and 14:33) and "give to the poor" and only then "will you have treasure in heaven." Then, to make a commitment fully clear, "come, follow me" (18:22). One must use the old adage: If Jesus is not Lord *over all* he is not Lord at all. He's called this man to turn from his privilege to a life of provisions for the poor. Generosity to the poor, especially from the rich, derives from the Old Testament law and is not unique to Jesus.

And recognition of our comfortable lives maybe needs to come to life. As Peggy Noonan, no stranger to wealth herself, reminded in an essay written in 2007:

> We are living in the second great Gilded Age, a time of startling personal wealth. In the West, the mansion after mansion with broad and rolling grounds; in the East, the apartments with foyers in which bowling teams could play. Or, on another level, the week's vacation in Disneyland or Dublin with the entire family—this in a nation in which, well within human memory, people with a week off stayed home and fixed things in the garage, or drove to the beach for a day and sat on a blanket from one of the kid's beds and thought: This is the life (Noonan, *The Time of Our Lives*, 357).

We were not poor and neither were we flush with funds when I grew up in the home of a public school teacher. But the dramatic shifts of wealth—both toward the wealthy and away from the poor—from the Reagan years onwards have imbalanced us, and we no longer recognize where we are located in history's and the world's economy. We might then consider identifying ourselves with the rich man more than we otherwise would.

It is a fact that the earliest circles around Jesus did not give up everything. Jesus continued to gather in their homes, showing that these kinds of absolute sayings of Jesus are hyperbole. As exaggerations they challenge us to a deeper surrender of our possessions. As they challenged the rich man.

The rich leader "became very sad" (18:23), and this gives Jesus an opening to instruct his apprentices one more time about holistic redemption in the kingdom. The hearts of the rich are stubbornly stuck to mammon, making their path into the kingdom (hyperbolically) impossible, like threading a camel through the eye of a needle (18:24–25). So clear was this saying of Jesus that the disciples wonder aloud "who then can be saved?" (18:26). Jesus reveals to them that such commitment is an act of God's empowerment, not human achievement (18:27).

The apprentices, one step slow, get Peter to make the truthful claim that they have in fact, unlike that rich man, left all for him. Jesus says that not only will such persons enter the future kingdom, but they will experience in the present life ("in this age") an abundance of provisions and in the kingdom ("in the age to come") "eternal life," precisely the terms of the rich man's opening question (18:18, 30).

Holistic redemption, let it be said, is wide enough to include the wealthy who learn to put their possessions in their rearview mirror. They are not excluded but given a stern challenge of what costly grace means.

Apostles

The Twelve's commitment to Jesus, as expressed with a self-pat on the back by Peter (18:28), is now challenged in a surprising way (18:31–33). The Jesus for whom they have surrendered is on his way to Jerusalem where he will be handed over, mocked, insulted, spat upon, flogged, and killed. Kingdom commitment includes suffering with Jesus.

Luke spins no fairy tale about the golden days of the apostles as if they were wholly on board all the time. He describes them as utterly clueless what Jesus meant by his prediction about his death (18:34). Let's give them a break. *We know* what's going to happen, they didn't. Better yet, they heard Jesus say such things (9:22, 43–45) but it didn't register—after all, Messiahs rule; they don't get killed. Luke has his compass pointed at Jerusalem from 9:51 on, and every now and then he reminds us of that point.

God's wide mercies include the twelve apostles who hear but don't comprehend, and there is no reason for us not to expect the same of followers of Jesus today.

Blind

Jericho, at the intersection of the Jordan River and the road to or from Jerusalem, closes in on Jerusalem for Luke's journey (9:51; 18:35). Entering Jericho, Jesus encounters a disabled man, a blind beggar, who pleads for mercy with Jesus (18:36–38). Disability entails dimensions that impede persons from entering the fabric of society. As the disciples thought children were below Jesus' concerns (18:15), so the same group ("those who led the way") apparently thinks a blind beggar doesn't rise on the social ladder high enough to merit Jesus' healing graces. Like the widow demanding justice, the blind man pleads all the more (18:39; cf. 18:3).

"What do you want me to do for you?" Jesus asks the man. "Lord, I want to see," he answers (18:40–41). So Jesus gives light to his eyes. He, like the grateful Samaritan leper (17:15–16), praises God and, unlike the rich man (18:23), follows Jesus (18:43).

God's mercy is wide enough to redeem the blind.

Rich Tax Collector

God's mercy is also wide enough to transform a tax collector into an agent of economic redemption (19:1–10). We all love the story about Zacchaeus, and I have since it was a flannel graph favorite. Fred Craddock, one of America's most well-known preachers, called Zacchaeus "the patron saint of yuppies or those essentially going-to-be-rich people." Why, because "he was rich. He was mildly irreligious. He was ingenious and he was enterprising" (*Sermons*, 286).

The issue at hand fits into the holistic redemption theme. He's rich, which has been a theme already in our passage (18:18–30). What sticks out is that he's a collaborator with Rome because he's a tax collector—he bids for a job, he gets the job, he collects funds for Rome, and the extra he collects is his to keep. He's rich because he charges more than he needs to. The NIV reads "short," but the term may well mean "short in years" and thus "young (and therefore not of adult size yet)." He has to climb a tree to see Jesus. He, like the blind man, had trouble seeing Jesus (19:3–4).

Jesus knows what seems unknowable: he not only sees Zacchaeus in the tree, but he knows him and invites himself to the man's home (19:5–6), which the locals find offensive because the man was a "sinner" (19:7). God's mercy, remember, is wide enough to include and transform sinners.

Now at the home, food in the belly, conversation developed, the meal has ended, and Zacchaeus stands up with an amazing announcement. Unlike the rich man, Zacchaeus comprehends the depth of the kingdom challenge for those who experience the wideness of God's redemption. Like the tax collector in the temple (18:9–14), Zacchaeus is also humble and confessing. Zacchaeus's words explain what those severe words in 12:33 and 14:33 actually looked like in real life: "Lord . . . I give half of my possessions to the poor, and *if I have cheated anybody out of anything* . . .". Hold on, we assume, don't we, that he was the paradigmatic cheater and thief. The text is not so sure. For those who were defrauded, Zacchaeus says he'll pay back four times what he had stolen (19:8). Did he need to? I ask one question: Does the text actually say he had to?

The issue is much less the man's cheating than the man's collaboration with Rome. Either way, Jesus' response is priceless: "Today salvation has come to this house." This rich collaborator and now generous tax collector is also a "son of Abraham." And Jesus announces that conversions, redemptions, and transformations like this man's are why he has come: "to seek and save the lost" (19:9–10).

Questions for Reflection and Application

1. What is the value and importance of children in the kingdom?

2. What does holistic redemption mean to rich people (among which we should probably count ourselves)?

3. How does the response of Zacchaeus differ from the response of the earlier rich man?

4. How mono-cultural is your church? What is the economic, racial, and educational makeup of your congregation?

5. Do we have the eyes of Jesus who sees all as worthy of the blessing of Jesus? How can we cultivate that better in our lives?

FOR FURTHER READING

Fred Craddock's sermon in William H. Willimon, ed., *Sermons from Duke Chapel: Voices from "A Great Towering Church"* (Durham: Duke University Press, 2005), 282–287.

Peggy Noonan, *The Time of Our Lives: Collected Writings* (New York: Twelve/Hatchette, 2017).

REDEMPTION RESISTANCE

Luke 19:11–27

11 While they were listening to this, he went on to tell them a parable,
because he was near Jerusalem and the people thought that the
kingdom of God was going to appear at once. 12 He said: A man of
noble birth went to a distant country to have himself appointed king
and then to return. 13 So he called ten of his servants and gave them
ten minas. 'Put this money to work,' he said, 'until I come back.'

14 But his subjects hated him and sent a delegation after him to
say, 'We don't want this man to be our king.'

15 He was made king, however, and returned home. Then he
sent for the servants to whom he had given the money, in order to
find out what they had gained with it.

16 The first one came and said, 'Sir, your mina has earned ten
more.'

17 'Well done, my good servant!' his master replied. 'Because
you have been trustworthy in a very small matter, take charge of
ten cities.'

18 The second came and said, 'Sir, your mina has earned five
more.'

19 His master answered, 'You take charge of five cities.'

20 Then another servant came and said, 'Sir, here is your mina;
I have kept it laid away in a piece of cloth. 21 I was afraid of you,
because you are a hard man. You take out what you did not put in
and reap what you did not sow.'

22 His master replied, 'I will judge you by your own words, you
wicked servant! You knew, did you, that I am a hard man, taking
out what I did not put in, and reaping what I did not sow? 23 Why
then didn't you put my money on deposit, so that when I came
back, I could have collected it with interest?'

24 Then he said to those standing by, 'Take his mina away from
him and give it to the one who has ten minas.'

25 'Sir,' they said, 'he already has ten!'

26 He replied, 'I tell you that to everyone who has, more will be
given, but as for the one who has nothing, even what they have will
be taken away. 27 But those enemies of mine who did not want me
to be king over them—bring them here and kill them in front of me.'

As now, so then. One can't turn the kingdom of God into the subject of all conversations and expect people not to ask the big question: Is it arriving soon? In fact, over the years I've had several pastors ask me about the meaning of kingdom because their "When?" question dominates what they think the kingdom is all about. It goes like this: "The younger generation of leaders all talk about the kingdom of God. What do they mean by that?" Yes, for many, "kingdom" replacing terms like "justification" and "salvation" has become commonplace Christian language. The reason why so many today ask about the meaning of kingdom is because, like me, they grew up thinking God's kingdom was the same as heaven, the climactic eternity of the future. Jesus hoisted the idea of kingdom high above his shoulders with perfect, beautiful balance: God's kingdom is both here and there, now and future, launched with more to come, inaugurated but not yet consummated. Some in Jesus' day were captured with hope that it would come soon and were speculating when and where and how, and Jesus is about to jolt them into a shocking story.

The journey theme of Luke (9:51), now coming to its end with Jesus about to arrive in Jerusalem, provokes some to ask the "how soon?" question (19:11). They had high hopes. In fact, they expected the kingdom of God to appear supernaturally and instantly. So Jesus uses a parable to adjust their imagination away from speculation about "How soon?" toward, well, I don't want to give you any spoilers. But I do think you will be surprised.

The Story

Jesus adapts a Roman colonial practice of a man of good stock (NIV: "noble birth"; 19:12) going off to a "distant country" where he will be appointed "king" and then return to his homeland as king (as all those listening knew Herod the Great had done in going off to Rome). Before going off, however, he loaned to ten of his slaves (NIV again has "servants") "ten minas," a very significant amount, with the responsibility of investing the funds for a good return when he comes back (19:13).

Here comes the crux of this parable, and we need to open our eyes because we're in the habit of excusing the violence of this king. No one hearing Jesus talk about a king taking over their land was vibrating with warm, fuzzy thoughts. A foreign king was known for exploitation. Let's read on.

Unsurprising to anyone who had a memory of Herod the Great and his successors, the appointed king's citizens *hate* the noble man. No surprise there. While the man-to-become-king is away, the locals hatch a plan to unseat the king by sending a delegation to the more powerful party (the

Roman emperor, perhaps) to inform him that they don't want that man as king. I consider this element of the story crucial to reading this parable. At the end of this parable the king violently kills these resisters (19:27). So savage is the king that he wants them slaughtered "in front of me."

This is not God, this is not Jesus. This is the way of Rome. Once you see this, the entire parable shifts its meaning (see too Gonzalez, *Luke*, 222–225).

These are our clues to read this parable as a subversive satire on the rulers of Judea and Galilee with some slaves participating as collaborators and others as dissidents.

Collaborators and Dissidents

Now comes a reckoning of what the slaves did with their loaned three months of money. And we should not be afraid to think of these as slaves to a foreign, abusive, violent power—that is, Rome. Three different slaves with three different yields: the first one increased his investment and so was given ten cities in the king's kingdom (19:16–17); the second one upped the investment by five times and so was given five cities (19:18–19); and the third one failed to take the risk of an investment and buried his mina because he considered the king a severe, austere lord (19:20–21).

The king loves the first two because they collaborated with him in the increase of his power. The king remonstrates with the third slave, rebuking him for not even putting the money "on deposit" where it could collect interest, and then taking back the mina and giving it to the first slave (19:22–24). Some observe this and wonder why the king would give it to the man who already had ten minas. The king informs them that to the one "who has, more will be given" while he will remove what those with "nothing" have, which has to mean the little that they did not invest. That form of recompense was a brutal reality for Judeans and Galileans under Roman power. The approval of a Rome-appointed king is not the approval of God.

His Followers Needed This Parable

The story is harsh as it involves an almost tit-for-a-tat measurement, which is also not the way of Jesus. Nor is the savagery that ends the parable worthy of Jesus. Instead, Jesus wants those expecting the imminent kingdom to know that entering into Jerusalem will mean the powers of Rome are about to take over, and it will mean tough years of slavery and challenges to their faithfulness.

We need to push the parable away from our individual lives and learn to think more nationally about the brutality of Rome and its colonial client kings. The third slave's so-called failure was only a failure to his emperor-based client king. For locals, it was an act of resistance. The nobleman, then, is not a positive image of a returning Jesus but a negative image of an exploiting colonial king. The violence of the king as the end of the parable, then, is the violence of Rome, not of God.

Yes, to be sure, many read the parable as an exhortation to faithfulness and see here that God has given gifts to his people and they are responsible to nurture the gifts so the people can flourish. But the use of a client king who got his appointment in Rome would not have connected Jesus' followers with God or himself. Nor did they connect themselves to a client king. No, they connected most easily with the "subjects" who hated the king. The foot-dragging resistance of the third slave made Jesus' listeners say some "youbetchas." And the savagery of the king killing those who opposed him neither surprised the audience of Jesus nor gave them any chance of thinking of their God. They saw the king of his parable not as God, but as an agent of Rome bent on their exploitation.

This parable gave the disciples a graphic imagination of the troubles his disciples were about to see: Rome's power over the land, exploitation of Jews as slaves of Rome, and the complicity or resistance of the people as the options they would face—for a full generation. Instead of an imminent arrival of the kingdom, they were about to face a tribulation of sorts.

This parable is followed by Jesus' own foot-dragging entry into Jerusalem as a protest of the ways of Rome, a protest that would lead to a crucifixion at the hands of powers who had become puppets of Rome.

Questions for Reflection and Application

1. Had you previously thought of kingdom being the same as heaven? How is this study reshaping your ideas of kingdom?

2. How does your understanding of the parable change when you think of some of the slaves as collaborators and some as dissidents?

3. How does your understanding change to think of this parable as being about the power and violence of Rome?

4. Who do you identify with in the parable?

5. What are your acts of resistance and dissent to the powers of empire today?

REDEMPTION'S ARRIVAL

Luke 19:28–48

[28] After Jesus had said this, he went on ahead, going up to Jerusalem.
[29] As he approached Bethphage and Bethany at the hill called the Mount of Olives, he sent two of his disciples, saying to them, [30] "Go to the village ahead of you, and as you enter it, you will find a colt tied there, which no one has ever ridden. Untie it and bring it here.
[31] If anyone asks you, 'Why are you untying it?' say, 'The Lord needs it.'"

[32] Those who were sent ahead went and found it just as he had told them. [33] As they were untying the colt, its owners asked them, "Why are you untying the colt?"

[34] They replied, "The Lord needs it."

[35] They brought it to Jesus, threw their cloaks on the colt and put Jesus on it. [36] As he went along, people spread their cloaks on the road.

[37] When he came near the place where the road goes down the Mount of Olives, the whole crowd of disciples began joyfully to praise God in loud voices for all the miracles they had seen:

[38] "Blessed is the king who comes in the name of the Lord!"
"Peace in heaven and glory in the highest!"

*39 Some of the Pharisees in the crowd said to Jesus, "Teacher,
rebuke your disciples!"*
*40 "I tell you," he replied, "if they keep quiet, the stones will cry
out."*
*41 As he approached Jerusalem and saw the city, he wept over
it 42 and said, "If you, even you, had only known on this day what
would bring you peace—but now it is hidden from your eyes. 43 The
days will come upon you when your enemies will build an embank-
ment against you and encircle you and hem you in on every side.
44 They will dash you to the ground, you and the children within
your walls. They will not leave one stone on another, because you
did not recognize the time of God's coming to you."*
*45 When Jesus entered the temple courts, he began to drive out
those who were selling. 46 "It is written," he said to them, " 'My house
will be a house of prayer'; but you have made it 'a den of robbers.'"*
*47 Every day he was teaching at the temple. But the chief priests,
the teachers of the law and the leaders among the people were trying
to kill him. 48 Yet they could not find any way to do it, because all
the people hung on his words.*

All the way to its end, this biography is about Jesus—what he did and said, and what was done to him and said of him. One fundamental and profound truth for following Jesus emerges line by line from the entrance into Jerusalem to his ascension, namely, *this is the Jesus whom we are to follow.* The one who offered the kingdom, the one opposed and crucified by the powers, the one raised from among the dead, and the one who ascended to the Father. Nearly 25% of this Gospel tells that story, and any gospeling that erases any of this is not communicating the full gospel.

Each event masterfully builds upon the previous and leads to the next event, and all shape the story toward the crucifixion, resurrection, and ascension. These are the events of redemption by the redeemer, who enters Jerusalem in our passage to propel the last week.

	Matt	Mark	Luke	John
Arrival in Bethany				12:1
Entry in Jerusalem	21:1–11	11:1–10	19:29–44	12:12–19
Weeping			19:41	
Observes temple		11:11		
Returns to Bethany		11:11		
Curses fig tree	21:18–19	11:11–18		
Temple action	21:12–13	11:15–18	19:45–46 (47–48)	
Return to Bethany		11:19		
Fig tree	21:20–22			
Authority question	21:23–27	11:27–33	20:1–8	
Parable of two sons	21:28–32			
Parable of vineyard	21:33–46	12:1–12	20:9–19	
Parable of wedding	22:1–14			
Taxes for Caesar	22:15–22	12:13–17	20:20–26	

	MATT	MARK	LUKE	JOHN
RESURRECTION QUESTION	22:23–33	12:18–27	20:27–40	
GREATEST COMMAND		12:28–34		
WHOSE SON QUESTION	22:41–46	12:35–37	20:41–44	
WOES	23:1–39	12:38–40	20:45–47	
WIDOW'S OFFERING		12:41–44	21:1–4	
PROPHESYING ON OLIVET	24:1–36	13:1–32	21:5–36	
DAYS OF NOAH	24:37–41			
TEN VIRGINS	25:1–13			
PARABLE OF BAGS OF GOLD	25:14–30	13:33–37		
PARABLE OF SHEEP & GOATS	25:31–46			
SUMMARY			21:37–38	
SANHEDRIN PLOT	26:1–5	14:1–2	22:1–2	
MARY ANOINTS JESUS	26:6–13	14:3–9		12:2–8
JUDAS' PLOT	26:14–16	14:10–11	22:3–6	

(continued)

	MATT	MARK	LUKE	JOHN
PREPARATION	26:17–20	14:12–17	22:7–14	
GREATEST QUESTION			22:24–30	
JUDAS IDENTIFIED	26:21–25	14:18–21	22:21–23	13:21–30
LAST SUPPER*	26:26–29	14:22–25	22:15–20	
SINGING	26:30	14:26		
PETER'S DENIAL PREDICTED	26:31–35	14:27–31	22:31–38	13:36–38
GETHSEMANE PRAYER	26:36–46	14:32–42	22:39–46	
ARREST	26:47–56	14:43–52	22:47–53	18:2–12

John's Gospel has four extra chapters of conversation, instruction, and prayer (13–17).

Notice how our passage opens: "after Jesus had said this" (19:28), "having delivered the parable" that warned of Rome's vicious destructions (19:11–27). Rome's lions were roaring, and Jesus publicly and prophetically paraded into their presence. The passage reveals the courage of Jesus to stick to his message and mission in spite of systemic public opposition. Only one word captures Jesus' entry into Jerusalem: provocation. The client king of the previous parable contrasts even more now with the suffering king who enters Jerusalem.

He Knows about a Colt

Jesus, on the western brow of Olivet, approaching an unknown hamlet called Bethpage as well as Bethany, sends two of his apprentices into the "village" where he informs them they will find a tied-up colt. How he knows about this colt is not clear, but I suspect those who were preparing the way for Jesus had arranged this (cf. 9:52; 10:1). They are to fetch it, explain that the (seemingly known) Lord needs it, and lead it to him for his (nothing less than) staged entry into Jerusalem (19:29–34).

It was as easy to walk into Jerusalem as it was to ride, so this act is intentional and, besides that, it fits Zechariah perfectly (Zechariah 9:9). What is even more intentional is that he is about to enter Jerusalem as a staged royal entry, but he chooses to ride not on an impressive, decorated, symbol-of-power steed but on an unridden "colt." His way of power is not Rome's; his kingdom is not their empire; his kingship is not the emperor's.

He Hears the Responses

Three responses shape the descent into the Kidron Valley and up the incline into a gate on the eastern side (or, less probably, the northern side). His followers, and again we can think of those whom he had sent in advance to prepare for his arrival, "threw their cloaks" on the colt and seem to have lifted Jesus onto the colt (19:35). The "people" tossed their cloaks onto the rocks and marble stones forming the path into the city (19:36). As he begins the rocky descent of the Mount of Olives, where Zechariah locates God's ultimate redemption (14:4), "the whole crowd of disciples" erupts into a chorus of loud praise music. As those who knew their psalms, they cite Psalm 118:26 and then echo the words of the angels from the birth of Jesus (Luke 2:14). Both of these poetic songs indicate the arrival of Israel's king, that is, the Messiah.

The third response counters the words of the first two: "Teacher, rebuke your disciples!" the Pharisees exclaim (19:39), but Jesus counters their counter by explaining that so deep is creation's groaning for peace that if the disciples had not sung, the rocks themselves would have broken into a lament (19:40). The Pharisees, it needs to be said, understood the political furor that such actions could provoke, especially at Passover when liberation from Egypt was the heart of the holiday.

He Laments over the City

The rocks did not lament but Jesus does, and his lament contrasts with the acclaim of the disciples. As he descended into his entry "he wept over" Jerusalem (19:41) because—as his previous parable explained—the people of the city do not recognize its true Messiah of peace (19:42). Because of this, judgment from Rome will rain down on Jerusalem and utterly destroy the temple (19:43–44; notice again 19:27). All that remains to this day is the western wall.

He Protests Corruption

The famous report of the so-called "cleansing" of the temple is reduced in Luke's biography of Jesus to two verses (19:45–46). Jesus counters the temple system, not simply its commercialization. His systemic protest takes on specific form when he opposes some kind of "selling" in the temple courts, which suggests he thought their motives for profit were contaminating the temple. His prophetic words from Isaiah 56:7 and Jeremiah 7:11, which he appropriates for clearing them out of the temple courts, make his intent doubly clear.

Jesus knows Jeremiah connected temple corruption with injustice for the poor (7:6, 9). The action of Jesus then subverts the system's injustices. He protects the sanctity of the temple; he opposes their mixed motives—and his action is nothing less than a public prophetic action, like others done by Isaiah, who protested sin by walking around in his birthday suit, or Jeremiah, who once broke a pot to symbolize destruction.

He Teaches

Jesus' protest in Jerusalem includes a week-long, intense set of engagements with Jerusalem's leaders. What he teaches, which Luke will record in the next two chapters, summarily generates intense opposition to his kingdom vision, so intense Luke tells us they wanted to kill him (19:47). The challenge for the opposition is the adoring response of the "people," that is, ordinary Jews who are in Jerusalem for Passover (19:48). One could easily think this refers to those from Galilee who had heard Jesus there and those from Judea who had encountered Jesus in his previous annual visits.

From the first step of the colt to Jesus' return that evening to Bethany, the sweep of this event stuns the reader as a deliberate provocation of the leaders in Jerusalem. You don't stage a royal entry on a donkey unless you want people to take notice, and you don't then stage a prophetic symbolic act in the temple unless you want the leaders to give your message immediate attention. This day sets the stage for a week of public preaching by Jesus.

It doesn't look like Jesus expects capitulation to him as king.

Questions for Reflection and Application

1. How does Jesus' arrival in Jerusalem contrast with the presence of the Roman authorities and their client kings in the city?

2. What are the three different responses to Jesus' entrance and what does each one signify?

3. Why does Jesus weep and lament? Why do you think Luke is the only Gospel writer who records this show of emotion?

4. How and why does Jesus confront injustice in the temple system?

5. In what ways could you cultivate some of Jesus' emotions in your own life? When could you express lamentation, zeal for God's house, and action-taking compassion for those suffering from injustice?

REDEMPTION'S FIRST SET OF CHALLENGES

Luke 20:1–26

*[1] One day as Jesus was teaching the people in the temple courts
and proclaiming the good news, the chief priests and the teachers
of the law, together with the elders, came up to him. [2] "Tell us by
what authority you are doing these things," they said. "Who gave
you this authority?"*

*[3] He replied, "I will also ask you a question. Tell me: [4] John's
baptism—was it from heaven, or of human origin?"*

*[5] They discussed it among themselves and said, "If we say,
'From heaven,' he will ask, 'Why didn't you believe him?' [6] But if
we say, 'Of human origin,' all the people will stone us, because they
are persuaded that John was a prophet."*

[7] So they answered, "We don't know where it was from."

*[8] Jesus said, "Neither will I tell you by what authority I am
doing these things."*

*[9] He went on to tell the people this parable: A man planted a
vineyard, rented it to some farmers and went away for a long time.
[10] At harvest time he sent a servant to the tenants so they would
give him some of the fruit of the vineyard. But the tenants beat
him and sent him away empty-handed. [11] He sent another servant,
but that one also they beat and treated shamefully and sent away*

empty-handed. 12 He sent still a third, and they wounded him and
threw him out.

13 "Then the owner of the vineyard said, 'What shall I do? I
will send my son, whom I love; perhaps they will respect him.'

14 "But when the tenants saw him, they talked the matter over.
'This is the heir,' they said. 'Let's kill him, and the inheritance will
be ours.' 15 So they threw him out of the vineyard and killed him.

"What then will the owner of the vineyard do to them?

16 He will come and kill those tenants and give the vineyard to
others."

When the people heard this, they said, "God forbid!"

17 Jesus looked directly at them and asked, "Then what is the
meaning of that which is written:

> *" 'The stone the builders rejected*
> *has become the cornerstone'?*

18 Everyone who falls on that stone will be broken to pieces;
anyone on whom it falls will be crushed.

19 The teachers of the law and the chief priests looked for a way
to arrest him immediately, because they knew he had spoken this
parable against them. But they were afraid of the people.

20 Keeping a close watch on him, they sent spies, who pretended
to be sincere. They hoped to catch Jesus in something he said, so
that they might hand him over to the power and authority of the
governor. 21 So the spies questioned him: "Teacher, we know that
you speak and teach what is right, and that you do not show par-
tiality but teach the way of God in accordance with the truth. 22 Is
it right for us to pay taxes to Caesar or not?"

23 He saw through their duplicity and said to them, 24 "Show
me a denarius. Whose image and inscription are on it?"

"Caesar's," they replied.

25 He said to them, "Then give back to Caesar what is Caesar's,
and to God what is God's."

[26] They were unable to trap him in what he had said there in public. And astonished by his answer, they became silent.

Prophets provoke, and provocateurs expect pushback. To call someone a "prophet" is, for those of us who study the Bible, a serious label. A prophet was someone who (1) is called by God, (2) to speak for God, (3) to the people of God, (4) about both redemption and judgment, (5) in light of the people of God's current way of life, and, because the prophet's message cuts into the people of God's corrupted way of life, the prophet (6) experiences opposition, rejection, and at times martyrdom. In one simple expression, a prophet *mediates special revelation from God to God's people.* Many today claim the prophet's mantle and speak of their prophetic calling, and I'm not the one to make the judgment. But this must be said: being critical of the church does not a prophet make. One has to claim revelation from God and a mission from God to wear the prophet's mantle with authenticity. A blog, a twitter handle, an Instagram account are not the platform for the prophet. The church is.

Jesus fits all six elements of a prophet, and Luke 20 perfectly features a prophet.

A Prophet's Authority

Jesus, like some street evangelist in a major city, is "teaching the people in the temple courts" and gospeling. Three of the main groups of religious authorities—which today would be like a theologian, a pastor, and a denominational authority—approach Jesus with a requirement that he provide credentials for his gospeling in the temple courts (20:1–2).

In true rabbi fashion, Jesus turns his response into a question, and the answer will declare their capacity to judge Jesus:

"John's baptism—was it from heaven, or of human origin?" (20:3–4). If they affirm John as sent by God, they implicate themselves for their response to John, which means, did they get baptized?! If they deny John's prophetic calling, "all the people will stone us" (20:5–6). This reveals something vital to the last week of Jesus: the powers of Jerusalem, tied as they are to Rome's powers, and the people of Jerusalem form into Team Rome vs. Team Jesus and John. The Gospel writers exaggerate at some level.

Luke makes the powers gutless. Their "we don't know" was a cop out.

So Jesus refuses to declare the source, which is divine, of his authority.

This is not dodgy for Jesus. Prophets spin words like this in ways that probe in order to provoke. The chapter could have a "Who's next?" caption at the end of the episodes.

A Prophet's Parable

He turns to Team Jesus and John, to the "people" (20:9). Jesus tells them a parable like the parable of the minas (19:11–27). Instead of a nobleman who becomes a client king authorized by Rome, our new lead character is a man who planted a vineyard and, like some of the mega-farms of our day, hired some farmers to farm the vineyard, and "went away for a long time" (20:9).

The drama of the story occurs when he sends three different slaves (NIV's "servants") to collect some grapes. The "tenants" beat the first slave, beat and "treated shamefully" the second, and the third they "wounded and threw him out" (20:10–12). The people know what kind of power the wealthy farmer has, the story is boilerplate for them, and they are themselves nodding in agreement and waiting for Jesus to deliver his own perspective.

Shockingly, the owner sends his son, believing they will respect his son (20:13). The hired workers huddle and hatch a plot to kill the son so the inheritance will fall to them—and they did toss the son out and kill him. The people are rhetorically asked by Jesus what the owner ought to do, and Jesus answers it: that owner will kill the workers. Furthermore, he will give the vineyard to others and start all over again (20:15–16). Jesus' parable reveals that the workers will not in fact inherit the vineyard. Their risk was as rash as their behaviors were brutal.

Jesus turns now to the people with a subtle Bible quiz. He quotes Psalm 118:22 and asks them to identity who the "stone" was whom the "builders" rejected, and who has become the "cornerstone" (Luke 20:17). He adds a line: those who "fall on that stone" will break apart and those upon whom that stone "falls will be crushed" (20:18).

It's a not-very-subtle riddle because prophets want their message to be clear. For Luke the powers knew the parable was about them. They are Israel's farmers; God is the owner of the vineyard, which is a common image for Israel among the prophets; they have not only rejected those whom God has sent over the centuries, but also they have now rejected the son, who is Jesus.

Gutless again. They get the story but are afraid to respond to Jesus because "they were afraid" of, you guessed it, Team Jesus and John (20:19).

His authority is from God, which makes him a prophet.
Who's next?

A Prophet's Riddle

Jesus turns now to some planted "ringers in the audience" (Spencer, *Luke*, 520), which evokes the image of someone embedded in his circle of listeners, that is, among the people who adore his kingdom vision (20:20). Their job was to pretend in order to trap.

One of them, using the skill of buttering-up, affirms how often he teaches "what is right," that is, according to the law of Moses, and how he's impartial in judgment (20:21). Now the buttering-up turns into a trap question: Is it observant to "pay taxes to Caesar or not"? (20:22). Talk about authority! Who's got more in that world than Ceasar?

Turnabout is fair play. Jesus forced the powers to decide on John's authority, so they now force Jesus to declare if he's Republican or Democrat, or the first century's Jewish equivalent. Jesus discerns what the NIV calls their "duplicity." The Greek term is stronger: their "trickery" or even their "wickedness" or "villainy." He asks for a coin, obtains one, flips it in his fingers and asks about "whose image and inscription are on it" (20:23), and they give the orthodox answer: "Caesar's" (20:24).

His answer unravels their questions. "Give back to Caesar what is Caesar's, and to God what is God's" (20:25). Do they comprehend his riddle? If he had said pay taxes, the ordinary "people" who love Jesus would have wondered about the politics of Team Jesus and John; if he had said not to pay taxes, they were with him, but big trouble would follow. To pay taxes declares allegiance to Caesar. The coin, too, is Exhibit A of violating the commandment about making images (Exodus 20:4), and if it is the coin most think, it inscribed Caesar as "divine Augustus." Is giving the coin back a summons to avoid the idolatry? Jesus, you observe, does not have a coin himself. Is he saying give the filthy stuff back to Rome and you learn to serve God apart from images? If so, the riddle poses a choice: Either God or Caesar. This is not about separation of church and state—give God's money to God and Caesar's money to Caesar. It is a riddle that rhetorically reaches into their hearts for a decision about "entire allegiance to God" without "compromises" (González, *Luke*, 233). His answer subverts their question and challenges their allegiance to Caesar. Team Jesus and John or Team Rome? Some who heard what Jesus said here will soon put forward allegations against Jesus that he "opposes payment of taxes to Caesar" (23:2), and that verse deserves to be part of how we understand the riddle of Jesus.

Three questions: Who gave you this authority? (20:2), What shall I do? (20:13), and, Is it right to pay taxes to Caesar or not? (20:22). Three responses: I won't tell you, the vineyard will shift to others, and choose God.

A prophet is someone who (1) is called by God, (2) to speak for God, (3) to the people of God, (4) about both redemption and judgment, (5) in light of the people of God's current way of life, and, because the prophet's message cuts into the people of God's corrupted way of life, the prophet (6) experiences opposition, rejection, and at times martyrdom. Jesus is that kind of prophet, and his message to all is, "Choose today whom you will serve."

We're only halfway through the challenges of his day in the temple courts, but the "ringers" in the audience, bested by Jesus, go "silent" (20:26).

Questions for Reflection and Application

1. What qualifies someone as a prophet?

2. In what ways does Jesus meet the criterion as a prophet?

3. How does Jesus push the religious authorities to make a decision about whether they are Team Rome or Team Jesus and John?

4. How do the religious authorities and their ringers try to get back at Jesus rhetorically and ideologically?

5. Evaluate yourself for allegiance to the ruling powers versus allegiance to God. Which team would someone guess you are on if they were to look at your life?

REDEMPTION'S SECOND SET OF CHALLENGES

Luke 20:27–21:4

*27 Some of the Sadducees, who say there is no resurrection, came to
Jesus with a question. 28 "Teacher," they said, "Moses wrote for us
that if a man's brother dies and leaves a wife but no children, the
man must marry the widow and raise up offspring for his brother.
29 Now there were seven brothers. The first one married a woman
and died childless. 30 The second 31 and then the third married her,
and in the same way the seven died, leaving no children. 32 Finally,
the woman died too. 33 Now then, at the resurrection whose wife
will she be, since the seven were married to her?"*

*34 Jesus replied, "The people of this age marry and are given in
marriage. 35 But those who are considered worthy of taking part in
the age to come and in the resurrection from the dead will neither
marry nor be given in marriage, 36 and they can no longer die;
for they are like the angels. They are God's children, since they
are children of the resurrection. 37 But in the account of the burning bush, even Moses showed that the dead rise, for he calls the
Lord 'the God of Abraham, and the God of Isaac, and the God
of Jacob.' 38 He is not the God of the dead, but of the living, for to
him all are alive."*

*39 Some of the teachers of the law responded, "Well said, teach-
er!" 40 And no one dared to ask him any more questions.*
*41 Then Jesus said to them, "Why is it said that the Messiah is
the son of David? 42 David himself declares in the Book of Psalms:*

> *" 'The Lord said to my Lord:*
> *"Sit at my right hand*
> *43 until I make your enemies*
> *a footstool for your feet." '*

44 David calls him 'Lord.' How then can he be his son?"
*45 While all the people were listening, Jesus said to his disciples,
46 "Beware of the teachers of the law. They like to walk around in
flowing robes and love to be greeted with respect in the marketplaces and have the most important seats in the synagogues and the
places of honor at banquets. 47 They devour widows' houses and
for a show make lengthy prayers. These men will be punished most
severely."*
*21:1 As Jesus looked up, he saw the rich putting their gifts into
the temple treasury. 2 He also saw a poor widow put in two very
small copper coins. 3 "Truly I tell you," he said, "this poor widow
has put in more than all the others. 4 All these people gave their gifts
out of their wealth; but she out of her poverty put in all she had to
live on."*

Everything, and please do avoid diminishing that word, was at risk for the redemption Jesus was bringing in the last week. By "risk," I mean Jesus, and his entire kingdom vision, were being challenged to the point of some wanting to put him away. Because of the seriousness and comprehensiveness of those challenges, Luke puts on display a series of Jesus' verbal victories. What was remembered about Jesus' last week then was not just the redemptive events of entry, last supper, crucifixion, resurrection, and ascension, but also the verbal mastery Jesus displayed in the courts of the temple. He contends with the leading priests and experts in the law, spies sent by the priests and experts, and, in today's passage, the Sadducees and, once again, the "teachers of the law" (20:27, 39). Having met their challenges, Jesus turns to his disciples for a warning and an example (20:45–21:4).

A Prophet's Reminder

Teachers of the Bible can become so defensive of one idea they neglect the balancing ideas the Bible teaches. The temple authorities, the Sadducees, comparable to today's intelligent, wealthy, and powerful class of priests or ministers—think of the Pope, the Archbishop of Canterbury, the president of the Southern Baptist Convention, and other pastors and leaders with household names—were convinced "there is no resurrection" (20:27). A contemporary historian, Josephus, observes the same, saying of the Sadducees that they believe "souls die with the body" and that they like to argue about theology (*Antiquities* 18.16).

Jesus, they knew, believed in the resurrection, and he expressed his belief as the Age to Come, the kingdom of God, and eternal life. The Sadducees, like those trained to give bite-sized responses, upload a riddle-like contradiction of resurrection for Jesus to consider. A woman had married, in complete observance of the law of what is called "levirate marriage" (Deuteronomy 25:5–6), seven brothers who died in succession, one at a time. Exaggeration is fair play. In the resurrection, they ask him: Whose wife will she be? It's very Jewish to think of the kingdom in physical, familial, and material terms (Luke 20:28–33).

Jesus responds, but his response can be read in two ways. First, he may be saying in the kingdom of God no one will be married because (a) they will possess immortality and not die, and (b) they will be like angels, who do not die either. Sadducees don't believe in angels, so that must have been said with a twinkle in his eye. Second, he may be more precisely saying there will be *no new marriages* in heaven, but present-day families will remain intact. The actual wording of Luke 20:35 reads "neither marry nor be given in marriage," and that is language for new marriages. In Judaism the second option is more likely than the first because not only are families intact but angels are not uniformly sexless in Judaism (notice Genesis 6:4). (I discuss this in my book *The Heaven Promise,* 162–170.) However, one can wonder if the second option answers the Sadducees' question. In fact, some see here a liberation of women-as-wives from being defined by and constrained by being married-to-a-man (Thomas Long, "Jesus' Final Exam," 267).

To this Jesus adds one of the standard defenses for first century Jews who believe in the resurrection: when God spoke to Moses, God said he was the God of Abraham, Isaac, and Jacob, who were dead. But Jesus observes if he's still their God, then they are alive! (Exodus 3:6; Luke 20:37–38).

Flummoxed, and standing next to the spies of the experts and leading priests, the Sadducees put it on mute and decide it's best not to ask Jesus questions (20:39–40). In fact, some of the "experts in the law," after hearing Jesus' response, say, "You spoke beautifully, Teacher" (my translation). Either they're the Pharisee-sort who believed in resurrection and so sided with Jesus or they're experts who became convinced by Jesus. Either way, they perfectly set up Jesus for a profound-er question, one that presses them to ask who Jesus is.

A Prophet's Question

His question is a riddle for them: "Why is it said that the Messiah is the son of David?" (20:41). *Son* of David is standard Jewish language for the coming Messiah (notice 18:38, 39). Hang on to that word "son." Assuming that son of David works for the Messiah, Jesus turns back to Psalm 110:1, one of the early Christians' favorite psalms, where we read, "The Lord said to *my Lord*." David's view of the Messiah is that he is the Lord. In that psalm David refers to God as Lord and then calls the Messiah his "Lord." Which leads to the riddling question: How can the Messiah be both David's Lord and his son (apart from preexistence)? Or, perhaps, how can the Lord be David's Lord and David's son?

Crickets.

The challenges are finished, so Jesus turns to his disciples.

A Prophet's Instruction

With Team Jesus and John listening ("all the people"), Jesus warns his disciples to avoid the "teachers of the law" because of three of their faulty ways of life: they love high-status honor and respect in public (20:46), they gobble up the resources of widows like televangelists do today, and they pray publicly to gain attention (20:47).

That subtle "devour widows' houses" was matched, providentially, by a public display of the very problem. He "looked up" and spotted the glaring contradiction of a rich people donating "gifts" in the "temple treasury" and, at the same time, a "poor widow" dropping in "two small copper coins" (21:1–2). One often hears in sermons that there was a trumpet blast when someone donated to the temple, but as Levine and Witherington have noted, there's not a shred of evidence for such a practice, though some receptacles for donations were shofar (ram's horn) shaped (Levine-Witherington, *Luke*, 556). Ever attentive to the piety of the poor, Jesus instructs his disciples that her giving was generously disproportionate to her poverty while the rich fellas' donations were disproportionate to their wealth. Maybe their bilking of the poor, which topped up their donations, led the widow to such a small donation.

The challenges now over, the prophet Jesus returns to the parable he gave back in 19:11–27 and predicts the coming destruction of Jerusalem at the hands of the brutal powers of Rome.

Questions for Reflection and Application

1. What does it add to our remembrance and understanding of Jesus' last week when we include his verbal victories in addition to the major action points?

2. What rhetorical moves does Jesus make with the Sadducees regarding marriage and heaven?

3. If you view the three faulty ways of life of the teachers of the law as red flags to avoid in religious leaders today, how could that help you evaluate churches for their safety and health?

4. How does the widow serve as an illustration of those who wickedly gobble up the resources of the poor?

5. In what ways do you struggle with any of these faulty ways of life: loving public honor, mistreating poor people, or seeking attention with religious behavior?

FOR FURTHER READING

Thomas G. Long, "Jesus' Final Exam," in *Sermons from Duke Chapel: Voices from "A Great Towering Church"*, ed. William H. Willimon (Durham: Duke University Press, 2005), 264–269.

Scot McKnight, *The Heaven Promise: Engaging the Bible's Truth about Life to Come* (New York: Water Brook, 2015).

REDEMPTION'S PROPHETIC WARNING

Luke 21:5–38

*5 Some of his disciples were remarking about how the temple was
adorned with beautiful stones and with gifts dedicated to God. But
Jesus said, 6 "As for what you see here, the time will come when not
one stone will be left on another; every one of them will be thrown
down."*

*7 "Teacher," they asked, "when will these things happen? And
what will be the sign that they are about to take place?"*

*8 He replied: "Watch out that you are not deceived. For many
will come in my name, claiming, 'I am he,' and, 'The time is near.'
Do not follow them. 9 When you hear of wars and uprisings, do not
be frightened. These things must happen first, but the end will not
come right away."*

*10 Then he said to them: "Nation will rise against nation, and
kingdom against kingdom. 11 There will be great earthquakes, fam-
ines and pestilences in various places, and fearful events and great
signs from heaven.*

*12 "But before all this, they will seize you and persecute you.
They will hand you over to synagogues and put you in prison, and
you will be brought before kings and governors, and all on account
of my name. 13 And so you will bear testimony to me. 14 But make*

up your mind not to worry beforehand how you will defend your-
selves. 15 *For I will give you words and wisdom that none of your*
adversaries will be able to resist or contradict. 16 *You will be be-*
trayed even by parents, brothers and sisters, relatives and friends,
and they will put some of you to death. 17 *Everyone will hate you*
because of me. 18 *But not a hair of your head will perish.* 19 *Stand*
firm, and you will win life.

20 *"When you see Jerusalem being surrounded by armies, you*
will know that its desolation is near. 21 *Then let those who are in*
Judea flee to the mountains, let those in the city get out, and let those
in the country not enter the city. 22 *For this is the time of punishment*
in fulfillment of all that has been written. 23 *How dreadful it will be*
in those days for pregnant women and nursing mothers! There will
be great distress in the land and wrath against this people. 24 *They*
will fall by the sword and will be taken as prisoners to all the na-
tions. Jerusalem will be trampled on by the Gentiles until the times
of the Gentiles are fulfilled.

25 *"There will be signs in the sun, moon and stars. On the earth,*
nations will be in anguish and perplexity at the roaring and tossing
of the sea. 26 *People will faint from terror, apprehensive of what is*
coming on the world, for the heavenly bodies will be shaken. 27 *At*
that time they will see the Son of Man coming in a cloud with power
and great glory. 28 *When these things begin to take place, stand up*
and lift up your heads, because your redemption is drawing near."

29 *He told them this parable: "Look at the fig tree and all the*
trees. 30 *When they sprout leaves, you can see for yourselves and*
know that summer is near. 31 *Even so, when you see these things*
happening, you know that the kingdom of God is near.

32 *"Truly I tell you, this generation will certainly not pass away*
until all these things have happened. 33 *Heaven and earth will pass*
away, but my words will never pass away.

34 *"Be careful, or your hearts will be weighed down with car-*
ousing, drunkenness and the anxieties of life, and that day will
close on you suddenly like a trap. 35 *For it will come on all those*

who live on the face of the whole earth. [36] *Be always on the watch, and pray that you may be able to escape all that is about to happen, and that you may be able to stand before the Son of Man."*

[37] *Each day Jesus was teaching at the temple, and each evening he went out to spend the night on the hill called the Mount of Olives,* [38] *and all the people came early in the morning to hear him at the temple.*

Passages predicting the future have been abused in the church in at least two ways. Some use, bend, break, and then refit the predictions into our day so they can *speculate* about our future. Others *weaponize* predictions like this and—this is not exaggeration—terrorize some persons, hoping they'll give their hearts to Jesus to escape some apocalyptic scenario where cars will careen out of control and some beastly antichrist will impose slavery on the whole world and force atheism with a knife at one's throat. We need to speak to this situation before we can even begin to consider our passage.

Kathleen Norris can be our guide. "The literature of apocalypse is scary stuff, the kind of thing that can give religion a bad name, because people so often use it as a means of controlling others, instilling dread by invoking a boogeyman God." Yes. Instead, this kind of literature "is a wake-up call, one that uses intensely poetic language and imagery to sharpen our awareness of God's presence in and promise for the world." If only we could get more convinced that the rhetoric of Jesus here is exactly that: designed to awaken the sleeping so they will become faithful disciples. She's right on this, too: "Maybe we're meant to use apocalyptic literature in the same way: not as an allowance to indulge in otherworldly fixation but as an injunction to pay closer attention to the world around us." She makes another very important observation that socks us in the nose: "In America, those who most cherish the language of apocalypse have traditionally come from the margins of society" because "despite considerable evidence to the contrary, in the end it is good that will prevail" (*Amazing Grace*, 318, 319, 320, 321).

One additional word she forgot before we move on: when Jesus entered Jerusalem, he wept (19:41–44). He didn't, as many do today, take glee over the destruction of his beloved Jerusalem or his beloved temple. He wept. We should read this passage, and those behind us and ahead of us, with sorrow and not *Schadenfreude*. The prophetic words that follow flow from the lamenting heart of Jesus. Instead of imagining a Jesus with fire in his eyes and words barking from his mouth, we need read this passage—and others like it—imagining a Jesus with tears flowing down his cheeks.

INSTEAD . . .

So, instead of reading our passage so we can speculate about Israel and the USA and who the antichrist might be, or so we can weaponize it into terrorizing us into spine-tingling scenarios so we can scare people into the kingdom, let us remember this is the language of minorities who both find hope in the future judgment of God to make things right and who, in the here and now, find courage to resist systemic oppressions and injustices. Amen?

Here's the big scenario for Jesus: Jerusalem will be sacked by Rome (and it occurred under the Roman general Titus) and the faithful will survive (and some did), but they need to be ready for opposition (and some were, some were not). Do we have eyes like the prophet Jesus to discern corruptions in our world that will cause institutions and nations to collapse? Are we ready to speak up and speak out about the corruptions and face the oppositions? Are we lamenting the injustices of our world as Jesus did his? Are we ready for the final return of Christ?

Think of This Passage like This

We can learn to rethink about this passage in a way that is faithful to what Jesus was saying and in a way that sheds light on discipleship today. First, this passage makes predictions about the temple in Jerusalem in the first century. "Some" ask a question (NIV translates with "disciples") about the temple, and Jesus predicts the temple's demise (21:5–7, 20–24). Second, he reveals to them indicators of Jerusalem's demise, indicators like fake claims to be Messiah, wars, natural disasters, persecutions, betrayals, difficult days, and cosmic signs (more below; 21:8–28). Third, their allegiance to Jesus will be tested to witness to Jesus under the threats of persecution, but their witness will be empowered by God's Spirit (21:8, 13–19, 34–36). Fourth, Jesus explicitly says "all" these predictions will happen soon, that is, they will occur with surprise to "this generation" (21:32–33; 21:27–36).

Finally, let's look at the cosmic signs. Jesus predicts "signs in the sun, moon and stars" and the shaking of "heavenly bodies" and the "Son of Man coming in a cloud with power and great glory" (21:25–27). Luke says the Son of Man's coming is near (21:27, 31). For many this is a descent to earth from heaven, but the very language Jesus uses for "coming" quotes from Daniel 7:13's describing *an ascent before the Ancient of Days*! These apocalyptic images are used in the prophets, like Joel 2:28–32 and Amos 8:7–14, for judgment on sin and the vindication of God's people in victory over the powers of this world, as well as for the dramatic presence of God's kingdom in judgment and redemption. The Son of Man's ascent symbolizes the victory of God over injustice in this world.

Prophets spoke like this: they envisioned the next big

event on God's calendar as if it were the last event in history. They were not mistaken or false prophets. No, the prophet's style was to invest the next big event with ultimate, final significance. Our political news does this *every day of the week, world without end!* American politicians have done this since the colonial days (Mathewes and Nichols, *Prophesies of Godlessness*).

Live like This

There is one clear implication, not discounting the courage of a prophet to speak up like this in the temple courts: difficult days are coming, and they are called to faithful witness in the face of persecution. It is wise to see sinful behaviors—like our egregious contamination of the earth's water supplies—leading to their own consequences without reducing divine judgments to natural consequences. No, these are spelled out as divine judgment on sinful behaviors, but that does not require us to cut out the natural consequences element. If you court rebellion against Rome, eventually Rome's might will be displayed. A leads to B.

God will make all things right, but the right-making way of God includes the elimination of injustice. Before God makes the world right, the wrong of this world has to be overcome and overturned and redeemed. How can we look into our world with corruptions in the church, pastoral failures, the chaos of severe tensions between citizens, the church losing respect in society—how can we see these and more and not be on our knees, invoking the Spirit for discernment for how best to live in our day in a way that pleases Jesus? Amen?

Kathleen Norris is right: this appeals most to those who experience injustices now, and it gives them courage to be faithful witnesses who resist the injustices by fighting for justice. With tears in their eyes.

Questions for Reflection and Application

1. So far, what has Luke told us about who Jesus is?

2. How does it change your reading of this passage to image Jesus with tears on his cheeks rather than fire in his eyes?

3. What is Jesus' message to his followers in this passage?

4. When and how have you experienced passages about the future being abused by speculation or weaponization?

5. What can you learn from oppressed people about interpreting Jesus here? How can you find hope for the future and courage for the present to resist injustice?

FOR FURTHER READING

Charles Mathewes, Christopher McKnight Nichols, eds., *Prophesies of Godlessness: Prediction of America's Imminent Secularization from the Puritans to the Present Day* (New York: Oxford University Press, 2008).

REDEMPTION'S UNFORGETTABLE EVENTS

Luke 22:1–38

[1] Now the Festival of Unleavened Bread, called the Passover, was approaching, [2] and the chief priests and the teachers of the law were looking for some way to get rid of Jesus, for they were afraid of the people. [3] Then Satan entered Judas, called Iscariot, one of the Twelve. [4] And Judas went to the chief priests and the officers of the temple guard and discussed with them how he might betray Jesus. [5] They were delighted and agreed to give him money. [6] He consented, and watched for an opportunity to hand Jesus over to them when no crowd was present.

[7] Then came the day of Unleavened Bread on which the Passover lamb had to be sacrificed. [8] Jesus sent Peter and John, saying, "Go and make preparations for us to eat the Passover."

[9] "Where do you want us to prepare for it?" they asked.

[10] He replied, "As you enter the city, a man carrying a jar of water will meet you. Follow him to the house that he enters, [11] and say to the owner of the house, 'The Teacher asks: Where is the guest room, where I may eat the Passover with my disciples?' [12] He will show you a large room upstairs, all furnished. Make preparations there."

[13] *They left and found things just as Jesus had told them. So they prepared the Passover.*

[14] *When the hour came, Jesus and his apostles reclined at the table.* [15] *And he said to them, "I have eagerly desired to eat this Passover with you before I suffer.* [16] *For I tell you, I will not eat it again until it finds fulfillment in the kingdom of God."*

[17] *After taking the cup, he gave thanks and said, "Take this and divide it among you.* [18] *For I tell you I will not drink again from the fruit of the vine until the kingdom of God comes."*

[19] *And he took bread, gave thanks and broke it, and gave it to them, saying, "This is my body given for you; do this in remembrance of me."*

[20] *In the same way, after the supper he took the cup, saying, "This cup is the new covenant in my blood, which is poured out for you.* [21] *But the hand of him who is going to betray me is with mine on the table.* [22] *The Son of Man will go as it has been decreed. But woe to that man who betrays him!"* [23] *They began to question among themselves which of them it might be who would do this.*

[24] *A dispute also arose among them as to which of them was considered to be greatest.* [25] *Jesus said to them, "The kings of the Gentiles lord it over them; and those who exercise authority over them call themselves Benefactors.* [26] *But you are not to be like that. Instead, the greatest among you should be like the youngest, and the one who rules like the one who serves.* [27] *For who is greater, the one who is at the table or the one who serves? Is it not the one who is at the table? But I am among you as one who serves.* [28] *You are those who have stood by me in my trials.* [29] *And I confer on you a kingdom, just as my Father conferred one on me,* [30] *so that you may eat and drink at my table in my kingdom and sit on thrones, judging the twelve tribes of Israel.*

[31] *"Simon, Simon, Satan has asked to sift all of you as wheat.* [32] *But I have prayed for you, Simon, that your faith may not fail. And when you have turned back, strengthen your brothers."*

[33] But he replied, "Lord, I am ready to go with you to prison and to death."

[34] Jesus answered, "I tell you, Peter, before the rooster crows today, you will deny three times that you know me."

[35] Then Jesus asked them, "When I sent you without purse, bag or sandals, did you lack anything?"

"Nothing," they answered.

[36] He said to them, "But now if you have a purse, take it, and also a bag; and if you don't have a sword, sell your cloak and buy
one. [37] It is written: 'And he was numbered with the transgressors'; and I tell you that this must be fulfilled in me. Yes, what is written about me is reaching its fulfillment."

[38] The disciples said, "See, Lord, here are two swords."

"That's enough!" he replied.

Had you been a disciple who had traveled with Jesus on the journey to Jerusalem (remember 9:51), you also would have wondered (at least privately) just what he would do once he arrived. His entry stunned and confused and forced one to consider what he might do next. They expected more than a staged entry and a set of public debates that finished off with Jesus the prophet predicting the demise of the city. The disciples were thinking kingdom, and for them kingdom meant power, control, God's will being done, sending Romans back to Rome, and an era of justice and peace. In other words, liberation. Kingdom and liberation are as tight as ligament and joint, land and crop, sky and sun.

What happened next were two unforgettable events. Just after one of Jesus' closest followers, Judas, furtively plotted to turn Jesus over to the Roman powers for money, Jesus celebrated a meal with his followers, including Judas. The colt on which Jesus entered the city, which mocked Rome's military might and steeds, anticipated the Passover banquet

Jesus celebrated with a few chosen followers, a Passover that anticipated nothing less than the final banquet in the kingdom. Let us not miss the point: this meal, which we call the Last or the Lord's Supper, embodies the very kingdom Jesus launched when he rode that colt up that fateful incline into the city of Jerusalem, a banquet unlike any other. One we celebrate every time we take Communion.

An Unforgettable Deal

Jews celebrated Passover, which combined the Feast of Unleavened Bread and Passover proper, for one week in the capital with one's family and friends. The climactic event was Passover itself, which celebrated the liberation of the children of Israel from Pharoah. The city swelled in numbers, and the crowding always worried the powers in Jerusalem lest a rebellion break out. Hotheads always found the week conducive to radical plots.

The leading priests and legal experts, Luke informs us, had their eyes on Jesus and were plotting how they might nab him and his kingdom-vision-loving followers. They knew they'd have to be sly because Team Jesus and John surrounded Jesus (22:1–2). What they didn't perceive was the darker forces at work. Luke turns the betrayal into a cosmic plot against Jesus when he says, "Satan entered Judas" (22:3). Empowered with darkness, Judas goes to the leading priests and to the "offices of the temple guards" and arranges a deal to betray Jesus for money (22:4–6). Luke is hard on the Jewish leaders, and his depiction of them as the instigators has led to horrific acts of anti-Semitism, including medieval people on Good Friday leaving churches in gangs to murder Jews (Winner, *The Dangers of Christian Practice*, 19–56).

Jesus' followers experienced the betrayal. For them it was the ultimate deceit, plot, seizure of a vulnerable moment, and the death of the one they loved most. No one experienced the baring of the vulnerable heart or the destruction of trust as Jesus did. The deal, combined as it will be in this Gospel a page or so later with the actual handing over, was etched into their memory forever.

An Unforgettable Meal

Not long after Judas's deal, Jesus arranged for his disciples to celebrate Passover in a reserved large upper room. Peter and John were sent to ready the room (22:7–13).

It is nothing short of cool for some teachers to fit the last supper into the present order of a Passover Seder, but the modern Passover Seder was not in its present form in the first century. The Passover celebration goes back to Exodus 12–13 and Deuteronomy 16, but we learn bits and bobs in other places, like Exodus 23:14–17 or Joshua 5:10–12 or Josephus or the Dead Sea Scrolls or Philo or the full tractate on Passover celebrations in the *Mishnah*. Plus, we've got our text and its parallels in Mark, Matthew, John 13, and 1 Corinthians. Remember this: we don't know exactly what the order, or Seder, looked like in the first century for there was no standardized liturgy for the event at the time. We can at least say Luke's text looks like it fits into a Seder-like meal, which eventually had four separate cups of celebration accompanied by prepared words. But which cup is mentioned in 22:17–18 or 22:20, or even at Mark 14:23–25? We don't know. Truth be told, the events of Luke 22 fit any meal of Passover week, and there is a glaring absence of lamb at this meal, which is the center of the Passover meal itself. Having said that, the mention of the day of the lamb's sacrifice in 22:7 and "eat this Passover" in 22:15 both suggest the Passover meal itself, which means you and I can guess why no one mentions the lamb!

Details aside, what was so unforgettable about this meal? First, Jesus' opening words inform his disciples both that he has ached to eat this Passover meal with them "before I suffer" (22:15) and twice that he will not have a meal with them again until they share the table "in the kingdom of God" (22:16, 18). For them our *Lord's* supper was their *last* supper, but a last supper that anticipated the *final banquet's supper*! Which is why the apostle Paul has "until he comes" inscribed in his version of the words of institution (1 Corinthians 11:26).

Second, it was unforgettable in that he connected his body and his blood to the bread and to the wine (Luke 22:19, 20). Let's not forget the march to Jerusalem and their anticipation of God's kingdom. Jesus, instead of talking glorious kingdom come down to earth, explains it all as about his own body, blood "poured out for you" (from Isaiah 53:12), and death. Third, Jesus wants them to remember this meal and to do it over and over "in remembrance of me" (22:19), which means he informed the disciples—surely it whizzed right over their heads—that he would die, he would be gone a good while, and they'd be eating without him but remembering him. Fourth, Jesus reveals that this very meal is "the new covenant" that is "in my blood" (22:20). And his death establishes the long-anticipated kingdom redemption.

What we call "atonement"—what God has done to expose sin and remove sin and reconcile us to God, to ourselves, and to one another—explodes into a multitude of redemptive meanings in the early church, all of it *from this cup and this bread* as the new covenant. The act of eating and drinking unfolds into a theology of forgiveness, reconciliation, redemption, justification, and union with Christ.

Fifth, a spine-straightening and face-elongating moment arrives when Jesus informs them a betrayer is at the table—and he slaps this statement onto the words of redemption!

"But the hand of him who is going to betray me with mine on the table" (22:21), to which Jesus adds a severe warning: Oy! "to that man" (22:22). A few spines curve toward one's companion to ask who it might be (22:23).

From redemption to betrayal to, sixth, an unforgettable, foolish argument. From, Who is the most dangerous among us?, the disciples now ask, Who is the most important among us?! (22:24–30). I confess I like that Matthew and Mark put this earlier in their Gospels (Matthew 20:25–28; Mark 10:42–45). It's so irreverent for this to show up in Jesus' last supper after Jesus has revealed the presence of a betrayer. But perhaps this reveals the foolish distractions into which even committed followers of Jesus can enter. Anyway, it gives Jesus a great opportunity to connect his suffering to their discipleship of serving one another. In spite of their foolishness, Jesus promises them a place in the kingdom's royal room (22:29–30).

Yet another unforgettable moment: Jesus predicts Satan's involvement yet again, this time in Peter's denials, at this last supper (22:31–34). You may have listened to a friend tell a story and afterwards reflect to yourself—*how could that many stunning actions happen in such a short time?* One has to wonder also how long it took for the disciples to pull from their memories all these unforgettable moments.

Finally, Jesus turns to provisions for what's ahead, an "ahead" only he seems to know with any clarity. He presses the days when others provided for them in their missions (Luke 9, 10) against the present night when they're going to need provisions. An unforgettable item mentioned was "sword" or a dagger or a short sword, "evidently" for protection. Peter, now extra vigilant to prove Jesus' prediction of his denials wrong, was sure to have grabbed one of the swords, and it will appear later that night (22:35–38).

Unforgettable from beginning to end.

Questions for Reflection and Application

1. How do kingdom and liberation connect with each other?

2. How does the celebration of Passover set the right backdrop for the events of Jesus' finale in his liberating work?

3. In what ways was the betrayal of Jesus a human plot and in what ways was it a cosmic plot?

4. Think of various ways you have taken Communion or celebrated the Eucharist. What layers of meaning do different approaches give you for understanding this story?

5. What is most unforgettable to you about the story of this night?

FOR FURTHER READING

Lauren F. Winner, *The Dangers of Christian Practice: On Wayward Gifts, Characteristic Damage, and Sin* (New Haven: Yale University Press, 2018).

REDEMPTION REQUEST

Luke 22:39–46

39 Jesus went out as usual to the Mount of Olives, and his disciples
followed him. 40 On reaching the place, he said to them, "Pray that
you will not fall into temptation." 41 He withdrew about a stone's
throw beyond them, knelt down and prayed, 42 "Father, if you are
willing, take this cup from me; yet not my will, but yours be done."
43 An angel from heaven appeared to him and strengthened him.
44 And being in anguish, he prayed more earnestly, and his sweat
was like drops of blood falling to the ground.

45 When he rose from prayer and went back to the disciples,
he found them asleep, exhausted from sorrow. 46 "Why are you
sleeping?" he asked them. "Get up and pray so that you will not fall
into temptation."

One cannot but be overwhelmed by the intensity of that last supper event with so much swirling in and around the upper room. Jesus, knowing the gravity of his kingdom mission's final days, needed to pray so he "went out as usual to the Mount of Olives" with his confused and expectant disciples in tow, all along wondering what would happen next (22:39).

He urges them to pray for themselves—"That you will not fall into temptation" (22:40), which sounds like what Judas was doing at that very moment. But the term behind "temptation" is the same term used in Luke's version of the Lord's prayer (11:4), where it is suggested that it can mean "tribulation" as in God's final testing of the nation. What is more is that the NIV's "fall into" is more than a stretch: the term means "enter into" and not "fall into" (*eiserchomai*). I prefer this translation of what Jesus said twice to them in Gethsemane: "Pray that you not enter into the Test."

Jesus then prays for himself and, surprisingly for most of us, that the Father "take this cup from me." So intimate is his relationship with the Father that he then, in spite of what he has requested, surrenders to the Father's will. The "cup" symbolizes his destiny, which Jesus faces with his eyes open to the horrors of the crucifixion, desertion, as well as the depths of death (22:42) and, so intense is his anguish or agony, Luke tells us he had sweat "like drops of blood falling to the ground" (22:44). Scott Spencer, a specialist on the emotions of Jesus, describes it like this: "intense . . . , soul-wrenching, pore-draining supplication" (Spencer, *Luke,* 566). No wonder the Father sent a comforting angel (22:43).

Though Jesus urged his disciples to pray, they fall asleep "exhausted from sorrow" or asleep "from the pain" they were experiencing from the unforgettable moments of the Passover meal with Jesus' predictions of betrayal, denial, and death (22:45). Jesus' emotion of anguish is paired with the disciples' emotion of intense pain or grief. Frustrated, he does not approve of their sleeping and orders them to get up. Once again, he urges them to pray so they will not "enter into the Test" (22:46).

Questions for Reflection and Application

1. What do you gather from this passage differently when you consider the disciples praying against "temptation" versus praying against "tribulation/testing"?

2. What does the cup symbolize in Jesus' prayer?

3. What is going on emotionally for Jesus in this scene?

4. What is going on emotionally for the disciples?

5. How can this scene be encouraging or instructive for your own emotional life?

REDEMPTION ABUSED

Luke 22:47–23:25

*[47] While he was still speaking a crowd came up, and the man who
was called Judas, one of the Twelve, was leading them. He approached Jesus to kiss him, [48] but Jesus asked him, "Judas, are you
betraying the Son of Man with a kiss?"*

*[49] When Jesus' followers saw what was going to happen, they
said, "Lord, should we strike with our swords?" [50] And one of them
struck the servant of the high priest, cutting off his right ear.*

*[51] But Jesus answered, "No more of this!" And he touched the
man's ear and healed him.*

*[52] Then Jesus said to the chief priests, the officers of the temple
guard, and the elders, who had come for him, "Am I leading a rebellion, that you have come with swords and clubs? [53] Every day I
was with you in the temple courts, and you did not lay a hand on
me. But this is your hour—when darkness reigns."*

*[54] Then seizing him, they led him away and took him into the
house of the high priest. Peter followed at a distance. [55] And when
some there had kindled a fire in the middle of the courtyard and
had sat down together, Peter sat down with them. [56] A servant girl
saw him seated there in the firelight. She looked closely at him and
said, "This man was with him."*

57 But he denied it. "Woman, I don't know him," he said.
58 A little later someone else saw him and said, "You also are
one of them."
"Man, I am not!" Peter replied.
59 About an hour later another asserted, "Certainly this fellow
was with him, for he is a Galilean."
60 Peter replied, "Man, I don't know what you're talking about!"
Just as he was speaking, the rooster crowed. 61 The Lord turned and
looked straight at Peter. Then Peter remembered the word the Lord
had spoken to him: "Before the rooster crows today, you will disown
me three times." 62 And he went outside and wept bitterly.
63 The men who were guarding Jesus began mocking and beating him. 64 They blindfolded him and demanded, "Prophesy! Who
hit you?" 65 And they said many other insulting things to him.
66 At daybreak the council of the elders of the people, both the
chief priests and the teachers of the law, met together, and Jesus
was led before them. 67 "If you are the Messiah," they said, "tell us."
Jesus answered, "If I tell you, you will not believe me,
68 and if I asked you, you would not answer. 69 But from now on,
the Son of Man will be seated at the right hand of the mighty God."
70 They all asked, "Are you then the Son of God?"
He replied, "You say that I am."
71 Then they said, "Why do we need any more testimony? We
have heard it from his own lips."
23:1 Then the whole assembly rose and led him off to Pilate.
2 And they began to accuse him, saying, "We have found this man
subverting our nation. He opposes payment of taxes to Caesar and
claims to be Messiah, a king."
3 So Pilate asked Jesus, "Are you the king of the Jews?"
"You have said so," Jesus replied.
4 Then Pilate announced to the chief priests and the crowd, "I
find no basis for a charge against this man."
5 But they insisted, "He stirs up the people all over Judea by
his teaching. He started in Galilee and has come all the way here."

*6 On hearing this, Pilate asked if the man was a Galilean.
7 When he learned that Jesus was under Herod's jurisdiction, he
sent him to Herod, who was also in Jerusalem at that time.*

*8 When Herod saw Jesus, he was greatly pleased, because for
a long time he had been wanting to see him. From what he had
heard about him, he hoped to see him perform a sign of some sort.
9 He plied him with many questions, but Jesus gave him no answer.
10 The chief priests and the teachers of the law were standing there,
vehemently accusing him. 11 Then Herod and his soldiers ridiculed
and mocked him. Dressing him in an elegant robe, they sent him
back to Pilate. 12 That day Herod and Pilate became friends—
before this they had been enemies.*

*13 Pilate called together the chief priests, the rulers and the
people, 14 and said to them, "You brought me this man as one who
was inciting the people to rebellion. I have examined him in your
presence and have found no basis for your charges against him.
15 Neither has Herod, for he sent him back to us; as you can see, he
has done nothing to deserve death. 16 Therefore, I will punish him
and then release him."*

*18 But the whole crowd shouted, "Away with this man! Release
Barabbas to us!" 19 (Barabbas had been thrown into prison for an
insurrection in the city, and for murder.)*

*20 Wanting to release Jesus, Pilate appealed to them again.
21 But they kept shouting, "Crucify him! Crucify him!"*

*22 For the third time he spoke to them: "Why? What crime
has this man committed? I have found in him no grounds for
the death penalty. Therefore I will have him punished and then
release him."*

*23 But with loud shouts they insistently demanded that he be
crucified, and their shouts prevailed. 24 So Pilate decided to grant
their demand. 25 He released the man who had been thrown into
prison for insurrection and murder, the one they asked for, and
surrendered Jesus to their will.*

If Jesus is the Messiah, God's Son and the people's Savior, then the separable incidents of today's passage are nothing less than abuse of God's agent of redemption. If Jesus is the Messiah, the actions and results of these various stages of investigation are an injustice. And hear me on this one, if Jesus is the Messiah, there is especially no reason to demonize or degrade any of these people. They are not evil; they collectively enacted a social injustice. Guilty? Yes. Evil? No. Protecting the city? Yes. If true, Jesus was abused relationally, physically, verbally, socially, familial-ly, and legally—by Judas, by Peter, by Jewish officials, by the guards, and by the Roman appointed authorities, Pilate and Herod Antipas. The exposure and rejection are so comprehensive one must see that Jesus was utterly alone before God and utterly rejected by the authorities.

God, in spite of the irony and the paradox of Jesus' rejection, turns the injustice of humans into justice-making. Justification undoes, then, both the acts of the unjust and the injustice itself. God turns rejection into redemption and reconciliation and overcomes the wrath of humans with the love of God. The beauty of God's power to unmake what humans make should not lead us to minimize the injustice or the brutality of these events. Rather, God's work on the other side gives us eyes to see the depth of human sin and the human condition. The rejections are not just by the Jewish leaders or by the Roman leaders, but also by two followers of Jesus with whom Luke begins today's passage.

Judas and Peter

All the Gospels predict and document the betrayal by Judas surrounded by the representatives of power in Jerusalem. Luke puts it like this: "a crowd came up, and the man who was called Judas, one of the Twelve, was leading them" (22:47). He did so with a kiss. An act of intimate friendship becomes a betrayer's means of identification.

I now reuse, with only minor edits, what I wrote in the guide for the Gospel of John about betrayal. It's a bit too easy for us to counter our intuitions by saying, *Well, the betrayal was all part of God's plan*. It is one thing to think God turned nightmare into Easter, but it is another to brush off the horrors of betrayal, a betrayal that led to a brutal, public crucifixion, by claiming this is how God works in the world. No, by all means, we must learn to see the betrayal as a diabolical act perpetrated by a greedy man who sold the Savior for money.

Jesus felt it. Betrayal assaults the heart and soul of one who trusts. Painful disagreements and group-dividing decisions do not always rise to the level of betrayals. Betrayals suddenly erase intimacies and love and collapse the foundations of relationships. Betrayals destroy the moral fibers of trust. One should never dismiss a betrayal by minimizing the act or the wounds. Betrayals require emotional strength to face, to endure, and to process. Betrayals may be forgiven, but regaining trust requires time. Here is an abstract of a technical study of the psychological impact of betrayal:

> Betrayal is the sense of being harmed by the intentional actions or omissions of a trusted person. The most common forms of betrayal are harmful disclosures of confidential information, disloyalty, infidelity, dishonesty. They can be traumatic and cause considerable distress. The effects of betrayal include shock, loss and grief, morbid pre-occupation, damaged self-esteem, self-doubting, anger. Not infrequently they produce life-altering changes. The effects of a catastrophic betrayal are most relevant for anxiety disorders, and

> OCD and PTSD in particular. Betrayal can cause mental contamination, and the betrayer commonly becomes a source of contamination (S. Rachman, "Betrayal: A Psychological Analysis").

Betrayal today is betrayal then, so this modern analysis describes the betrayal by Judas. Jesus was betrayed but so too were the other eleven and the various circles of Jesus' followers, not least his mother and brothers. They all *felt* betrayal.

What to make of the dagger? Jesus' words back in the upper room were not metaphors, that's for sure. Nor was the way of the sword the way of Jesus. Luke, perhaps out of kindness to Peter, does not mention that Peter did the deed (John 18:10), but he did. Jesus seems to say, "Let this arrest happen," and then healed the man (Luke 22:51). Jesus abruptly counters the choice of Peter to wield a dagger when he queries the authorities with a penetrating question: "Am I leading a rebellion" that you need all your weapons? Why did you not nab me in the temple courts this week? Jesus answers his own question with an apocalyptic answer ("this is your hour") and a cosmic image ("when darkness" has its authority; 22:52–53 [NIV has "reigns," but the word is "authority"]). The darkness includes Judas' penetrating the inner ring in Jerusalem.

Nabbed, Jesus was led into the high priest's residence (22:54). Peter followed, and from that distance he did exactly what Jesus predicted: he denied association with, and broke allegiance to, Jesus. Were we not so familiar with the story we'd find it heinous. Only a thin line separates Judas's betrayal and Peter's denials. The words of Peter look like this: (1) "Woman, I don't know him," (2) "Man, I am not!" and (3) "Man, I don't know what you're talking about!" (22:57, 58, 60). He denies association with Jesus and with other Galileans who followed Jesus.

Luke masters the moment with two dramatic effects: instantly, "as he was speaking, the rooster crowed," and then Jesus "turned and looked straight at Peter" (22:60–61). The NIV's "looked straight at" brings front stage the directness of the term Luke chose to use; it's as if Jesus looked into Peter. Peter's bitter weeping contrasts with Judas's non-response. Judas disappears at this point from Luke's Gospel because he will describe Judas's demise in the first chapter of Acts (1:18–20).

The Guards and the Inner Ring

Not much is said about the men guarding Jesus but what is said matters: they abused him socially ("mocking," "insulting") and physically ("beating" 22:63, 65). Ridiculing his reputation as a prophet and making him more vulnerable and unable to look into the eyes of others for support, they covered his eyes and then demanded he lean into his supernatural knowledge to tell them who struck him (22:64).

Before Jesus is led to the procurator Pilate and the tetrarch Herod Antipas, there's a huddle of the "elders" and the "chief priests and teachers of the law" so they can delineate specific allegations against Jesus (22:66). Then Jesus is brought before them and they go for the allegation they know will land: "If you are the Messiah, tell us" (22:67).

Jesus won't play well in their Yes or No drama. His answer begins with an evasion but then jumps lanes to his ultimate vindication. So, the evasion works with what we call today confirmation bias—they will believe what fits their existing beliefs (and biases), which cannot accept that he is Messiah. So Jesus says, "If I say to you, you will never trust," and then, "If I ask, you will never respond" (my translations; 22:68). His words have a tinge of open-endedness that puts the weight on "you will never trust" and "never respond."

Like his questions of the other authorities during the week, his questions provoke dead silences. It is what Jesus does next that seized the attention of his interrogators and gave them the words they needed for their filed charges: "But from now on, the Son of Man will be seated at the right hand of the mighty God" (22:69). He hereby claims not only to be the son of man of Daniel 7, but he makes it clear his vindication and enthronement before the Ancient of Days is on the verge of happening right now.

No wonder they shift terms without changing senses. Their "Are you the Son of God?" (22:70) means "Are you the Messiah, the king of Israel?" His response is only slightly less evasive: "You say that I am." They got what they wanted out of him (22:71). They believe he has claimed to be Messiah, and don't forget this means he's the king of Israel. The scene depicts a huddle of leaders working to get the right words out of the man, even if Jesus did not say what they wanted him to say, at least not directly. And why would he? They cart him off to the Rome-based leaders next because their powers are restricted by the Roman leaders.

The Procurator and the Tetrarch and the Procurator

Pilate and then Herod Antipas and then Pilate again.

First, Pilate. The first round sounds like a Sanhedrin ("whole assembly" in the NIV) investigation of three allegations: "subverting our nation," resisting "payment of taxes to Caesar," and he "claims to be Messiah, a king" (23:2). Pilate avoids the Jewish language about Messiah and directly asks Jesus to say whether he is "king of the Jews" or not, and Jesus does what Jesus does. He says, "You say" (23:3; my translation), which is more evasive than the NIV's "You have said so." Jesus wants Pilate to carry the weight of the decision. In a leap of logic, Pilate, interpreting Jesus' words as a denial, finds Jesus innocent (23:4). The "chief priests and the crowd" will have none of it, so they move from the presented allegation to reports that Jesus is a Galilean rebel, a false prophet, an anarchist, or something of that order (23:5). Galilee had a reputation for some as a place for rebels, so Pilate asks Jesus if he's a Galilean, which permits him then to transfer Jesus to Herod Antipas, the tetrarch over Galilee (23:6–7).

Second, Herod Antipas. Having heard all about Jesus from others up in Galilee, he pesters Jesus with all sorts of questions and hopes to see him do some of his supposed miracles. (It feels like Moses and Aaron before Pharaoh a bit.) Jesus is Jesus and refuses to answer his questions (and we don't know exactly why). More allegations lead to another leap of logic on Herod's part who, with his "soldiers ridiculed and mocked" Jesus. They outfit him with royal robes and send him back to Pilate, which—in another leap of logic—leads to their permanent friendship (22:8–12).

Third, Pilate again. Instead of interrogating Jesus again, this time, uncharacteristic of a man with his power, Pilate takes a poll of his audience, explaining that their charge is "rebellion." Pilate admits neither he nor Herod find a basis for their allegations. Frankly, even a casual reading of this passage evokes a Pilate who just doesn't care. Pilate did not like or get along with the Jewish authorities, so his viewpoint that Jesus has done nothing wrong may well be a plot to subvert their authority. So he proposes to "punish him," which would involve an abusive lashing, and then "release him" (22:13–16). Such a decision creates a foment from the "whole crowd" who want Jesus put down and the rebel-murderer Barabbas released. Ironically, "Barabbas" means "son of the father." Pilate appeals to them for reason but they want Jesus crucified, to which he says in effect "For what?" and they push back even more. The tragedy of injustice is a crowd overcoming law in the highest court in the land of Israel. This back-and-forth is not only unusual in a court scene like this, but it virtually diminishes all of Pilate's power.

"So Pilate decided to grant their demand," and "surrendered Jesus to their will" (22:25).

Questions for Reflection and Application

1. In what ways can this passage be understood as a narrative of abuses against Jesus?

2. How does justice undo injustice in God's plan?

3. How does Pilate respond to Jesus and the allegations against him? How does Herod?

4. What is the role and impact of betrayal in this narrative?

5. Have you ever experienced betrayal from a trusted friend or authority figure? Have you ever betrayed a loved one? Who do you most relate to in these scenes?

FOR FURTHER READING

S. Rachman, "Betrayal: A Psychological Analysis," *Behaviour Research and Therapy* 48.4 (April, 2010): 304–11. @ doi: 10.1016/j.brat.2009.12.002. Epub 2009 Dec 24. PMID: 20035927.

REDEMPTION CRUCIFIED AND BURIED

Luke 23:26–56

*26 As the soldiers led him away, they seized Simon from Cyrene,
who was on his way in from the country, and put the cross on him
and made him carry it behind Jesus. 27 A large number of people
followed him, including women who mourned and wailed for him.
28 Jesus turned and said to them, "Daughters of Jerusalem, do not
weep for me; weep for yourselves and for your children. 29 For the
time will come when you will say, 'Blessed are the childless wom-
en, the wombs that never bore and the breasts that never nursed!'
30 Then*

" 'they will say to the mountains, "Fall on us!"
and to the hills, "Cover us!" '

*31 For if people do these things when the tree is green, what will
happen when it is dry?"*

*32 Two other men, both criminals, were also led out with him to
be executed. 33 When they came to the place called the Skull, they
crucified him there, along with the criminals—one on his right, the
other on his left. 34 Jesus said, "Father, forgive them, for they do*

not know what they are doing." And they divided up his clothes by
casting lots.

35 The people stood watching, and the rulers even sneered at
him. They said, "He saved others; let him save himself if he is God's
Messiah, the Chosen One."

36 The soldiers also came up and mocked him. They offered
him wine vinegar 37 and said, "If you are the king of the Jews, save
yourself."

38 There was a written notice above him, which read: THIS IS
THE KING OF THE JEWS.

39 One of the criminals who hung there hurled insults at him:
"Aren't you the Messiah? Save yourself and us!"

40 But the other criminal rebuked him. "Don't you fear God,"
he said, "since you are under the same sentence? 41 We are punished
justly, for we are getting what our deeds deserve. But this man has
done nothing wrong."

42 Then he said, "Jesus, remember me when you come into your
kingdom."

43 Jesus answered him, "Truly I tell you, today you will be with
me in paradise."

44 It was now about noon, and darkness came over the whole
land until three in the afternoon, 45 for the sun stopped shining. And
the curtain of the temple was torn in two. 46 Jesus called out with a
loud voice, "Father, into your hands I commit my spirit." When he
had said this, he breathed his last.

47 The centurion, seeing what had happened, praised God and
said, "Surely this was a righteous man." 48 When all the people
who had gathered to witness this sight saw what took place, they
beat their breasts and went away. 49 But all those who knew him,
including the women who had followed him from Galilee, stood at
a distance, watching these things.

50 Now there was a man named Joseph, a member of the
Council, a good and upright man, 51 who had not consented to their

*decision and action. He came from the Judean town of Arimathea,
and he himself was waiting for the kingdom of God.* [52] *Going to
Pilate, he asked for Jesus' body.* [53] *Then he took it down, wrapped
it in linen cloth and placed it in a tomb cut in the rock, one in
which no one had yet been laid.* [54] *It was Preparation Day, and the
Sabbath was about to begin.*

[55] *The women who had come with Jesus from Galilee followed
Joseph and saw the tomb and how his body was laid in it.* [56] *Then
they went home and prepared spices and perfumes. But they rested
on the Sabbath in obedience to the commandment.*

If you are tempted to dive in with my reflections and skip the reading of the Bible verses, I ask you to resist the temptation, roll your eyes up, and read the text from top to bottom first. There is no substitute for reading and knowing the story of our Lord's crucifixion and burial. It is our story, a tragic injustice turned into a glorious act of justice and vindication. Our story is one in which the hero Jesus dies but is raised from among the dead. Each element of the story has to be told for Easter to make sense. Luke portrays four basic elements in today's passage: the walk to the place of the Skull, the crucifixion of Jesus, the death of Jesus, and the burial of Jesus. He fills in details as he was able to determine them, but nothing replaces the major elements: death by crucifixion and burial.

What could the followers of Jesus have made of these unforgettable, shocking, and tragic events? They had hopes that the kingdom would come when Jesus rode into Jerusalem, but one event after another jolted them from side to side as if they were back on a boat on a stormy Sea of Galilee. They were now tossed from the boat, lost at sea, and without words to express their wonderings. We join them now in those last events.

To the Skull

Luke is a master of the short vignette of otherwise unknown characters. Here we meet the conscripted "Simon from Cyrene" (modern Libya) and the weeping "daughters of Jerusalem" who, though wailing over the decision of Pilate, are given a unique word of warning from Jesus. Simon carries the crossbeam of the cross because Jesus has wilted under the physical and social abuse. The wailing women are told by Jesus *don't cry for me, Jerusalem,* but to weep for themselves and their children because, as he told them all in parables and direct warnings, the city will be destroyed (23:30). To which he adds a riddle-like word: "if people do these things when the tree is green, what will happen when it is dry?" (23:31). I like this explanation: "If the innocent Jesus [green wood] can be killed, how much easier it will be for the guilty Jerusalem [dry wood] to go up in flames" (Levine-Witherington, *Luke,* 630). Or perhaps it's even more directly for these women: "if your children [green wood] can be kindled, how much more when they age and turn into firebrands opposing Rome [dry wood]" (N.T. Wright, *Jesus and the Victory of God,* 567–570). Jesus' own death then anticipates the horror that awaits the children of these women.

Crucified

The facts are simply stated: by Roman-appointed officials Jesus was crucified, most probably on a cross as we know one, probably nailed to the wood, and his death involved a slow suffocation. "Two other men, both criminals" were "executed" alongside Jesus. The location is "the place called the Skull" (Aramaic *Golgotha,* Latin *Calvary*), most likely now under the Church of the Holy Sepulchre. At the cross

Jesus continues to be the agent of God's holistic redemption as Jesus pronounced forgiveness on "them," and we cannot be sure who "them" is, "for they do not know what they are doing" (23:32–34).

Humiliated, Jesus observes as his clothing was divided between those who wanted them, and this occurs prior to his death in full view of the one crucified. One group mocked him as one who claimed to be able to save but couldn't save himself (23:35), and another group offered him "wine vinegar" and repeated the line about not being able to save himself.

The titulus above him, which records the reason for the crucifixion, returns to the Messiah query posed by both of the powers at work in Jerusalem (22:67; 23:3)—"THIS IS THE KING OF THE JEWS" (23:38). One criminal trades in the same language: "if you are the king of the Jews, save yourself" while the other, reverent before God and repentant for his actions, looks at Jesus, pleading for him to "remember me when you come into your kingdom" (23:39–41). Jesus, being Jesus to the end, assures the man he will be with him in paradise (23:43).

Crucifixions were exploited by the powerful as a deterrent to further crime, but sadism, revenge, brutality, and grisly displays of power generated this form of punishment. Crucifixions and executions, designed as public theater, attracted throngs of people. Luke perhaps thinks of it as theater (23:48: NIV translates *theōrian* with "sight" but could be translated with "spectacle" or less dramatically with "observance"). Crucifixions publicly shamed and degraded the victim and all who knew the victim. The tortures of crucifixion outstrip any sense of justice, leaving all bystanders stunned at what humans can do to humans, which is why some returned home pounding their chests (23:48).

DEAD

The facts of the story make up the story as they fit into a plot. From "about noon until three in the afternoon" there is a cosmic shadow "over the whole land." The shadow is matched by a schism in the temple's curtain. Both of which anticipate the voice of Jesus who commits himself into the "hands" of his Father, and he dies (23:44–46).

Three responses are recorded by Luke. First, either the cosmic signs or the voice of Jesus, or both, impress a Roman "centurion" so much he offers nothing less than a confession: he "praised God" and declared that Jesus was "a righteous man" (23:47), which is a Roman man declaring Jesus innocent, the verdict against him unjust, and his relationship with God right. Second, Luke tells us the crowd witnessing Jesus' hideous crucifixion "beat their breasts" before returning home (23:48). This act indicates grief and even perhaps repentance for the complicity in such a barbaric deed. And third, the followers of Jesus, either out of fear of being too closely associated with the one crucified between criminals or to avoid having to see the gruesome affair up close, remain at a distance "watching these things" as witnesses (23:49).

BURIED

At least one member of the original group, usually called Sanhedrin (22:66), by the name "Joseph," was from the village called "Arimathea." He was both *tov,* or good, and law-observant, or righteous. He was plugged into the kingdom vision of Jesus and was "waiting," like Simeon and Anna, "for the kingdom of God" (23:50–51). Out of respect for Jesus he requests from Pilate permission to bury Jesus in a brand new "tomb cut in the rock" (23:53). It was Friday, called here the "Preparation Day" for the Sabbath, and leaving a body unburied was irreverent.

Some women from Galilee were watching and so knew where Jesus' body was entombed. To ready his body they went home, observed the Sabbath rest, and "prepared spices and perfumes" for the corpse of Jesus (23:55–56). Normally the body was prepared with spices prior to burial. It is possible Luke simply failed to tell us they prepared spices *and then returned to the tomb to anoint the body,* and then rested on Sabbath. But Luke is about to tell us in 24:1 they planned on anointing the body on Sunday morning.

Questions for Reflection and Application

1. How does God use the injustice of Jesus' crucifixion to work cosmic justice?

2. How does Luke present Jesus' death as a theatrical spectacle?

3. What are the various responses of the witnesses to the crucifixion?

4. What is the role and importance of women here?

5. How does this story strike you anew on this reading?

FOR FURTHER READING

N.T. Wright, *Jesus and the Victory of God* (Minneapolis: Fortress, 1996).

REDEMPTION RAISED

Luke 24:1–12

1 On the first day of the week, very early in the morning, the wom-
en took the spices they had prepared and went to the tomb. 2 They
found the stone rolled away from the tomb, 3 but when they entered,
they did not find the body of the Lord Jesus. 4 While they were
wondering about this, suddenly two men in clothes that gleamed
like lightning stood beside them. 5 In their fright the women bowed
down with their faces to the ground, but the men said to them, "Why
do you look for the living among the dead? 6 He is not here; he has
risen! Remember how he told you, while he was still with you in
Galilee: 7 'The Son of Man must be delivered over to the hands of
sinners, be crucified and on the third day be raised again.' " 8 Then
they remembered his words.

9 When they came back from the tomb, they told all these things
to the Eleven and to all the others. 10 It was Mary Magdalene,
Joanna, Mary the mother of James, and the others with them who
told this to the apostles. 11 But they did not believe the women, be-
cause their words seemed to them like nonsense. 12 Peter, however,
got up and ran to the tomb. Bending over, he saw the strips of linen
lying by themselves, and he went away, wondering to himself what
had happened.

Something beyond comprehension happens to the crucifixion of Jesus when it gets turned into "Good" Friday. That something is the resurrection, which transforms crucifixion from hideous injustice into redemptive event. That transformation does not undo the hideousness or permit us to put paid to the cross. No, resurrection makes the crucifixion all the more unjust and hideous—and redemptive!

The best words of the Gospel of Luke are, "On the first day of the week" because I know those words roll the stone and reveal the empty tomb. Let's get the facts before us: they return to the tomb, the stone is rolled away, the tomb is empty, and they encounter "two men" in dazzling clothing, and they are called "a vision of angels" in the next passage (24:23). They were overawed so much they fell to the ground where they hear, "Why do you look for the living among the dead?" Whaaaaa?!?! The men keep talking, saying, "he has risen!" and then they remind the women what Jesus had said. "Remember . . . on the third day be raised again" (24:1–7).

These women then return to tell the "Eleven" and "all the others" (24:9). Women witnesses, beginning with Mary Magdalene and including Joanna and Mary the mother of James—and "the others with them" (24:10), that is, a retinue of women become the vanguard of the Easter gospel about Jesus. The apostles don't trust the vanguard (24:11), not because they heard it from women (Levine-Witherington, *Luke*, 653–654) but because dead bodies don't come back to life. Peter, worked up about their words, hightails it to the tomb where he finds "strips of linen." He exits the tomb "wondering to himself what had happened" (24:12).

What happens is God raised Jesus from among the dead.

When I'm asked about the best evidence for the resurrection, I offer the following kinds of "evidence": (1) *objective*: the tomb was empty; (2) *eyewitnesses:* many claimed to have seen Jesus in the earliest days after the crucifixion; (3) *multiple witnesses*: all four Gospels record stories about the resurrection; (4) *Roman*: a decree was later given by a Roman emperor about Galilee, that capital punishment would be enacted for anyone guilty of tomb spoilation, and this in response no doubt to the many claiming for their growing faith that Jesus had been raised from the dead; (5) *friendly fire*: none of the opponents of the earliest Christians produced a rotting corpse to prove Jesus had not been raised, and had there been one they would have produced it; (6) *experiential*: millions witness to their own experience of knowing Jesus as one who is alive speaking to them; and (7) *Jesus*: he said he'd be raised, which is what Luke tells us in this passage (24:6–8).

I believe.

Questions for Reflection and Application

1. How does our knowledge of resurrection transform our understanding of the cross?

2. How do the female disciples factor into the narrative?

3. What evidence do we have for the reality of Jesus' resurrection?

4. Do you ever struggle to believe that Jesus truly rose from the dead? Why or why not?

5. What experiences have you had in your life with Jesus that compel your belief?

REDEMPTION APPEARS

Luke 24:13–49

[13] Now that same day two of them were going to a village called Emmaus, about seven miles from Jerusalem. [14] They were talking with each other about everything that had happened. [15] As they talked and discussed these things with each other, Jesus himself came up and walked along with them; [16] but they were kept from recognizing him.

[17] He asked them, "What are you discussing together as you walk along?"

They stood still, their faces downcast.

[18] One of them, named Cleopas, asked him, "Are you the only one visiting Jerusalem who does not know the things that have happened there in these days?"

[19] "What things?" he asked.

"About Jesus of Nazareth," they replied. "He was a prophet, powerful in word and deed before God and all the people. [20] The chief priests and our rulers handed him over to be sentenced to death, and they crucified him; [21] but we had hoped that he was the one who was going to redeem Israel. And what is more, it is the third day since all this took place. [22] In addition, some of our women amazed us. They went to the tomb early this morning [23] but didn't find his body. They came and told us that they had seen a vision of angels, who said he was alive. [24] Then some of our companions

went to the tomb and found it just as the women had said, but they did not see Jesus."

25 He said to them, "How foolish you are, and how slow to believe all that the prophets have spoken! 26 Did not the Messiah have to suffer these things and then enter his glory?" 27 And beginning with Moses and all the Prophets, he explained to them what was said in all the Scriptures concerning himself.

28 As they approached the village to which they were going, Jesus continued on as if he were going farther. 29 But they urged him strongly, "Stay with us, for it is nearly evening; the day is almost over." So he went in to stay with them.

30 When he was at the table with them, he took bread, gave thanks, broke it and began to give it to them. 31 Then their eyes were opened and they recognized him, and he disappeared from their sight. 32 They asked each other, "Were not our hearts burning within us while he talked with us on the road and opened the Scriptures to us?"

33 They got up and returned at once to Jerusalem. There they found the Eleven and those with them, assembled together 34 and saying, "It is true! The Lord has risen and has appeared to Simon." 35 Then the two told what had happened on the way, and how Jesus was recognized by them when he broke the bread.

36 While they were still talking about this, Jesus himself stood among them and said to them, "Peace be with you."

37 They were startled and frightened, thinking they saw a ghost. 38 He said to them, "Why are you troubled, and why do doubts rise in your minds? 39 Look at my hands and my feet. It is I myself! Touch me and see; a ghost does not have flesh and bones, as you see I have."

40 When he had said this, he showed them his hands and feet. 41 And while they still did not believe it because of joy and amazement, he asked them, "Do you have anything here to eat?" 42 They gave him a piece of broiled fish, 43 and he took it and ate it in their presence.

[44] He said to them, "This is what I told you while I was still with you: Everything must be fulfilled that is written about me in the Law of Moses, the Prophets and the Psalms."

[45] Then he opened their minds so they could understand the Scriptures. [46] He told them, "This is what is written: The Messiah will suffer and rise from the dead on the third day, [47] and repentance for the forgiveness of sins will be preached in his name to all nations, beginning at Jerusalem. [48] You are witnesses of these things. [49] I am going to send you what my Father has promised; but stay in the city until you have been clothed with power from on high."

Jesus was raised from among the dead in the flesh, with a body, and not just as a soul or in the spirit. The Christian witness about the resurrection and eternal life is not, as Tom Wright quippingly has said often, a belief in "life after death" but in bodily "life after life after death" (Wright, *Surprised by Hope*, 148–152). Christians are not just alive after they die, which is true, but they have an embodied life after surviving death. Today's passage from Luke 24 time after time reveals an embodied Jesus. He was raised not into some general life-after-death sphere but through death into a glorified new body that is both fully a body and a body fit for new creation.

This chapter makes the gospel what the gospel is: good news. The resurrection of Jesus, to remind ourselves, flips the script from a tragic, unjust death to a tragic, unjust death that launches new creation. Two of the first to experience the new world Jesus brings were on a road to Emmaus, and their story is one of the most favorite stories in the Bible.

To Two from Emmaus

On the road "two of them," and we don't know who "them" is, but it includes a man named Cleopas[1] and another person, who could have been his wife. So, it's two of those in Jerusalem who observed what happened to Jesus with a keen interest in who he was. The NIV's "talking" and "what had happened" (24:14) make a little more plain what Luke says in more sophisticated language. Perhaps we can translate "sharing with" what had "coalesced." They are going back and forth with one another in a deep communion that involves some disagreement when someone suddenly joins them in their journey to their home in Emmaus (24:15). For God's own purposes, "they were kept from recognizing him" (24:16; look at 9:45 and 18:34). We can't know for sure, but God's hiding Jesus' identity from them seems to permit them to be drawn into a deeper faith. Jesus asks them about their topic of conversation and they, devastated, express surprise.

So they give a recap of the Gospel of Luke: Jesus was a "prophet, powerful in word and deed before God and all the people" (24:19) but the powers of Jerusalem handed him over to crucifixion. That shattered their hope "that he was the one who was going to redeem Israel" (24:21). They bring up "third day" to echo the predictions of Jesus about his resurrection, and then they support his prediction with the reports of the women and some who had been with them (24:24).

On the verge of telling us their back-and-forth was about whether or not Jesus had been raised, Jesus, without identifying himself, interrupts them and rebukes them for not having paid sufficient attention to what *the prophets had said about the Messiah,* which included that the Messiah would both "suffer" and only "then enter his glory." Since they didn't have the skill set yet to perceive this in their own Scriptures, he went through the Bible explaining how it spoke of himself, though he must not have said it quite that directly (24:25–27). The road trip arrives at Emmaus, they invite Jesus to overnight with them—a very Jewish act of hospitality—and so he stays.

Not only stays, but he makes himself the host when they are at the table where "he took bread, gave thanks, broke it and began to give it to them"—sounds like the feeding stories, sounds like the last supper—and "then their eyes were opened and they recognized him" (24:30—31). At the table with Jesus, in his way of praying and cracking the (flat)bread and distributing it, he was suddenly recognized.

Then—of all things—he disappears. All alone at the table, the two, and not saying one thing about Jesus' sudden disappearance as if it were common experience, realized their hearts were aflame with the truths of God, not just at the Table, but especially in his exposition of Scripture (24:32). Jesus was a stranger, then a prophet, then an interpreter, then a host, and then an interpreter of Scripture for them.

Like the women, they have to tell the Eleven that they had seen Jesus and that he was "alive," and that means he's got a living, raised body, and that they did not recognize him until he became the host at their table (24:33–35).

To Thirteen Plus in Jerusalem

The two from Emmaus are in Jerusalem with the Eleven with others (24:33) when, all of a sudden, the disappeared Jesus appeared "among them." This kind of materiality both transcends our embodied life and points us to the kind of body we will have in the kingdom of God. Jesus speaks words of peace, words we utter each Sunday: "Peace be with you" (24:36).

Again with slightly raised vocabulary, Luke tells us they were terrified and over-awed because they wondered if they had not just seen a "spirit" (NIV has "ghost"). He recognizes their fear, so he offers them a physical experience of an actual raised body—give that some thought. "Touch me and see" because spirits like that don't have bodies (24:37–39). There is no record anyone reached out and touched him. (Would you have?)

In fact, they were so bedazzled by this sudden presence of Jesus they "still did not believe"! What happens next is for the thirteen-plus in the room. He asked for food, they gave him food, and he ate "a piece of broiled fish," and he did so "in their presence" so they could see for themselves he was not only raised but he was a body (24:41–43).

As he did with the two from Emmaus, he now does for all them. He taught them the Bible's fundamental storyline that ran from Genesis 1:1 to Jesus—the one from Galilee, the one who did miracles and taught in parables, the one who traveled to Jerusalem where he challenged the leaders and was crucified, the one who was raised, and the one who just ate in their presence (24:44). Which he now explains to them more than he had done on the road to Emmaus. As he had opened their eyes he now "opens their minds" to comprehend the sacred writings by teaching them the fundamental storyline: the Messiah will come, will suffer, and will rise from the dead. The only genuine response to the Messiah is "repentance," and those who repent will experience a holistic redemption that is expressed as "forgiveness of sins." This storyline, this summons to repentance, and this holistic redemption is for them to gospel "to the nations, beginning at Jerusalem" (24:47; cf. Acts 1:8). The thirteen have a calling in life: they are "witnesses," which means in word and deed they are to exhibit and explain Jesus to all. The promise, and here Jesus in Jerusalem itself promises "what my Father has promised," and Luke, knowing what he was about to write in Acts 2, anticipates witnesses empowered by the Jesus-sent Holy Spirit (Luke 24:48). So, he tells them, stay right here until it happens.

Little did they know.

Questions for Reflection and Application

1. Why does it matter that Jesus was raised with a body and that we will be raised with new bodies?

2. Compare Luke 24:16 with 9:45 and 18:34. What similarities do you see in the passages?

3. Scott Spencer observes the two disciples from Emmaus moving from hopelessness to heart-slowness to heartburn (Spencer, *Luke*, 619–623). When have you experienced similar progressions in yourself as you learn the story of Jesus?

4. Do you think you would have reached out and touched the risen body of Jesus if given the chance? Why or why not?

5. How does the summary of the Scriptures here at the end function as a complete message that can be gospeled to others? How can you use this message to gospel people today?

REDEMPTION ASCENDED

Luke 24:50–53

*50 When he had led them out to the vicinity of Bethany, he lifted
up his hands and blessed them. 51 While he was blessing them, he
left them and was taken up into heaven. 52 Then they worshiped
him and returned to Jerusalem with great joy. 53 And they stayed
continually at the temple, praising God.*

The gospel biography of Luke tells the full story of the life of Jesus and cannot be reduced either to his teaching or to his death. It includes his earthly ministry, from birth to baptism to preaching and teaching and doing miracles to Jerusalem's tragic events that are turned on their head by the resurrection. But it also includes his ascension, and Luke provides two accounts of the ascension, both here and in Acts 1:9–11.

In Bethany

The ascension is surrounded by Jesus' blessing because he knows they will need that blessing in their mission. Before he ascends, he blesses them with God's redemptive blessings.

While blessing them, he parted from them and was carried up or lifted up "into heaven," to be at the right hand of the Father.

In Jerusalem

The ascension is followed, not by fear or by sorrow but by worship, joy, temple presence, and praise. Luke here sets us up for Acts 1's reprisal and Acts 2's Pentecost gift of the Spirit to launch the holistic redemption mission of the apostles Peter and Paul. Just like Jesus.

Questions for Reflection and Application

1. What do you think is significant about the disciples' "great joy"?

2. Which events should be included in a full telling of the story of Jesus?

3. What do you think the contents of Jesus' blessing might have been?

4. Look at Acts 1:9-11. What are the similarities and differences between the ascension accounts?

5. As this study concludes, what has Luke told us about who Jesus is?

NOTES

Chapter 6: Redemption's Son

1. The census mentioned in Luke 2:1–3 creates tension with the historical record since Quirinius, the governor who supervised the census, did not become governor until 6 AD, at which time he did require a census. There is no solution to this problem.

Chapter 7: Two More Redemption Witnesses

1. An observation to keep in mind always when purification comes up: most people were impure most of the time. Impurity was ritual, not moral; impurity was not sin but made one unfit for temple access.

Chapter 10: Redemption and the Son of God

1. The word "son" appears only in 3:23 (for Jesus); all the others in the NIV are implied and filled in by the translators. The Greek text is one long series of "of's": of Joseph . . . of Heli, of Matthat, etc.

Chapter 11: Redemption through the Wilderness

1. The Hebrew term *ha-satanas,* which we translate "Satan," was translated into Greek with *diabolos,* which we translate into English as "devil." Both the Hebrew and Greek terms mean "accuser."

Chapter 17: Redemption's Job Description

1. This scroll is designated as 4Q521, or Qumran Cave 4, item 521.

Chapter 18: Responses to Redemption

1. Every time Mary appears with "Magdalene" it could be translated "*the* Magdalene." It is possible, but by no means certain, that this could mean "the magnificent" or "the tower."

Chapter 23: Redemption Challenges Disciples

1. For discussion, see https://quoteinvestigator.com/2017/09/22/bible/#f+16920+1+5.

Chapter 24: Redemption's Agents Expand

1. http://www.earlychristianwritings.com/text/didache-roberts.html

Chapter 27: Redemption Praying

1. http://www.earlychristianwritings.com/text/didache-roberts.html
2. Everything in this parabolic story hangs on the meaning of "impudence," one viable translation of *anaideia*. The term can mean "shamelessness" but not "persistence" or "avoidance of shame." It counters friendship in this verse.

Chapter 28: Redemption's Oppositions

1. Baal-zebub, which occurs in some manuscripts, means "lord of the flies" and was ridicule of the god of Ekron in 2 Kings 1:2.

Chapter 50: Redemption Appears

1. Perhaps a variant spelling of Clopas, who is mentioned in John 19:25. If true, it is likely the other person with Cleopas was Mary, his wife.

New Testament Everyday Bible Study Series

In the **New Testament Everyday Bible Study Series**, widely respected biblical scholar Scot McKnight combines interpretive insights with pastoral wisdom for all the books of the New Testament.

Each volume provides:

- Original Meaning. Brief, precise expositions of the biblical text and offers a clear focus for the central message of each passage.
- Fresh Interpretation. Brings the passage alive with fresh images and what it means to follow King Jesus.
- Practical Application. Biblical connections and questions for reflection and application for each passage.

— AVAILABLE IN THE SERIES —

James and Galatians

Acts

Philippians and 1 & 2 Thessalonians

John

HarperChristian Resources

The Blue Parakeet

Rethinking How You Read the Bible

Scot McKnight, author of
The Jesus Creed

Why Can't I Just Be a Christian?

Parakeets make delightful pets. We cage them or clip their wings to keep them where we want them. Scot McKnight contends that many, conservatives and liberals alike, attempt the same thing with the Bible. We all try to tame it.

McKnight's *The Blue Parakeet* has emerged at the perfect time to cool the flames of a world on fire with contention and controversy. It calls Christians to a way to read the Bible that leads beyond old debates and denominational battles. It calls Christians to stop taming the Bible and to let it speak anew for a new generation.

In his books *The Jesus Creed* and *Embracing Grace*, Scot McKnight established himself as one of America's finest Christian thinkers, an author to be reckoned with.

In *The Blue Parakeet*, McKnight again touches the hearts and minds of today's Christians, this time challenging them to rethink how to read the Bible, not just to puzzle it together into some systematic theology but to see it as a Story that we're summoned to enter and to carry forward in our day.

In his own inimitable style, McKnight sets traditional and liberal Christianity on its ear, leaving readers equipped, encouraged, and emboldened to be the people of faith they long to be.

Available in stores and online!

ALSO AVAILABLE FROM SCOT MCKNIGHT

How to Know, Read, Live, and Show the Gospel

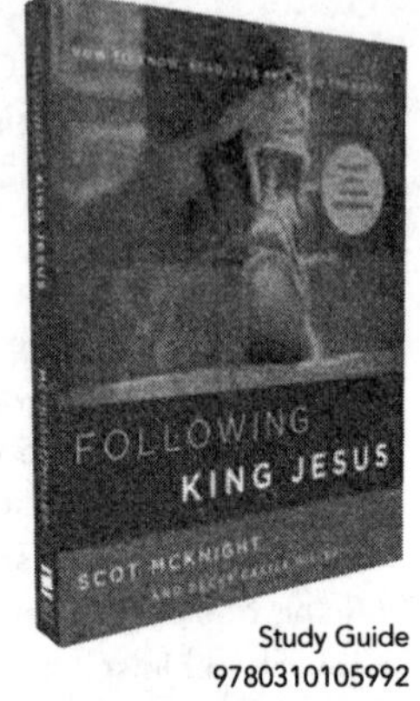

Study Guide
9780310105992

We want to follow King Jesus, but do we know how?

Author and professor Scot McKnight will help you discover what it means to follow King Jesus through 24 lessons based on four of his writings (*The King Jesus Gospel, The Blue Parakeet - 2nd edition, One.Life,* and *A Fellowship of Differents*). McKnight's unique framework for discipleship is designed to be used for personal study and within disciple-making groups of two or more. In this workbook, McKnight will help you:

- Know the biblical meaning of the gospel
- Read the Bible and understand how to apply it today
- Live as disciples of Jesus in all areas of life
- Show the world God's character through life together in the church

Each lesson, created by Becky Castle Miller, has both Personal Study and Group Discussion sections. The Personal Study section contains a dis-cipleship reading from Scot McKnight, an insightful Bible study, and a time for individual prayer, action, and reflection. The Group Discussion section includes discussion questions and activities to do together with a discipleship group. You'll share insights from your per-sonal study time with each other and explore different ways of living out what you're learning.

Whether you have been a Christian for many years or you are desiring a fresh look at what it means to be a disciple, this workbook is an in-depth guide to what it means to follow King Jesus and to discover how to put that kind of life into practice.